Insect Media

CARY WOLFE, SERIES EDITOR

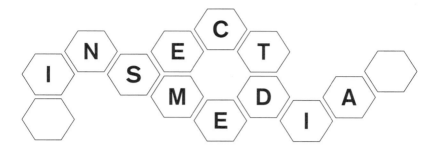

INSECT MEDIA

An Archaeology of Animals and Technology

Jussi Parikka

posthumanities **11**

University of Minnesota Press
Minneapolis
London

An earlier version of chapter 1 was published as "Insect Technics: Intensities of Animal Bodies," in *An [Un]Likely Alliance: Thinking Environment[s] with Deleuze/ Guattari,* ed. Bernd Herzogenrath (Newcastle: Cambridge Scholars Publishing, 2008), 339–62; reprinted with permission of Cambridge Scholars Publishing. Parts of chapter 2 were previously published in "Politics of Swarms: Translations between Entomology and Biopolitics," *Parallax* 14, no. 3 (2008): 112–24; permission to reprint is granted by Taylor and Francis, Ltd. Chapter 7 is a revision of "Insects, Sex, and Biodigitality in Lynn Hershman-Leeson's *Teknolust,*" *Postmodern Culture* 17, no. 2 (January 2007).

Published by the University of Minnesota Press
111 Third Avenue South, Suite 290
Minneapolis, MN 55401-2520
http://www.upress.umn.edu

Library of Congress Cataloging-in-Publication Data

Parikka, Jussi, 1976–
    Insect media : an archaeology of animals and technology / Jussi Parikka.
        p.   cm. — (Posthumanities ; v. 11)
    Includes bibliographical references (p.   ) and index.
    ISBN 978-0-8166-6739-0 (hc : alk. paper) — ISBN 978-0-8166-6740-6
(pb : alk. paper)
    1. Swarm intelligence. 2. Insects—Behavior—mathematical models.
3. Bionics. I. Title.
    Q337.3.P36 2010
    595.709—dc22

                                                                        2010035074

Printed in the United States of America on acid-free paper

The University of Minnesota is an equal-opportunity educator and employer.

17 16 15 14 13 12 11 10   10 9 8 7 6 5 4 3 2 1

CONTENTS

ACKNOWLEDGMENTS

Even if I do not particularly enjoy insects, working with this book was a joy. I had already had the chance to work with the underbelly of media theory with my earlier virus-related project and my more recent book on "spam cultures," but *Insect Media* gave me the opportunity to elaborate and continue theoretical and media archaeological ideas that were giving glimpses of their insectoid faces.

Nothing is possible without creative surroundings and a network of people with both intelligence and instinct who generously offer advice and support. Institutionally, this book started while I was finishing my Ph.D. thesis for the Department of Cultural History at the University of Turku in Finland, and my background in the department is still very much visible in this book. I have an obsession to "historicize," although I never felt like being a proper historian. I thank warmly many former colleagues and the excellent e-library collections that allowed me to find quirky sources from the nineteenth century (and earlier) and that supported me in my academic perversions. Via the Department of Media Studies, Humboldt University, Berlin, I moved to Anglia Ruskin University in Cambridge, where innovative colleagues ensured a good working atmosphere while I adjusted to the peculiarities of the British higher education system. A warm thank you to all of you who made me feel welcome and offered support with this project.

While Anglia Ruskin's Department of English, Communication, Film, and Media was my primary everyday context, through a range of other people and institutions I was able to obtain important feedback and tips that (in)formed my budding ideas into a book. In no particular order, I thank Milla Tiainen, Pasi Väliaho, Katve-Kaisa Kontturi, Ilona Hongisto, Teemu Taira, Olli Pyyhtinen, Matthew Fuller, Michael Goddard, Joss Hands, Sean Campbell, Eric Kluitenberg, Charlie Gere, Seb Franklin, Thomas Elsaesser, Jukka Sihvonen, Trond Lundemo, Juri Nummelin, Erkki Huhtamo, Alan Winfield, Craig Reynolds, Steven Shaviro, Tony D. Sampson, Floris Paalman, Lynn Hershman-Leeson, Garnet Hertz, Gary Genosko, Tina Kendall, Tanya Horeck, and Sarah Barrow. I hope I did not forget too many; as always, there is a swarm.

Without the supportive feedback of Douglas Armato at the University of Minnesota Press and Cary Wolfe's supportive and perceptive role as the series editor for Posthumanities, I would have been lost. Thanks also to Danielle Kasprzak for responding to my endless questions so promptly. I also thank the anonymous referees for critical but affirmative and encouraging comments.

Financially, I thank the Finnish Cultural Foundation for a six-month research grant during the early phases of research.

A special and warm thank you goes as always to Milla: we hate insects and spiders together but love things material, not least cultural theory.

INTRODUCTION
Insects in the Age of Technology

> ... cultural and technical phenomena providing a fertile soil, a good soup, for the development of insects, bacteria, germs, or even particles. The industrial age defined as the age of insects. ...
>
> —Gilles Deleuze and Félix Guattari, *A Thousand Plateaus*

> There is an entire genealogy to be written from the point of view of the challenge posed by insect coordination, by "swarm intelligence." Again and again, poetic, philosophical, and biological studies ask the same question: how does this "intelligent," global organization emerge from a myriad of local, "dumb" interactions?
>
> —Alex Galloway and Eugene Thacker, *The Exploit*

FROM CYBORGS TO INSECTS

First, a practical exercise. Pick up an entomology book; something such as Thomas Eisner's *For the Love of Insects* from a couple of years back will do fine, or an older book from the nineteenth century, like John Lubbock's *On the Senses, Instincts, and Intelligence of Animals with Special Reference to Insects* (1888) suits the purpose as well. However, do not read the book as a description of the biology of those tiny insects or solely as an excavation of the microcosmic worlds of entomology. Instead, if you approach it as media theory, it reveals a whole new world of sensations, perceptions, movements, stratagems, and patterns of organization that work much beyond the confines of the human world.

Of course, in a way this has already been done. Some years ago the

American research agency DARPA (the Defense Advanced Research Projects Agency), in the past responsible for various high-tech army gadgets, revealed information about its aspirations to fabricate cyborg insects. DARPA was criticized and ridiculed quite soon because of this imaginative, to say the least, plan of harnessing these simple forms of life as part of the most developed military machine the world has ever seen. The idea was to insert electronic devices into insect pupae. The so-called MEMS (microelectromechanical systems) system was designed to smoothen as part of the body structure of the animal during later metamorphoses. The cyborg insect could be then controlled and used as a spy tool for army covert operations. Who would suspect a lone moth or a bumblebee?[1]

The connection between insects and high-tech war was not altogether new. Some years earlier, in the midst of fears of terrorists and cyber-hackers, swarms were identified as future models of conflict: "from ants and bees and wolf packs, to ancient Parthians and medieval Mongols."[2] Insect organization was creeping into the most high-tech area of the contemporary world, the U.S. military, which was making use of ideas of nonlinearity, small tactical units, and network-oriented models of action. Not only the military was picking up entomology books; insects were being discussed in various other fields of media, communication, and digital design and theory as well. In visual systems, insects' compound eyes represented a powerful example of biologically inspired computation. Biomimetics was opening up a new field in engineering naturelike behavior such as locomotion, navigation, and vision.[3] Insects' wide field of view was attracting a great deal of research interest from players developing medical, industrial, and military applications.[4] Artists such as Garnet Hertz (designer of a cockroach-controlled robot), Toshio Iwai ("Music Insects"), and Mira Calix (a composer working with insect sounds) were engaging with similar questions as well, using insects to think through high-tech creation. Experimental video works such as the bizarre narrative of David Blair's online film *Wax, or The Discovery of Television among the Bees* (1991) ties together military development, insects, and high-tech telecommunications media.[5]

Suddenly the cyborg as imagined since the 1980s in theory and fiction seemed quite old-fashioned. This shift was not altogether dismissing the human being and its perceptive and cognitive capabilities: the two-handed and -legged brainy animal was seen to demonstrate distinct powers in visual (recognizing edges, seeing contrasts, differentiating between dimensional entities) and tactile (the hand) faculties. Yet a much less brainy entity, the insect, was a powerful new kind of model for designing artificial agents that expressed complex behavior, not through pre-programming and centralization but through autonomy, emergence, and distributed functioning.[6] Since the 1980s, such terms as swarms, distributed intelligence, and insect models of organization have infiltrated both the design of digital technologies and cultural theoretical analysis of such media systems. Yet, as researchers commented, "The most talented roboticist in the world is not going to come close to what a cockroach can do."[7]

One of the most discussed contexts for such a cultural and scientific reorientation in terms of design practices and plans was artificial intelligence (AI) research. New ideas in cognitive science seemed to offer the most convincing explanations of the potential for tapping into the simple architectures already developed by nature. "Intelligence is overrated," such research paradigms seemed implicitly to suggest. The approach, which focused on the redundancy of numerous "dumb" machines, emphasized that

1. there is no need for planning;

2. no need for central representation;

3. our traditional ways of modeling the world for the actors are impractical and unnecessary;

4. we should pay more close attention to biology and evolution;

5. One should focus on building real, concrete solutions, not merely theoretical models.[8]

In robotics, MIT professor Rodney Brooks noted in the late 1980s that artificial agents do not have to resemble or act like humans; there are much more efficient ways of doing complex tasks than by modeling intelligent machines. Brooks designed insectlike robots, and in his 1989 paper "Fast, Cheap, and Out of Control," coauthored by Anita Flynn, he introduced the idea of using insectlike mobots as space exploration agents instead of large "intelligent" ones.[9] Douglas Hofstadter had already used the notion of the ant colony to pave the way for a rethinking of cognition as distributed "mass communication" between miniagents,[10] but Brooks deployed a similar insect metaphor: no central command but massive parallelism and cooperation.

Such research in "new AI" had many parallels in the emerging artificial life sciences, which, however, dealt mostly with software. The approaches were kicked off by researchers such as Christopher Langton. In that context, and in the midst of the emerging digital software culture of the 1980s, the field of programming also gained much from the scientific theories of artificial life. In software and network processes, simple but interconnected agents had been planned since the 1960s. Nowadays everybody knows viruses and worms by name, but the fact that we are thinking them in terms of parallel processing and artificial life is often less emphasized. Yet such program types, which span computer boundaries as "parasite computing," are exemplary of software that acts in a manner reminiscent of insect colonies: individually dumb, but highly efficient when coupled with their environment. The ideas of distributing artificial actors into insectlike colonies of part functions and parallel processing represented a move toward situatedness but also embodiment: robots are in the world, and their actions are enabled and controlled by the very present environment. This could be seen as signaling a kind of ethological turn in creating artificial agents, because such ideas were reminiscent of those of animal ethologists such as Jakob von Uexküll's in work from the 1920s: artificial actors are embedded in a perceptual world, which implies that what we perceive is what we are, and animals and artificial agents are defined by the capabilities of perception, sensation, and orientation in their environment.[11]

The ethological and ecological interests spread quickly to cultural and media theory as well, with writers embracing swarms and termites as relevant to leftist politics (Hardt and Negri), insects as figures important for material feminism (Braidotti), and notions such as packs and "nonanthropomorphic intelligence" as key terms for a biophilosophy of the contemporary network culture (Thacker).[12]

Strange Sensations of Insect Media

The aim of *Insect Media* is to dig into this field of insects and media and cultural theory that seems to have emerged during recent decades. Yet, because I am infected with a historical obsession, my aim is to dig deeper. It might be more coherent to offer an analysis of the interconnections of such models, concepts, and diagrams of insects, viroids, and media since the 1980s, but my contention is that it proves fruitful to stretch this analysis on a wider temporal scale and begin with an analysis of animal worlds of the nineteenth century. In other words, the fascination with simple forms of life such as insects, viruses, and the like has been interfaced with media design and theory for years now, but nineteenth-century entomology, and various other cultural discourses and practices since then, have hailed the powers of insects as media in themselves, capable of weird affect worlds, strange sensations, and uncanny potentials that cannot immediately be pinpointed in terms of a register of known possibilities. Hence the task of the book is twofold: first, to look at media as insects and see what kinds of theoretical modulations we can come up with if we extend further the recent decades of obsession with insectlike models of media, and second, to analyze the archaeology of the recent figurations in terms of "insects as media," a cultural historical theme that can be catalyzed into media theoretical implications as well.

My aim is not to write a linear history of insects and media but to offer some key case studies, all of which address a transposition between insects (and other simple forms of life) and media technologies. The translations among different modern sciences (biology, entomology, technology) are coupled with a philosophically tuned cultural analysis that offers new ways to think of the bestiality of media technologies as intensive potentials. So when I refer to a work of "translation," it is not to awaken ideas of the metaphoricity of technology but to point to how specific figures such as "insects" are continuously distributed across a social field not merely as denotations of a special class of icky animals but as carriers of intensities (potentials) and modes of aesthetic, political, economic, and technological thought. Translation, then, is not a linguistic operation without residue but a transposition,[13] and a much more active operation on levels of nondiscursive media production, as becomes especially evident when approaching the end of the twentieth century and the use of insect models of organization in computer science and digital culture.

In a parallel move, the book implicitly questions the definition of media in itself. In fact, the notion of media is broadened from technologies and uses of mass communication to various processes that are often not even mentioned in media studies textbooks. Yet faculties of transmission, recording, and connecting can be found in various places. Stones and geological formations are recordings of the slow passing of time and the turbulence of matter-energy. Plants and animals constitute their being through various modes of transmission and coupling with their environment. They contract the forces of the cosmos into environmental relations, couplings, which is perhaps not a reflective (human) relation but is still a lived one of relations actual and virtual (potential).[14] Media, then, in this book, are not only a technology, a political agenda, or an exclusively human theme. Media are a contraction of forces of the world into specific resonating milieus: internal milieus with their resonation, external milieus affording their rhythms as part of that resonation. An animal has to find a common tune with its environment, and a technology has to work through rhythmic relations with other force fields such as politics and economics. In this context, sensations, percepts, and affects become the primary vectors through which entities are co-created at the same time as their environmental relations.

In other words, there is a whole cosmology of media technologies that spans much more of time than the human historical approach suggests. In this sense, insects and animals provide an interesting case of how to widen the possibilities to think media and technological culture. They are contractions of the world and organizations into environmental relations and milieus. This is not meant to be read as a sociobiological celebration of the superiority of nature as a deterministic machine to which we should adapt. Nature is not a model to be followed but a toolbox or a storehouse of invention, as has been voiced since the nineteenth century in the context of biology but also that of experimental work in technological discourses.

A MEDIA ARCHAEOLOGICAL TWIST

This idea of focusing on the joint history of media and nature can be seen as a kind of twisted media archaeology.[15] It does not try to excavate lost histories of present technologies but rather, by its temporal realigning, looks for conceptual cuts through which to open up new agendas of research and analysis. In my take, this methodological clue leads to a rethinking of the various senses and rationalities inherent in techno-logy and bio-logy. *Bestial media archaeology, as addressed in this book, is a means by which to look at the immanent conditions of possibility of the current insect theme in media design and theory; to question the supposed newness of the coupling of (seemingly) simple animal behavior with media technologies; to look for the longer duration of this phenomenon; to present important case studies of this history of insect media that do not merely represent the past of this specific "idea" but offer important philosophical interventions into how we habitually think about media, technology, and the conjoining and differences of animal and nonorganic life.* The chapters that follow demonstrate how insects have been short-circuited as part of philosophical, engineering, and scientific concerns regarding media systems since the nineteenth century.

Examples from nineteenth-century popular discourse are illustrative. In 1897 the *New York Times* addressed spiders as "builders, engineers and weavers" and also as the "original inventors of a system of telegraphy." For such Victorian writers, spiders' webs offered themselves as ingenious communication systems that do not merely signal according to a binary setting (something has hit the web or has not hit the web) but transmit information regarding the "general character and weight of any object touching it."[16] Similar accounts have abounded since the mid-nineteenth century. Insects sense, move, build, communicate, and even create art in various ways that raised wonder and awe, for example, in U.S. popular culture. An apt example of the nineteenth-century insect mania is the story about the "cricket mania" of a young lady who collected and trained crickets as musical instruments:

> 200 crickets in a wirework-house, filled with ferns and shells, which she called a "fernery." The constant rubbing of the wings of these insects, producing the sounds so familiar to thousands everywhere seemed to be the finest music to her ears. She admitted at once that she had a mania for capturing crickets.[17]

In the nineteenth century, insects infiltrated popular culture as fashion figures—literally, as in the case of the beetle dresses and insect hats of the Victorian era (especially between the 1850s and the 1880s).[18] In popular entomology books such as the classic *An Introduction to Entomology; or, Elements of the Natural History of Insects: Comprising an Account of Noxious and Useful Insects, of Their Metamorphoses, Food,*

Stratagems, Habitations, Societies, Motions, Noises, Hybernation, Instinct, etc. etc. (originally four volumes, 1815–1826), insects are approached as engineers, architects, and tinkerers of the microscopic world. They are marveled at due to their powers of affect, sensing, and motion—for instance, their ability to fly, for which they were appropriated as models of the aspiring branch of motion engineering, as were spiders (which were back then counted as insects):

> What will you say, if I tell you that these webs (at least many of them) are airballoons and that the aeronauts are not "lovers who may bestride the gossamer / That idles in the wanton summer air / And yet not fall," but *spiders,* who, long before Montgolfier, nay, ever since the creation, have been in the habit of sailing through the fields of ether in these air-light chariots.[19]

In another passage of the book, spiders are referred to as having electric capabilities, with the authors arguing that "there is a mode . . . in which some geometric spiders shoot and direct their threads, and fly upon them; by which it appears that as they dart them out they guide them as if by magic, emitting at the same time a stream of air, . . . or possibly some subtle electric fluid."[20]

Modern media were constantly present in the animal world and in the physiological research of animal bodies, understood as wire systems.[21] It is no wonder, then, that the famous entomologist J. H. Fabre speculated in 1911 whether moths, too—the great peacock moths, to be exact—were capable of wireless telegraphy, of "Hertzian vibrations of the ether."[22] Though Fabre quickly came to the conclusion that the curious communication of the moths did not result from modulating electric or magnetic waves, the mere fact that he considered such a link is worth mentioning.

Despite various examples, in most histories and theories of media the centrality of the human being has persisted since the early nineteenth century. Media technologies have, since their early modern roots, been perceived as crucial components in the emerging power structures of the nation-state and capitalist business, which has contributed to the need to view technologies as centrally run and controlled by and subject to top-down functional goals. Yet in recent years of technological "evolution," other things have been underlined, namely, a move toward invertebrate animals. According to Steven Shaviro, the nineteenth-century biological organic metaphors were based on the seemingly well-structured "verte-brate body plans," whereas those of our postmodern age are more closely related to the lives of insects and, for example, arthropods in their ability to generate distributed, experimental, and metamorphosing organiza-tions.[23] Yet the division is not so clear-cut, and there is a neglected his-tory to be excavated: to a certain extent, a history of "postmodern tech-nology" had already started in the nineteenth century with pioneering discourses on insect technics. The nineteenth- and twentieth-century history of media was already filled with such "hidden themes" of alterna-tive media. Within the majoritarian joining of technology–state–human being we find cracks and varia: the early modern media sphere incorpo-rated in its phases of emergence a panorama of ideas and views of media and technology (even though, one should note, the term "media" is much younger in its present usage) in which processes of transmission, calcu-lation, and storage were not restricted to forms of technical media that we would normally understand by the term (twentieth-century mass media from cinema and radio to television and network media such as the Internet).

To follow Akira Mizuta Lippit, the intertwining of animals and tech-nology was an inherent part of the modernization and emergence of technical media at the end of the nineteenth century. The disappearance of animals from urban cultures of technical media was paralleled by the appearance of animals in various discourses, from media (e.g., cinema) to modern subjectivity (e.g., psychoanalysis). As Lippit notes, from me-tonymies of nature animals became embedded in the new industrial en-vironment, where

> the idioms and histories of numerous technological innovations from the steam engine to quantum mechanics bear the traces of an incorporated animality. James Watt and later Henry Ford, Thomas Edison, Alexander Graham Bell, Walt Disney, and Erwin Schrödinger, among other key fig-ures in the industrial and aesthetic shifts of the late nineteenth and early twentieth centuries, found uses for animal spirits in developing their re-spective machines, creating in the process a series of fantastic hybrids.[24]

Siegfried Zielinski's anarchaeological approach has tried to delineate media history that has run away from its institutional and conventional definitions to neglected, "minor" phenomena; similarly, Jeffrey Sconce, for example, has mapped the anomalies haunting the normalized understanding of media since the nineteenth century, demonstrating how media mediate not merely between humans but also, on the imaginary media level, between ghosts and the living.[25] Again, the media archaeological method has proved apt as a cartography of media culture beyond the usual confines of technology and human intentions to encompass a variety of not only sources used but also analytical perspectives not confined to a narrow focus on actual technologies and their histories. Such work has already been done in the field of media archaeology, especially in mapping the histories of "imaginary media."[26]

In addition to scholarly contributions, recent decades of media art have also succeeded in deterritorializing media practices from a narrow understanding based on technologies to a wider and more innovative distribution—to organic, chemical, and other alternative platforms, where not only the established forms of transmission of perception count but also the realization that basically anything can become a medium— a realization that easily shakes our understanding of contemporary but also past media. Exemplary are the ideas proposed by former Mongrel art group members Harwood, Wright, and Yokokoji to consider the ecology as a medium in itself. The Cross Talk proposal explains ecosystems as communication networks, platforms of alternative agencies and sensoriums, in a fashion that subsequently also radicalizes the idea of "free" media. Exhibitions such as Bug City (2006) in Canada were as exemplary in discussing the insect question as crucial to modernity and postmodernity. Such exhibitions are good educations in the "becoming-insect" of contemporary culture and how to enter the swarm logic that seems to characterize network culture: we "enter the swarm" when using the bit torrent protocol, we are told, as much as when we enter the swarm space, whether visual or aural, in swarm art installations that introduce the move from static design to dynamic spaces and interaction with such processes.[27] A recent installation, Timo Kahlen's 2008 *Swarm* piece, is a good example of the way a sound object turns the whole space where it is placed into a vibratory, lived space with bee sounds that are modulated and recomposed.

Biomedia art pieces might often work through the centrality of the algorithmic, which creates "natural forms" in digital environments. However, at least as interesting is how they are able to reframe life in its wet materiality.[28] Genetic algorithms express complex processes that resemble Karl Blossfeldt's photographic art from the 1920s depicting "natural forms." Instead of just representing, digital media were creating forms in the 1990s of interest to evolutionary algorithms and have been followed by various biomedia projects that cross the boundary of digitality and the fleshy bodies of animality. In any case, the more interesting experiments not only showed the phenomenological resemblances in nature and art(ifice) but engaged in a more radical redistribution of the presumed division. This "art for animals," as Matthew Fuller has called it, does not represent or depict animals as objects but targets animals as audiences: it is "work that makes a direct address to the perceptual world of one or more non-human animal species."[29] Technologies and techniques of seeing, hearing, and transmission can be found in the most surprising places.

In the context of *Insect Media,* Zielinski's suggestion regarding the fundamental inhumanity of media is important. The earlier idea of technology as an organ stretching from the human being has been demonstrated as dysfunctional, as has the straightforward translation of the organic as the technological in the era of the computer: "Technology is not human; in a specific sense, it is deeply inhuman. The best, fully functioning technology can be created only in opposition to the traditional image of what is human and living, seldom as its extension or expansion."[30] I take this as referring to the impetus to steer clear of easy-going metaphorics and look for another, a more fundamental level, of molecular movements, intensities, which characterize potentials for media. This follows an earlier critical task of reorientation expressed by Friedrich Nietzsche, in which the human being and the valuation of consciousness as the highest level of evolution were questioned.[31] This anthropomorphic dream, or prejudice, tended to form trees of thought and progress in which the cognitive man was the primary reference point. There is an urgent need for a cartography of potential forces of inhuman kinds that question evolutionary trees and exhibit alternative logics of thought, organization, and sensation.[32]

This can also be understood as the immanent theme that runs throughout modernity and the animal–technology relationship, where animals seem to suggest a mode of communication and media beyond those of the human language. As Lippit argues, animals suggested, from the Darwinian revolution to Freudian psychoanalysis and in the midst of "the advances of the optical and technological media," a new understanding of technics beyond that of symbolic human communication.[33] This realization is something that should further be added to a methodological approach to animal technics.

Next, I will address the question of media as a milieu of intensive capabilities, an ethology, and hence illuminate more specifically the theoretical contexts of this book.

MEDIA ETHOLOGY

One might object that it's all nice and interesting, this talk about animals and biology, but remains irrelevant to the world of media technologies: it is in vain to transport biological models into the world of technology, which, in the age of digital computing, is more mathematical than biological. Yet mine is not a metaphoric suggestion but one committed to approaching media technologies not as a fixed substance but as a realm of affects, potentials, and energetics. It is my contention that contemporary analysis of media should furthermore underline the need to rethink the material basis of contemporary media condition and produce much more complex intuitions that take into account a certain "activity of matter," nonhuman forces expressing themselves as part of this media assemblage of modernity.

Coupling biology and technology and relying on concepts adopted from biology in cultural explanations have had their fair share of felicitous criticism in recent years. For example, Anna Munster and Geert Lovink note that we should argue "against biologism." Networks, for example, do not "grow" in the manner of teleological plants, nor do they "emerge"; contagions, memes, and epidemics are in constant danger of being pressed into metaphorical use by marketing departments that use them instead of providing a specific view of what goes on in networks and other cybernetic systems.[34] This relates to the question, What do we actually talk about when we address animals, insects, and media technologies? Do we think of them as predefined, discrete forms of reality in which natural beings are separated from cultural substance (and seen only through our discursive lenses)? Or would there be a chance for a view in which we would not have to assume a preparatory division but could approach things as intensive molecular flows, in which, for example, the notion of "media" was only the end result of connections, articulations of flows, affects, speeds, densities, discourses, and practices (namely, assemblages)?[35] Could we see media as a contracting of sensations into a certain field of consistency—whether called an environment or a media ecology? In other words, could we not (only) ask how nature is evident in our media cultures but what in media technology is already present in nature?[36] That seems to be the implicit question that various models of swarms and such projects as Craig Reynolds's 1980s work with boids pose: how can we reframe the natural to make it into a viable dynamic machine for the technological?

Whereas since the boom of network media in the 1990s there has been a constant danger of inflating the use of cultural theoretical concepts, there is also another a danger in loose metaphorics. By using analogy as a method of explanation, we often try to see one phenomenon in the use of some other, usually a familiar one. Take viruses. A computer virus might be explained as being "like" a biological virus, capturing the cells of the host, using them to spread its own code, and making new viruses (perhaps also killing the host). Despite the reasonable-sounding "analysis," the problem is that there is so much baggage that comes along metaphorics, and in the case of biological metaphors, it tends to "naturalize" a cybernetic construction. The phenomena are placed on an explanatory grid that has already stabilized the relations of nodes. What are neglected are the intensive processes of individuation out of which more stable formations emerge. In this sense, we should be interested not only in the actualized technological objects, animal beings or their combinations, but in approaching them as carriers of potentials, forces of individuation, expressions of "what bodies can do." Similarly, when I analyze literary examples or insect figures in popular cultural objects, I do not approach them primarily as metaphors but as relays in the wider structuration of the biopolitical regime of the technical media age.

In this context, Gilles Deleuze and Félix Guattari, who were reluctant themselves to think in terms of "media" (discarding it as a realm of communication), can offer media theoretical clues. Their neomaterialist ideas have been continued and developed by many other writers also mentioned in this book, such as Eugene Thacker, Alex Galloway, Tiziana

Terranova, Matthew Fuller, Elizabeth Grosz, John Johnston, Manuel DeLanda, Luciana Parisi, Rosi Braidotti, and Brian Massumi. In this context, this book approaches the translations and transpositions of insects and biology with technology and media in terms of the following three key terms: intensity, assemblage, and diagram.

Intensity

As an alternative to years of the hegemony of the signifier, the linguistic turn, and the various types of cultural constructionism that have placed "meaning" in its linguistic form as the key object of cultural studies, various new approaches have emerged. Within cultural studies, Lawrence Grossberg was among the first to address the shortcomings of meaning and draw from Deleuze, Guattari, and Spinoza for a more material approach tuned to affect. Indeed, *affect* is one of the key words used in thinking beyond both the signifier and the body as only an individualized entity and to grasp the interconnected nature of bodies of various kinds.[37] In what has been coined "material feminism,"[38] different strategies to counter the primacy of the linguistic have been proposed in order to adequately theorize the nonhuman and the intensity of the material. The list could go on, including Bruno Latour's theories of nonhuman networks, Langdon Winner's takes on science and technology studies, German "materialist" media theories from those of Kittler to those of more recent writers such as Wolfgang Ernst, notions of abstract materialism suggested by Luciana Parisi and other writers, or, for example, the critique of hylomorphism.[39]

Neomaterialist cultural analysis, in the context of this book, is an approach that tries to acknowledge the specificity of the material. The differential creativity of the material stems from a radicality of difference that is not only difference within a genus, a third general concept, as the Aristotelian tradition supposes (for there to be a difference, there must first be something common). Difference, in such a case, is in danger of residing merely on the actual level of already defined entities of the world. Instead, difference becomes an ontogenetic—and consequently heterogenetic—force.[40]

A differing force of creation, a becoming, an intensity creates what we perceive. The perceived takes place only through events in which both the subject and the object are formed. This is the intensity inherent in

Deleuze's thought and also in more recent formulations of neomaterialism: to see the divisible, the extensive, the named merely as a result of forces of intensive differentiation. The focus on the intensive does not mean that extensions are not real. On the contrary, they are very much real, imposing themselves, but only as one possible mode of being, on temporary end results in the intensive processes of individuation.[41] Differentiated entities tend to hide their history of differentiation, which in a way undermines the creative processuality of the world.[42]

The focus on intensities, in addition to being an ontological statement, refers to the crucial methodological need to understand the creative forces of the world. These forces mold our lived relations, which increasingly are characterized by the milieu of technology and nonhuman technological actors but also by new modulations of nature in the form of biodigital technologies, nanotechnologies, and biological computation, for example.[43]

In general, a new materialism addresses a micropolitics of matter, the nondiscursive manipulation of energetic material flows that have been captured in the bioproduction of modern media culture since the nineteenth century. This means there is a need to stay in tune with the ethics and politics of life and subrepresentational processes. As Braidotti writes, there is a whole history of thinking animals in terms of energetics and potentials, often reduced to a technological-industrial mode. Paraphrasing Braidotti, the idea of animals as machines is not reducible to the philosophical claim that both lack souls but to think both as workers and producers, like "an industrial production plant."[44] Raw material for production, but also producers, animals are much more than they are captured to be.

Thus biopower, the key theme of the book, is to be grasped not merely as the capture of life as the *object* of power, which Foucault analyzed meticulously in terms of the biological features of human populations. Instead, as Braidotti suggests, life is intensive, creative, and infinite in the Spinozan take, in which life became a subject as well. It is an agency that in its intensive creativity is coming up with new solutions and ways of engaging with the world. This viewpoint differs to some extent from the recent Heideggerian emphasis on life and biopolitics suggested by Giorgio Agamben, in which death is the continuous zero point and horizon of life. Beyond what Braidotti calls a narcissistic viewpoint that promotes loss and melancholia, a Spinozian version looks at life as something that surpasses the individual and is a nonpersonal force of creativity that contracts individuals as its attributes.[45] In Braidotti's take, life is the double articulation of *bios* (politics and discourse) and *zoe* (nonhuman intensity), a continuous intensive creation that is also continuously articulated on a social level of power and knowledge that, increasingly during modernity, has been a level of technical media: from technologies of the image and the cinema to games, software, and networks.

Assemblages

Seemingly stable bodies are always formed of intensive flows and their molecular connections. Bodies are not merely predefined organs and functions; they form as part of the environment in which they are embedded.[46] Gilbert Simondon talks about individuation and the (in)formative role of environmental milieus in this metastability of transductive relations; Deleuze and Guattari insist that we must get away from closed models of bodies and organisms and look at how bodies are continuously articulated with their outsides.[47]

Another way to take into account the ontological intensity of the world is to focus on the intensive qualities of beings, their capacities. In a mode of thought that also draws from Simondon's emphasis on individuation, this suggests a cartographical mapping of the qualitative modes of creation of forms of life defined not (only) by their stabilized forms of organization but by their potentials for experience, sensation, and becoming. Recently an increasing number of media theorists have drawn from Simondon, including Mark Hansen. For Hansen, too, Simondon offers a way to step further from social constructivism that stems from what Hansen describes as an externalist account of the body toward an ontology of the originary technicity of bodies.[48] Biological and technological bodies are not natural kinds, but they carry tendencies toward various relations, percepts, and affects.[49] Such points are later elaborated in this book not only in contexts of philosophy but, for example, through the "cybernetic zoology" of the 1950s and 1960s, including Karl von Frisch's research into bee dancing and W. Grey Walter's cybernetic turtles. These various discursive and technological constructions can be seen as environing and affective assemblages that operate through relating and responding to the fluctuations of their milieus.

This is where ethology becomes media theory. Such an ethological perspective (referring to Jakob von Uexküll) of the world leads us to evaluate bodies not according to their innate, morphological essences but as expressions of certain movements, sensations, and interactions with their environments. These are always intensive potentials, not pre-determined qualities, which underlines an experimental empiricism.[50] Assemblages are compositions, affects, and passages in a state of becoming and a relationality that is the stuff of experience. No assemblage stems from a prescribed relation hidden inside it, as if it were a seed; rather, an assemblage comes from the folding of the inside and the outside. An assemblage, whether classified as technology, animal, or a human being, is a product of the connecting relations, and what can become technological is not decided *before* the relations are entered into, something that Simondon refers to as the transductive relation. In other words, assemblages are always constituted by a relationality, but this does not mean a complete external constructivism but an ontogenesis of transindividual individuation. All relations are enabled by a pre-individual reality of potentials and virtuality, and this transindividual element that beings share is what affords collective assemblings as well.[51]

Affects are always in transit and hence contain an element of virtuality. Jean-François Lyotard refers to the "affect-phrases" of animals that do not fit into the communicative and discursive logic of human language but cut through it, opening up another, alternative, way of relating and communicating.[52] Animals are beyond language but not mute. They are stratified by but not reducible to the human signifying practices and hence offer a fruitful way of approaching affects. Beyond language, however, animals such as insects map territories, contract forces, fold their bodies, and establish relations. This is what I find a crucial point in the field of animal studies and posthumanism as well: we must not get stuck with the question concerning language and the defining differences (usually in terms of language) that remove the animal from the cultural. Instead we should map the differing modalities of expression of animal bodies that point toward asignifying semiotics. Animal studies joins forces with media theory of a nonhuman kind. Reproduction of culture takes as much into account those semiotics of intensive bodily interactions and fluctuations as it does the linguistic acts and discourses; indeed, it is increasingly urgent to recognize the different genealogy of thought that helps us to realize this regime of asignifying semiotics and nonlinguistic individuation that draws more from Spinoza, Bergson, Whitehead, Simondon, and Deleuze-Guattari than from Plato, Descartes, Hegel, and Heidegger or even Derrida.[53]

The asignifying regime of signs can be related to the notion of affect. Affects are not possessed by anyone, but blocs of them constitute individuals.[54] Affects are transitions, gateways, and passages between dimensions. As an artistic endeavor, however, affects are reducible not to human art but to art as creation, the art of relations, from animals to technics of various other kinds. This affinity with the primacy of affects (as indexes of relationality) is what distinguishes this project from some much-discussed positions in animal studies. Much of the agenda has been set in relation to the Western metaphysical tradition in which the intensity of the animal has been undermined by a lack of language of the beast. Even though writers such as Jacques Derrida have succeeded in pointing toward the "heterogeneous multiciplicity" in the animal itself, it is more often writers coming from Deleuzian or Whiteheadian traditions who have been able to grasp the vibrant materiality of the animality.[55]

In other words, mine is a kind of a milieu approach to the world and, in the context of this book, to media technologies. Also, media can be defined as assembled of various bodies interacting, of intensive relations. Media can be seen as an assemblage of various forces, from human potential to technological interactions and powers to economic forces at play, experimental aesthetic forces, conceptual philosophical modulations. Media contract forces, but also act as a passage and a mode of intensification that affords sensations, percepts, and thoughts. An assemblage is not, then, only a collection of already existing elements (technology taking the animal as its model, for example) but is in itself a mode of cutting flows. It consists of much more elementary things such as speeds and slowness, affects (potentials to connect) and qualities—a mode more akin to becoming than expressing a solid being (the becoming animal of technology, the becoming technical of the insect).[56]

The assemblage approach underlines a nonrepresentational cultural analysis. Becomings and machinic conjunctions are not about imitation and representation of forms or actors.[57] Instead they move on a plane of immanence that traverses the stable forms. An insect becoming media or a network becoming an insect swarm is not an imitation but a molecular expression of the affects that the assemblage is capable of. Suddenly, in a certain territorial situation, coupled to its environment, an insect might be seen as a modern media technology (the entomological translation of insects in terms of telegraphs, for example), or a network agency might be modeled as animal packs or insect swarms self-organizing in a certain environment. The questions of naturality or artificiality are bracketed, and the focus is placed on the nonrepresentational environment and the machinic assemblage in which the entities act.

In other words, media can be approached as intensive capabilities that are constitutive of worlds.[58] Also, animals live in and of media: their world is by definition formed of the constant interactional sensing, movement, and memory of their surroundings, much as the media environment in which we live is constituted of our ethological bodies interacting with bodies technological, political, and economic. Or, to put it a bit differently: we do not so much *have* media as we *are* media and *of* media; media are brains that contract forces of the cosmos, cast a plane over the chaos. Deleuze and Guattari wrote the seminal book *What Is Philosophy?* but someone should address the topic What Are Media? in a manner as extensive and original. What is the specific plane that media contracts, or is there even one? Do media work through elements from science, art, and philosophy, a crisscrossing of various modes of dealing with chaos? Furthermore, it is not clear that we can find the answer in books on philosophy, but perhaps we can find it in such works of fiction as the film *Teknolust* by Lynn Hershman-Leeson (analyzed in chapter 7).

Diagrammatics

Even though in this book I am continuously underlining the importance of an intensive focus on the plane of immanence on which particular bodies, organisms, and other stratifications (technologies, animal species, human characteristics) are formed, this is supplemented by a historical view. Any assemblage works on various spatial and temporal scales and hence as an "ecology" of a kind. In addition to their openness to new connections, there are what Manuel Delanda calls "universal singularities" that are the space of potential, of virtuality, which limits what any assemblage (body) can do (a diagram). Potentials are always articulated in and through specific historical situations. As will become evident in the book, the intensity of affects, whether animal, human, or media technological, is constantly captured as part of the productive machinery of media technological modernity. To be sure, this is what technoscience has been about: rationalizing modes of action, capturing the movement and interaction of bodies, controlling the future by standardizing the otherwise fluctuating animal affects. This relates to Michel Foucault's interest in analyzing the techniques of the spatialization and channeling of bodies and the creation of new diagrammatic maps that are not stable, closed structures but ways of distributing singularities: virtual elements that define the borders of a diagram and limit the turns and directions into which it can actualize.

Following Delanda's terms, diagrammatics can be understood, however, not only as a parasitical capture but as a tracking of the intensive singularities of body diagrams. These are spaces of possibilities or topologies of potential singularities that are the potential modes of actualization of a certain body plan. During evolution, vertebrates, crustaceans, and insects, for example, have developed and followed a certain diagrammatic space of possibility that defines (not as preexisting possibilities but as virtualities that need to be actualized in intensive, embodied processes) what a specific animal is capable of.[59] An animal phylum has a certain topology, a space of possibility, and a key feature of this book is its analysis of why technological modernity has gradually taken such an interest in the singularities of primitive life, especially insects. For me, this is also a historical question, which explains the focus on modern times. Insects have been discussed for a long time; the philosophers in ancient Greece were already contributing to the topic in various texts. But in order to question more specifically the biopolitics of technical modernity and technical media, I want to limit my book to developments not earlier than the birth of modern entomology and modern media.

In one crucial mode, the translation of animals into media has been part of the science of physiology in diagrams of translation par excellence that have created media technological sensations and perceptions severed from the observing, perceiving subject. As argued by several writers, the sciences of sensation and physiology contributed to the emerging technological media culture of the nineteenth century, which was keen on rationalizing procedures of perception, communication, and organization.[60] Animals, too, and even such seemingly irrelevant "dumb" forms of life as insects, were already then being translated through scientific research into constituents of media technologies and a conceptual opening to nonhuman affects as the potentialities of a media to come. The articulations of insects–media–technology were part of a larger diagrammatic field of excavation of the principles of (animal) life.

Hence diagrammatics refers to a mode of analyzing, defining, and reproducing animal affectivity (which spreads from the human sensorium measured as psychophysical quantities to insect organization and sensation) and distributing it from strict scientific contexts across a broad social field. Starting in the nineteenth century, insects spread from fashion garments to popular fiction in the form of amazing stories of alien insects with horrific capabilities. Of course, the diagramming is not unidirectional, from science to popular culture, but exists as a continuous feedback loop. This is why the book mixes such a variety of source materials, from the sciences of entomology and computers to, for example, media art and surrealism, popular science fiction, techniques of digital cinema, and concepts of late twentieth-century feminism. This is how diagrams always work: through mixing and transporting practices and discourses.

FROM ANIMAL AFFECT TO TECHNOLOGY

Referring to the title of the book—*Insect Media*—I wish to underline that I do not intend to write a whole history or a universal theory of media from the viewpoints of these small animals. The book works through transversal case studies that address issues I see as especially important in the present context of the insect media of network culture. The topics are chosen to represent a transversal link between various levels of knowledge production and culture. In other words, the chapters move from science (entomology and biology) to technical media, from popular culture to avant-garde arts, and touch various media from cinema to music, software, and literature. They act as condensation points for transversal networks of scientific discourses, popular cultural clues, and media theoretical notions. Hence they draw from a heterogeneous source base and work to illustrate through empirical examples the potentials in emphasizing the transdisciplinary relations of "the insect question."

Think of the first half of the book as a media archaeological parallel to the 1996 film *Microcosmos*. Through a magnifying cinematic lens, insect life is revealed to consist of industrious workers and factories, weird capacities and potentials, complex systems. The themes stretch from scientific research and biology to science fiction, the physiology of movement and perception, avant-garde aesthetics, and the non-Cartesian philosophy of the early twentieth century. The notion of media as technics is not reducible to technology as we normally understand it (tools and machines used by humans or technological systems ontologically different from living organisms). It is much closer to Simondon's idea of technicity as the "transformations and correlations that characterize technical objects."[61] A primary characteristic of insects, metamorphosis, is transported to the heart of technics, and technics becomes an issue of affects, relations, and transformations, not a particular substance.

The first chapter addresses the enthusiasm in insect analysis from entomology to popular culture and the philosophy of the nineteenth century. Moving from the early entomological classic of Kirby and Spence to *Alice in Wonderland* and *The Population of an Old Pear-Tree; or, Stories of Insect Life,* the chapter maps the fabulations of the insect world as a microcosmos of new movements, actions, and perceptions. These intensive potentials were tracked in the physiological research of, for example, Etienne-Jules Marey but also continued in Henri Bergson's biophilosophy. There the characteristic mode of life of insects, instinct, is contrasted with that of the intelligent tool-making animals. Despite this realization, the primitive insect is revealed as an alternative kind of technical assemblage, a technics of insects and nature in which the tools are not yet differentiated from the body of the animal. In a way, the chapter can be thought of as providing a "response" to Donna Haraway's call for a nonanthropological way of understanding reality beyond the human-centered notion of "culture" or the sociological emphasis on human groups—the need to turn toward animal societies, which also "have been extensively employed in rationalization and naturalization of the oppressive orders of domination in the human body politic"[62] and hence are a crucial part of the biopower of the contemporary technological world.

Chapter 2 continues the idea of natural technics in the context of architecture and organization. The idea of seeing insects and animals as builders, architects, and geometricians was widely discussed in the latter half of the nineteenth century and was also seen in the context of the early modernist architecture of the early twentieth century. For example, the comb structures of bees seemed to express a meticulous order, a theme that was widely used to underline the rigid and hierarchic social systems of insects. Yet in addition, a whole other contrasting theme should not be neglected, that of swarming and self-organizing systems. This idea gained much interest in the context of research into emergent systems, as with C. Lloyd Morgan, and here insects can offer indispensable lessons in the nonhierarchical modes of organization of network society, as Eugene Thacker has suggested.

Chapter 3 focuses on the work of the early ethological pioneer Jakob von Uexküll. His research into the affect and perceptive worlds of insects is a radical continuation (and also overturning) of Kantian philosophy and attracted much attention in philosophical discourse of the twentieth century from Heidegger to Deleuze and on to Agamben. The chapter analyses his ideas of animal perception and underlines the issue of temporality as a way to understand the variations and potential openness in perception. Ethological research works as a double of the 1920s and 1930s avant-garde discourse of technological (mostly cinematic) perception as radical anti-Cartesian probing.

The next chapter continues along the routes paved by the avant-garde. The early surrealist movement was very interested in insects, and the chapter uses the research of Roger Caillois into the spatial worlds of insects as an opening to discuss the metamorphosis of space, temporality, and devouring mimicry. Later adopted by Lacan in his theories of the mirror stage, the early surrealist discourses give a hint of how to move beyond the phenomenal affect worlds of the human being toward animality as a mythical but also intensive force. As Caillois's work on play and imitation has been adopted as part of game studies, what would a more elaborated "insect approach" to worlds of gaming and play look like, something that would again challenge the anthropomorphic way of looking at the genealogy of technics and evolution?

Mediated by a short theoretical intermezzo, the second half of the book focuses on post–World War II discourse relating to media as insects. The aim of this part is to articulate how insects and animal affects were directly addressed in technological contexts from research into the cybernetic loops between machines and animals, the perception qualities of machines and animals, the simulations of swarm behavior and semiintelligent systems, and, in recent years, media art from the feminist film *Teknolust* by Lynn Hershman-Leeson to some other key examples. The second half of the book tracks the technological synthesis of the affective qualities of animal and insect life, a contracting of the intensive ecological potential of animals as they were understood in the cybernetic and digital discourses of recent decades. A simulation of movement, perception, swarming, and even evolution amounted to a new kind of approach between biological and technological beings in which the intensive life of the hybrids was discussed not only in terms of cyborgs but increasingly in those of insectlike distributed systems.

In this context, chapter 5 moves from cybernetics to a related set of questions developed by researchers of animal perception. Cybernetics has been identified by a plethora of cultural theorists and historians as the crucial mode of interfacing animal affects and technological systems, with a special emphasis on, for example, Norbert Wiener's work. However, the ideas offered by Gilbert Simondon in his writings from the 1950s and 1960s offer a much more intensive and embodied understanding of information, communication, and individuation. In this context, the chapter discusses Karl von Frisch's research into bee dancing and communication in the 1950s as well as briefly reviewing the "cybernetic zoology" of W. Grey Walter with his robotic tortoise. The chapter addresses the need for an embodied understanding of communication that is promoted through the concepts of assemblage, individuation, and transduction.

Similar themes are continued in chapter 6, which analyzes new techniques of computer-generated imaging that spread from computer science and visualizing experiments (e.g., in artificial life research) to mainstream New Hollywood cinema. Addressing the theme of insects in 1980s and 1990s cinematic culture, the chapter thematizes the culture of the visual as a culture of calculation based on insect models of automated systems. The visual creations, "biomorphs," that were an example of nature's computational power harnessed to create complex forms in Richard Dawkins's work, provide the key example to connect the computational powers of nature to the swarms and flocks on the visual screen. However, to address the shortcomings of the neo-Darwinist discourse in digital culture, the chapter turns to the swarm algorithms developed by Craig Reynolds. In the 1980s, his "boids" figures emerged as key modes of programming collective behavior, and the chapter uses the idea of boids to address ethologies of software.

Chapter 7 continues along cinematic lines but engages with the film *Teknolust* (2002). It presents an alternative cinematic account of bio-technologies in contemporary culture through the lives of three self-reproducing automata. The automata break free from the home lab of bioscientist Rosetta (Tilda Swinton) and embark on a life of their own, trespassing the boundaries between worlds of computer-generated habitat and the analog world outside computers. The chapter analyzes the figurations of sex, sexuality, and reproduction in *Teknolust,* which presents a refreshing account of the biopower of contemporary digital culture. In the context of feminist sexual difference, Braidotti has been keenly promoting figurations of insects and animals as efficient philosophical concepts of nomadic cultural analysis. Such alien forms of affects and sensations offer a challenge to normalized figurations of the male body as the normalized mold of being. Insects, among other figures, creep into the supposedly intact but in fact crack-filled phantasm of the body of late modernity, revealing the distributed and assembled nature of any body taken to be natural. Insects, then, are a parallel mode of becoming in terms of bodily metamorphoses but also as carriers of nomadic, energetic thought that turn from an emphasis on metaphors and meaning to one on metamorphoses and temporal bodies.[63] We are constantly penetrated and accompanied by a panorama of nonhuman forces and "mutations of desire" (Parisi), something that the figure of the cyborgs perhaps tried to convey but of which more recent variations closer to animals have been more pertinent examples, as is also argued by Elizabeth Grosz. In this context, *Teknolust* demonstrates the new forms of subjectivity imagined and glued as part of the intimacy between female agency and new technologies.

The concluding epilogue draws together themes discussed earlier and addresses recent (new) media artworks in which the theme of insects is analyzed. Seeing insects as a powerful mode of distributed intelligence, harnessing nature and experimenting with nonhuman modes of sensation, such insect media can be also be seen as philosophical thought experiments. The epilogue also addresses some themes of new media art in recent media philosophy, for example, Mark Hansen's writings.

In closing, a few words of clarification. Insects are not the only phylum of animals I analyze in this book, but they provide a generic opening for my interests in this "bestial" media archaeology of animal affects. Why insects? Not only have animals been of media historical importance in general; insects can be seen as "the privileged case study,"[64] as Eugene Thacker notes: they are paradigmatic examples of the many, the emerging swarm order that questions notions of sovereignty, life, and organization that are so crucial for current articulations of politics, networks, and technology. If the human has been the starting point in most accounts of Western political philosophy (and also the philosophy of organization), insects provide a crucial difference within that mode of thought. Of course "insects" is a huge category that comprises in its modern definition a subclass of arthropods of more than 900,000 species from dragonflies to bees, grasshoppers to moths, flies to ants, bugs to praying mantises. This book tends to focus on just a few selected ones that have been dear to popular culture and designers of technology: bees, ants, wasps, spiders, and a few other examples, which exhibit a curious creative relationship with the world. Although the twentieth century has had its fair share of reductive accounts that see various "minuscule forms of life"—whether behavioral traits of social insects (sociobiology) or genes, for example—as the defining stuff of life, this book defines this "stuff" only through relations of externality and change and hence is far from suggesting that everything is already defined and set for us by and in nature.

In addition, there is a curious, nearly ephemeral side to insects. They are probably furthest from the image of domesticated animals that have been contained and rationalized as part of the pet culture of modern society.[65] Yet, as noted throughout the book, insects have also gradually been made part of the diagrammatics of the contemporary media condition as uncanny models of sensation and organization. However, they remain radically nonhuman: as often presented in science fiction, insects are from outer space; they remain alien to human life. They present a curious threat but perhaps also a possibility of a future nonhuman life. In the communist-fearing United States of the 1950s, insects were models of the cold other, this time seen through the lenses of cold war politics. For David Cronenberg, the connection and fear were more intimate: perhaps insects are already inside us, perhaps there is an uncanny animality within us. In his remake of the 1958 Kurt Neumann film *The Fly,* Cronenberg's 1980s vision presented the metamorphosis of the protagonist, Seth Brundle, as stemming from the molecular level. Despite the monstrous change, Brundle himself sees it as merely expressing the dormant continuity between the animal and the human: "I'm an insect who dreamt he was a man, and loved it. But now the dream is over, and the insect is awake." The molecular metamorphosis expresses itself on the level of affects and percepts, the way the Brundle-fly relates to his/its environment. What distinguishes this new hybrid from humans are its new strengths, energy, body hair, perceptual capabilities, and sexual appetite.[66] Cronenberg's film can be seen as a cartography of human and insect affects. The medium of film continues the work of the microscope in examining the worlds of animality. However, whereas the microscope was embedded in the scientific practices of recording, analyzing, and reproducing the motions, percepts, and capabilities of the animal, Cronenberg's project is much more poetic and works in terms of an ecosophy: a catalysis of animal forces for the society of technical media and a mapping of singularities of the new forces stemming from the assemblages of technics.[67]

Swarms, metamorphoses, and weird sensations are easily produced by digital technologies of imaging, but this theme is not reducible to technological possibilities. Hence, there is also a philosophical side to these simple animals, constantly present in this book as well. The insect becomes a philosophical figure for a cultural analysis of the nonhuman basics of media technological modernity, labeled not by the conscious unity of Man but by the swarming, distributed intelligence of insects, collective agents, and uncanny potentials of the "autonomity of affect."[68]

NINETEENTH-CENTURY INSECT TECHNICS
The Uncanny Affects of Insects

Man is inclined to congratulate himself upon his wonderful progress, forgetting that in many cases he has yet to reach the degree of perfection seen in numerous animals. The recently developed monoplane, for example, does not differ greatly in its general proportions from those of our hawk moths, and the biplane is almost a duplicate of a pair of dragon flies, one flying above the other; both models that have been favorites in the insect world for thousands of years. Dare any man say that our latest advancement in applied science, namely, the radio telephone, is more than a relatively crude modification of methods which have been used by insects for countless ages?

—E. P. Felt, "Bugs and Antennae"

This chapter offers key background for subsequent chapters and revolves around three themes, all of which characterize the nineteenth century:

1. The rise of modern biology from the start of the century, and the emergence of its now most prominent representative, Charles Darwin, with his theory of evolution. The Great Chain of Divine Being was gradually confronted with a temporally radical and materialist theory of evolution in which the continuity of life forms was intimately coupled with and restricted by their environment. This temporality also opened up a future for forms of life so far unknown.

2. The emergence of modern technical media, from photography to cinema and telegraphy, all of which presented a new sphere of capturing and reproducing sensations and communication. Psychophysiological scientific research into the bodily grounding of sensation was intimately

coupled with the new capitalist sphere of production of perceptions and communication.

3. The appearance of insects as a special topic of interest among trained professional entomologists and vast ranks of amateur devotees. There was continuous work on collecting, inspecting, and classifying insect genera and individuals in their capabilities, and the insect craze spread gradually as part of the popular culture of the century and also affected views on technology and modern society. Much as anthropology transported knowledge concerning primitive societies as part of the cultural discussion and theories of society in the nineteenth century, entomological research suggested how instinctive primitive forms of life might contribute to contemporary understanding of technical and rational life. In other words, such discourses pointed not only toward the fascinating pre- and nonhuman worlds of evolution but, through different pathways, to a pre-intelligent way of perceiving the creation of the artifice and hence technology.

Entomology spread much beyond its confines and interfaced its agenda with those of technology and philosophy. However, the science of insects was not part of physics or physiology or any of the key sciences of the century. It was often practiced by enlightened amateurs and enthusiasts. This makes it more interesting, however. In a way, it became a mode of minor knowledge, not only in terms of its objects, which needed new techniques of visual culture to make them visible, but also in terms of its transversal links. Entomology had direct economic links that made it a crucial enterprise of the century: to protect crops from insects. Yet there is also a much more fluid way to see entomology as a traveling science or a practice: a movement from insect research to theological meditations, philosophy, popular cultural narratives, and, for example, physiological mapping of the capacities and affects of animal bodies.[1]

This chapter focuses on what I call insect technics and addresses the idea of a history of technology in the primitive life of insects, a theme that emerged during the nineteenth century. This is evident from classics of entomology such as *An Introduction to Entomology; or, Elements of the Natural History of Insects: Comprising an Account of Noxious and Useful Insects, of Their Metamorphoses, Hybernation, Instinct* (1815–1826), by William Kirby and William Spence. The book was a huge success, published in four volumes, and published through several editions. It can be said to have been a popular classic, marked by a pre-Darwinian mix of science and religion. The two writers have often been referred to as the fathers of entomology; Spence founded the Society of Entomologists of London in 1833, and Kirby was well known for his extensive studies and the collections he made while working at the service of Higher Forces (the Christian God, that is). The example of Kirby and Spence evinces the early interest in this kind of an articulation.

From entomological discourses this chapter turns to the philosophy of technology and biopolitics, moving toward Henri Bergson's biologically inspired philosophy to shed light on the idea of animals as innovators. It is my aim to show that insect technics was a transversal theme articulated in a plethora of contexts throughout the nineteenth century and that the diagrammatic practices of biopower and notions of insect technics intertwined. In the midst of the nineteenth century, the importance of animal affects in the diagrammatic construction of modern technological culture was realized through various practical projects. At the same time, in philosophy the insect theme offered a way of understanding how to approach the instinctual worlds of contracting milieus into assemblages that function as technological elements. This is where short-circuiting Bergson's philosophy as part of current media theory suggests how to think media through its nonhuman forces.

THE MICROCOSMOS OF INSECTS

To a particular pair of theologically inspired naturalists, Kirby and Spence, insects, despite the normal opinion of them as noxious and filthy, expressed nature's fullest "power and skill." This power becomes evident via mimicry, with insects capable of robbing "the trees of their leaves to form for themselves artificial wings, so exactly do they resemble them in their form, substance, and vascular structure,"[2] or expressive of forms, colors, and mathematical figures that exceed the model they are imitating. Mimicry is here a passage or a vector that shows that all nature is connected, that there is a layer of intensity that characterizes all of the expressions of nature. Insects are expressive not only of their specific genealogical record and evolution but of a much broader field of nature— visual elements from peacocks' tails to the feathers of birds, movement of clouds and undulations of water, geometric forms and hieroglyphical symbols. It is as if insects were a microcosmical doubling of other animals, a kind of intensification of potentials of life: "The bull, the stag, the rhinoceros, and even the hitherto vainly sought for unicorn, have in this respect many representatives among insects."[3]

In *Introduction to Entomology,* this theme echoes quite evidently the idea of the Great Chain of Being, the order of nature guaranteed by God. Angels and "spirits of the just" might be the expressions of a higher order of perfection, but insects, according to Kirby and Spence, despite their tiny size and seeming irrelevance, are indexes of forces to be accounted for:

> That creatures, which in the scale of being are next to nonentities, should be elaborated with so much art and contrivance, have such a number of parts both internal and external, all so highly finished and each so nicely calculated to answer its end; that they should include in this evanescent form such a variety of organs of perception and instruments of motion, exceeding in number and peculiarity of structure those of other animals. . . . —truly these wonders and miracles declare to every one who attends to the subject, *"The hand that made us is divine."*[4]

The natural theological tradition that continued as an influential mode of argumentation in the natural sciences during the nineteenth century was keen to underline nature as an expression of divinity. Nature was a model for proper Christian education, organization, the values of society, and an industrious lifestyle.[5]

In the classical Great Chain of Being, below God, the angels, and man came the animals with their own hierarchies. Wild beasts reigned, then came useful animals, and below them were domesticated forms of life. Insects were not too high on this ladder. Spiders and bees were recognized as useful, but flies and beetles ranked at the bottom of the chain. So despite the affinities Kirby and Spence wanted to create with this *scala naturae,* their version was a bit different, with insects and angels at times exhibiting common traits.

In fact, at times religious attitudes went hand in hand with a celebration of the complexity of minuscule life. Étienne-Louis Geoffroy, in his *Histoire abrégée des insectes* (1765), argues for the centrality of insects and even for their philosophical inspection, because their minuscule and delicate composition exhibits the constructions of a marvellous design.[6] From Aristotle and Pliny the Elder to modern entomologists such as Muffet and Swammerdam, various researchers have contributed to excavating the microcosmos of insect characteristics. In 1824 Thomas Say, in his *American Entomology*, echoed a similar attitude in his motto: "Each moss, Each shell, each crawling insect, holds a rank Important in the plan of Him who framed This scale of beings."[7] In natural theological texts, insects were seen as a celebration of God's powers in their alternative and surprising habits, singular instincts, industrious nature, and various forms of work.[8] Insects and their ingenious and complex form of organization were sure proofs of the powers of the Creator.

The artist Kevin Murray has suggested in his brief overview of the insect media of the network age that there was a dualist enterprise in the nineteenth-century approaches to insects—the pious exploration ante Darwin and the materialist one after him.[9] Yet, as I argue, this dualism is not completely watertight, and there is a fundamental theme of technics that connects the earlier more religious takes on nature and primitive life with the Darwinian take. Like his predecessors, Darwin saw nature as a force of perfection even though he emphasised the material force of natural selection behind this evolution. Darwin himself did not renounce the Creator's impact in the *Origin of Species* (1859) but underlined using similar rhetoric that the machine of nature produces complex, interconnected perfection that has superseded man's achievements (expressed in domestic breeding):

> It is interesting to contemplate an entangled bank, clothed with many plants of many kinds, with birds singing on the bushes, with various insects flitting about, and with worms crawling through the damp earth, and to reflect that these elaborately constructed forms, so different from each other, and dependent on each other in so complex a manner, have all been produced by laws acting around us.[10]

Kirby and Spence's approach probably attracted the attention it did not only because of its catchy language but also because of what could be called its ethological touch (even though the term in its more modern usage became commonplace only after the turn of the century). Insects were approached as living and interacting entities that are intimately coupled with their environment, yet presented as active participants and constructors. Insects intertwine with human lives (via "direct and indirect injuries caused by insects, injuries to our living vegetable property but also direct and indirect benefits derived from insects") but also engage in ingenious building projects, stratagems, sexual behavior, and other expressive forms of motion, perception, and sensation. Instead of adhering to a strict taxonomic account of the interrelations between insect species by documenting the insects' forms, growth, or structural anatomy, the ethnography of insects in *An Introduction to Entomology* is traversed by the fantastical spirit of the curiosity cabinet. Insects are war machines, like the horsefly *(Tabanus L.),* for example: "Wonderful and various are the weapons that enable them to enforce their demand. What would you think of any large animal that should come to attack you with a tremendous apparatus of knives and lancets issuing from its mouth?"[11] The tools are described as intimate parts of the organism:

> Reamur [sic] has minutely described the ovipositor, or singular organ by which these insects are enabled to bore a round hole in the skin of the animal and deposit their eggs in the wound. The anus of the female is furnished with a tube of a corneous substance, consisting of four pieces, which, like the pieces of a telescope, are retractile within each other.[12]

EXPLORATIONS

Insofar as optical parallels were used, innate insect capacities paralleled another key nineteenth-century theme, that of artificial light. "The Age of Machinery" (as coined by Carlyle in 1829) presented new kinds of expressions of human intellect that put nature to its own use, but these were disparaged by our entomologists, who argued that the most perfect forms of illumination, tools, and artifice were found in simple forms of life:

> Providence has supplied them with an effectual substitute [for artificial light]—a luminous preparation or secretion, which has all the advantages of our lamps and candles without their inconveniencies; which gives light sufficient to direct their motions, while it is incapable of burning; and whose lustre is maintained without needing fresh supplies of oil or the application of the snuffers.[13]

Insects' powers of building continuously attracted the early entomological gaze. Buildings of nature were described as more fabulous than the pyramids of Egypt or the aqueducts of Rome. In this weird parallel world, such minuscule and admittedly small-brained entities as termites were pictured as akin to the inhabitants of ancient monarchies and empires of Western civilization. If the Victorian era valued the history of civilization, which, throughout the nineteenth century, increasingly became an integral part of museum collections in Europe, this analogy between insects and ancients suggested not a denigration of the ancients but a curious kind of a valuation that expressed a particular interest in microcosmical worlds. Indeed, insects were not seen as small, insignificant animals but were in Victorian England tokens of civilization and taste, with insect motifs found in dresses and jewelry.[14]

Whereas the imperialist powers of Europe, led by Britain, headed for overseas conquests, the mentality of exposition and mapping new terrains also impacted nongeographical fields. The seeing eye, a key figure of hierarchical analyzing power, could also be a nonhuman eye, like that of the fly, which, according to Steven Connor, can be seen as the recurring "radically alien mode of entomological vision,"[15] consisting of four thousand sensors. Hence, in 1898 one author toyed with the idea of "photographing through a fly's eye" as a mode of experimental vision— one also able to catch Queen Victoria with "the most infinitesimal lens known to science," that of a dragonfly.[16]

Jean-Jacques Lecercle notes that the Victorian enthusiasm for entomology and insect worlds was related to a general discourse of natural history that, as a genre, defined the century. Through the themes of exploration and taxonomy, Lecercle claims that *Alice in Wonderland* can be read as a key novel of the era in its evaluation and classification of various life worlds beyond the human. Like Alice in the 1865 novel, the reader experiences new landscapes and exotic species as an armchair explorer of worlds not merely extensive but also opened up by an intensive gaze into alien microcosmoses. Uncanny phenomenal worlds tie together the entomological quest; Darwin inspired both biological accounts of curious species and Alice's adventures into imaginative worlds of twisting logic. In taxonomic terms, the entomologist was surrounded by a new cult of archiving in private and public collections. New modes of visualizing and representing insect forms of life produced a new phase of taxonomy as public craze instead of scientific tool. But here again, the wonder worlds of Alice or the nonsense poet Edward Lear are the ideal points of reference for the nineteenth-century natural historian and entomologist:

> And it [nonsense] is part of a craze for discovering and classifying new species. Its advantage over natural history is that it can invent those species (like the Snap-dragon-fly) in the imaginative sense, whereas natural history can invent them only in the archaeological sense, that is discover what already exists. Nonsense is the entomologist's dream come true, or the Linnaean classification gone mad, because gone creative.[17]

For Alice, the feeling of not being herself and "being so many different sizes in a day is very confusing,"[18] which of course is something incomprehensible to the caterpillar she encounters. It is not queer for the caterpillar, whose mode of being is defined by the metamorphosis and the various perception-/action-modulations it brings about. It is only the suddenness of the becoming-insect of Alice that dizzies her. A couple of years later, in *The Population of an Old Pear-Tree; or, Stories of Insect Life* (1870), an everyday meadow is disclosed as a vivacious microcosmos in itself. The harmonious scene, "like a great amphitheatre,"[19] is filled with life that easily escapes the (human) eye. Like Alice, the protagonist wandering in the meadow is "lulled and benumbed by dreamy sensations,"[20] which, however, transport him suddenly into new perceptions and bodily affects. What is revealed to our boy hero in this educational novel fashioned in the style of travel literature (connecting it thus to the colonialist contexts of its age) is a world teeming with sounds, movements, sensations, and insect beings (huge spiders, cruel mole-crickets, energetic bees) that are beyond the human form (despite the constant tension of such narratives as educational and moralizing tales that anthropomorphize affective qualities into human characteristics). True to entomological classification, a big part of the novel is reserved for the structural-anatomical differences of the insect, but the affects of insects relating to their surroundings is under scrutiny.

ANTHROPOLOGIES OF TECHNOLOGY

As precursors of ethnology, the natural historical quests (whether archaeological, entomological, or imaginative) expressed an appreciation for phenomenal worlds differing from that of the human who was equipped with two hands, two eyes, and two feet. In a way, this entailed a kind of extended Kantianism interested in the a priori conditions of alternative life-worlds. Curiously the obsession with new phenomenal worlds was connected to the emergence of new technologies of movement, sensation, and communication (all challenging the Kantian apperception of man as the historically constant basis of knowledge and perception). Nature, viewed through a technological lens, was gradually becoming the new "storehouse of invention"[21] that would entice inventors into perfecting their developments. What is revealed is also a shift in the Victorian understanding technology—a shift that marks the rise of modern technology by the end of the nineteenth century. This could be also called an anthropological and an ethnological turn. As Georges Canguilhem notes, the new appreciation of technology as art decoupled it from a strictly rational way of seeing technology. In contrast to Descartes's understanding of the equivalence of mechanics and living organisms, at the end of the eighteenth century Kant suggested a reconsideration of technics in terms of human history. Skill preceded knowledge, just as machines preceded the scientific knowledge of them:

> Art, regarded as a human skill, differs from science (as ability differs from knowledge) in the same way that a practical aptitude differs from a theoretical faculty, as technique differs from theory. What one is capable of doing, as soon as we merely know what ought to be done and therefore are sufficiently cognizant of the desired effect, is not called art. Only that which man, even if he knows it completely, may not therefore have the skill to accomplish belongs to art.[22]

Canguilhem maps the rise of a philosophy of technology that sought to find the origins of the skill of art in the anthropological layers of human nature. As one of the key thinkers of early philosophy of technology, Ernst Kapp introduced his famous theories of technology as an extension of the human species in 1877 in *Grundlinien einer Philosophie der Technik: Zur Entstehungsgeschichte der Cultur aus neuen Gesichtspunkten.* In this early prime example of later cyborg theories and ideas of organ projection, Kapp proceeded to think of technology as based on the human body. The human being is the measure of all things *(Der Mensch das Maass der Dinge),* a proposition that was meant as a continuation of the Kantian theme of perceptual worlds. There was no way to break beyond what we as human beings perceive, which was not a reason for mourning but an instance of pride. For Kapp, loyal to the Western tradition of thought, the human being as the possessor of a self-conscious mind was the privileged caretaker of the natural world. Yet Kapp's image was more complex than a simple dualism of mind versus body. In fact, man is also his physiological body, which extends as part of the world, interfacing the inner with the outer reality. Kapp was highly appreciative of the physiological understanding of the bodily substance of being but regarded the human being not as emerging *from* the animal but as coming *after* the animal.[23] This paradigm relates to his curious interpretation of the recapitulation thesis, proposed by Ernst Häckel. Häckel believed that the embryo of any organism recapitulates in its ontogenesis the phylogenetic history of its species, a theory that underlined that every individual was in a way a perfect condensation of the whole history of its species. Kapp adapted this theory to an anthropological and world historical frame: each human being is a recapitulation of the whole of the animal kingdom, the potential of any animal whatsoever.[24]

Through the human form, technology and the animal kingdom are hence continuously connected. Yet for Kapp, the human hand remained the ur-form of technics. For this contemporary of Karl Marx and former student of the Prussian state education system, the creating and laboring man qualified as superior to the nonreflexive animal. The anthropological notion of technology valued the hand as the natural tool from which artificial creation stems. Human history was the history of labor, in which work was one mode of activity *(Thätigkeit),* but only conscious activity was work. Hence, for animals work does not exist, even though bees and ants might seem industrious.[25]

The eye provides the model for the camera obscura and other artificial modes of visualization, and the muscles work in concert with new machines of industry. The telegraph is formed in parallel with the nervous system as a coevolutionary system, thereby resonating with Kapp's general anthropology of human culture. This media technological exteriorization leads to a Hegelian kind of dialectical emergence to new levels of self-consciousness, echoing later twentieth-century views inspired by McLuhan and Teilhard de Chardin.[26] Canguilhem notes, however, that this theory of the parallels between the human and insect worlds encountered severe stumbling blocks with such technologies as fire and the wheel, which clearly do not stem from the human body.[27] In the context of contemporary network technologies that operate with distributed, nonhuman speeds and logic, questioning such parallels remains relevant and is perhaps a reason that the notion of insects has persisted in high-tech media environments.

In the physiological research so dear to Kapp, the thresholds of human sensation and perception became a crucial field of research for the aspiring media culture. This development emerged alongside the need to provide information for the new rationalization and organization of human labor and what spun off into new creations of modes of sensing in the form of audiovisual media culture. The physiological understanding of the human organism provided the necessary impetus for research focused specifically on perception severed from the human observer, leading to the subsequent rationalization, reproduction, and control of physiological events. Jonathan Crary's work stands out in its media archaeological focus on the capturing of perception in physiological studies of the nineteenth century.[28] In such analysis of the physiological body, the human being serves as the storehouse of sensation and perception, as in Johannes Müller's *Handbuch der Physiologie des Menschen* (1833–40). Müller's work exemplifies research that focused on the interfacing layer of sense organs between the outer world and the inner consciousness. Senses were seen as the indispensable layer that informed animals of the environment outside them, a layer that also determined the mode of orientation for a specific animal. Tones perceived are determined by the quality of the sense of hearing, just as light and colors are qualified by the specific energy of nerves of vision.[29] Senses are seen as tools with which to grasp the world, world-forming probes, modes of folding the inside with the outside.[30]

PHYSIOLOGIES AND BIOPOLITICS

As Crary explains, Müller understood the body as a factory of decentralized actions, "run by measurable amounts of energy and labour."[31] Life was primarily a set of interconnected physiochemical processes, and the body became an inventory of mechanical capacities.[32] Not just human beings but animals and insects also were part of this storehouse. In his early work *Zur vergleichenden Physiologie des Gesichtssinns* (1826), Müller addressed the sense thresholds of insects. The later work *Handbuch der Physiologie des Menschen* (1840), especially its second part, similarly addresses the visual capacities of insects, spiders, and other "lower animals," noting the peculiar aggregate vision of insects.[33] Consider Crary's observation of how Müller, also writing as part of the Kantian legacy concerning the perceptional apparatus of human beings, nevertheless already stood at the crumbling point of Kant's conception of apperception as the crucial and indispensable synthesis of perception:

> When Müller distinguishes the human eye from the compound eyes of crustacea and insects, he seems to be citing our optical equipment as a kind of Kantian faculty that organizes sensory experience in a necessary and unchanging way. But his work, in spite of his praise of Kant, implies something quite different. Far from being apodictic or universal in nature, like the "spectacles" of time and space, our physiological apparatus is again and again shown to be defective, inconsistent, prey to illusion, and, in a crucial manner, susceptible to external procedures of manipulation and stimulation that have the essential capacity *to produce experience for the subject.*[34]

Physiological research returned the material body to the agenda of perception. From soul to the transcendental subject and on to the physiological human being, Kant's agenda found a material platform that further radicalized its conclusions. In addition to Müller's early remarks concerning animal perception and movement, the famous later experiments by Etienne-Jules Marey are relevant to our topic as well. Marey, known for his pre-cinematic research on the nature of perception and movement, occupied himself early on with animal motion. In *La Machine Animale* (1873), the creator of various mechanisms for tracing the animal body comprehensively addressed the muscular and mechanical characteristics of movement and flight of numerous classes of animals. Even though Marey acknowledged the long history of analogies between machines and animals, he underlined the importance of this parallel for contemporary research. Marey wrote that it is not only a valid parallel but also of practical use: studying animals allows us to engage with the basic principles of how mechanics work, with the additional possibility of offering a synthetic counterpart to the moving, sensing animal.[35] In an age of technical speed and movement (via railroads but also navigation and flight), Marey's underlining of the importance of research on nature and natural movement for the progress of mankind seemed to offer insights into the physical interactions of bodies with their environment. Accurate research provided a tool for optimizing certain repetitive acts and movements. This resonated with the emerging sciences of optimized labor movements, for example. Sciences of the body in movement offered ways to map the thresholds of the material body—what a body is capable of in the context of physical and mental labor—and feed those results to those trying to meet the needs of the industrial society. Pruning the body was in isomorphic relation to a macro-level standardization that characterizes industrial modernity. In the works of Marey and such people as Frederick Winslow Taylor and Frank Bunker Gilbreth, we find a form of definition and optimization of the human body as a particular capacity.[36]

In addition to exploring a number of other interests, Marey stands as one of the early pioneers of insect media. For example, human bipedal locomotion remained merely one potential example of how movement could be achieved (contrasted with, for example, the four-legged movement of horse), opening up a panorama of natural creatures to be analyzed in their discrete moments of movement. For Marey, insects were a special case of flight, interesting because of the great speed of their wing movements and the sounds emitted. In *La Machine Animale,* the issues regarding insect flight addressed were (1) the frequency of wing movement, (2) the successive positions the wings take as part of the loop of movement, (3) and how the power of motion that produces and maintains the movement develops. The same key issues were also expressed in various other publications reporting Marey's insect studies.[37] The practical dilemma was how to record the movement that was beyond capability of the human eye to perceive. On the one hand, Marey saw the acoustic traces left by movement as indexes of its frequency, but on the other hand, more accurate research equipment was needed. Proceeding from observation to potential causes, the so-called graphic method, and especially Hermann von Helmholz's invention the myograph (early 1850s) for registering movement in graphical form, provided invaluable assistance in turning continuous movement into distinctive, analyzable units.[38] Here the actual wings of insects were taken as indexes and harnessed so as to leave wing marks on a blackened paper, traces of the

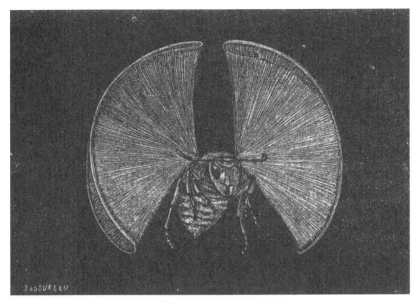

An image from Marey's *La machine animale* (1873) of a wasp exposed in motion between a ray of light and darkened paper.

points of the continuous movement.[39] The result was a graphical representation of various kinds of movements resembling beautiful abstract lithographic art. Thus it is no wonder, as Marta Braun argues in her study *Picturing Time,* that Marey's way of capturing temporal intensities in a media technological form found resonance later in modernist art, for example, in Marcel Duchamp's work, where Marey's positivism was turned into a fascination for temporal perception detached from the everyday habitual human way of seeing the world. A new way of seeing opened up in scientific and media technological contexts (later celebrated by such filmmakers and writers as Jean Epstein) that was connected to a search for new perception-/action-connections that moved beyond the human eye/hand couple.

A curious expression of Marey's interests was his artificial insect creation (1869), a tool for theoretical study. In a model construct of wings moved by an air pump and inserted on a drum, Marey was capable of reproducing the flight patterns of insects (wing-stroke patterns in the form of the numeral eight) that allowed him to measure the capacities of animals in their activity. The question was how the wings and their potential allowed such a "rapid translation of motive force."[40] Marey's experiments soon attracted interest beyond France. For example, various U.S. newspapers and publications were keen on reporting this curious interfacing of animal locomotion and artificial creation. The papers expressed the undoubted potential in Marey's research for the emerging topic of human flying. For example, *Scientific American* underlined how Marey's experiments were useful to aeronauts "and those aspiring to be aeronauts."[41] Certainly, war and the continuous effort put into finding aerial solutions to warfare was a key context in which to understand the interest in flight research. The United States had just come out of the Civil War, and France and Prussia were on the verge of their war around that time.[42]

In another example, *Harper's Monthly* underlined the fascinating prospects of Marey's apparatus, which also demonstrated the importance of coupling organs with their surroundings:

> By an improved artificial apparatus, Professor Marey has succeeded in simulating with entire accuracy the movement of the membranous wings of insects in flight, to wit: the raising of the body above a given level, and its forward motion in space. The apparatus shows clearly that it is the resistance of the air which imparts to the wings the figure-of-eight motion referred to, as the same curve was described by the wing of the artificial insect, which, of course, only received as its motor rectilineal movements of elevation and depression in the wings. It is, therefore, erroneous to say that a movement of torsion is voluntary on the part of the insect, and assimilated to the effect of the action of a helix, in screwing its way through the air.[43]

Around the 1880s, other writers were also celebrating the beauty and efficient grace of organic movement. Animals were seen in terms of smooth machines, but machines were similarly "animalized" in the works of Paul Souriau (*L'esthétique du mouvement,* 1889) and Jean Marie Guyau (*Les problèmes de l'esthetique contemporaine,* 1884). Besides analogies, the aesthetic was a realm beyond divisions into organic, inorganic, or technological spheres.[44] Similarly, the crucial techniques of walking,

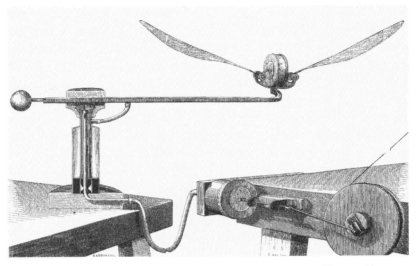

Marey's artificial insect creation pictured in *La machine animale*. The machine was designed to reproduce the insect's wing movement.

swimming, and flying stemmed from the animal locomotions, which were also of interest to James Bell Pettigrew. Pettigrew dedicated a whole book, *Animal Locomotion* (1874), to the issue of how animal physiology is tuned toward certain movements, as were some of the beetle wings he discussed in terms of "sustainers or gliders in flight."[45] The meticulous information Pettigrew gathered helped him to understand the physiological (or perhaps, in a sense, media technical) conditions of certain movements, something that was channeled into his dissertation on aeronautics.

Such research is of special interest in the context of the physiological capture of animal life, which was succinctly translated as part of the creation of new media technologies. As Pasi Väliaho has argued, Marey's stands as an interesting interface between the experimentalization of life (sensation, locomotion, etc.) and cinema. For Väliaho, both are defined by their quest to "quantify, enhance and perhaps even to (re)produce the 'animal machine.'"[46] Through the creation of measurability, measurable abstract yardsticks, the animal was translated from an intensive assemblage into an extensive, spatialized temporality that could be repeated—

even without the animal. In a corresponding fashion, Akira Mizuta Lippit has referred to the appropriation of animals by technical media "for the symbolic and actual powers they represented."[47] The disappearance of animals from the actual living worlds of urbanized Western societies was paralleled by the incorporation of animal affects and intensities in the emerging media technologies of modernity, cinema at the forefront.

The graphic inscription machines of Marey (and the whole field of physiology dedicated to excavating the energies of the body) worked beyond the hermeneutic register of meaning and obediently translated the language of nature into visual form. Väliaho notes that this was a creation of a certain kind of "degree zero" of perception, severed from the human observer, registering life before the intervention of hermeneutic meaning making. Writing of the registering machines, Marey noted:

> These machines are not only destined to replace the observer, in which case they perform their role with overwhelming supremacy, but they also have their own domain where nothing can replace them. When the eye ceases seeing, the ear hearing and the sense of touch feeling, or when our senses give us deceptive appearances, these machines are like new senses of astounding precision.[48]

But if the graphic method of registering animal life referred to and created a technological plane severed from the conscious observer, they also implied the intensity inherent in other forms of life than human. For Marey the machines marked a new mode of sensation of "astounding precision," but in parallel movement, animal life introduced the idea that the Kantian determination of the perceptive qualities of the human being were not the only ones possible. Instead, there was something akin to a foreign planet of perceptions waiting to be excavated and reproduced. This reflects perhaps the key alternatives of understanding technology in terms of either "intelligence" (as the ability to select and reproduce wanted actions) or instinct as nonreflexive, continuous folding with the world. The capturing of instinctive life by analytic intelligence is one way to express the interfacing of continuous life processes with quantified discrete units of analysis, a point to which I shall soon return with the aid of Bergson.

Despite a continuous interest in the physiological human being in experimental and theoretical analysis, storehouses for invention were continuously deterritorialized from the human body to include varying phenomenal worlds, researched both by physiologists but increasingly also by entomologists, who provided alluring newspaper stories of the uncanny perceptual capacities of insects, from vision through compound eyes to locomotion on six legs. As in the case of research on flying, the approximately 340-million-year-old insect innovation was much later turned into part of the technologies of movement of modernization.

Marey was one of most noted researchers, and his interest in the analysis of living processes of various kinds (from simple forms of vegetative life to complex expressions such as the human being) was connected to the agenda of biopower as a tracking of not only actual but also potential modes of action, sensation, and perception. As Foucault made evident, biopower was a new mode of taking the human species as the object of power and politics in its biological being.

Giorgio Agamben explains how the question of life and living became a crucial feature of the rise of modern state and biopower, emerging on the basic differentiation of animal life ("defined by its relation to an external world") and "organic life" (the repetitious processes of unconscious functions such blood circulation, respiration, excretion, etc.). Despite Foucault's emphasis on the human body, animals were also integrated, as species and as expressing nonhuman potentials, into the new networks of power and knowledge. The new apparatus of capture emerging during the nineteenth century did not focus solely on the social life of human beings but increasingly on life beyond a particular living body, life as an organic, anonymous process that could be analyzed, defined, and also reproduced beyond its particular substrate.[49]

However, what Rosi Braidotti has emphasized is that we should not see biopower merely as taking "life" as the object of new mechanisms of control and exploitation. The new regimes of biopower of modernity are not just parasitically objectifying life, which would lead to an unsupportable dualist position. Instead, life as the articulation of *bios* (social life) and *zoe* (animal life) is the subject of new modulations of life in the age of biotechnologies; the intensive regimes of life are never just exhausted in the capture that commodifies the minuscule intensive elements, but it is an inventiveness that exceeds the contemporary capitalist understanding of it.[50]

INSECT TECHNICS

Darwin had given the original and the still most famous impetus to think of nature as a force of "perfection" in the *Origin of Species*. For him, natural selection was a kind of immanent process that allowed structures to evolve into perfected forms. This evolution was a continuous and continuing process, implying nature as a kind of a perfection machine:

> When we see any structure perfected for any particular habit, as the wings of a bird for flight, we should bear in mind that animals displaying early transitional grades of the structure will seldom continue to exist to the present day, for they will have been supplanted by the very process of perfection through natural selection.[51]

Yet it was Henri Bergson, writing years later in his *L´évolution créatrice* (1907), who suggested that we could differentiate the diverse modes of organisms and tools to shed light on the problem of evolution. Bergson was a diligent critic of certain modes of Darwinism that were too keen on imposing passivity and habituation with the environment as the goals of organisms and evolution. Instead, as Elizabeth Grosz notes, in Bergson's view life has no goal or *telos*. It is a mode of differentiation whose future forms we are unable to decipher. Evolution works by mistakes and deviations and is far from a linear enterprise of smooth progress. This approach implies a radical openness to a variety of forms of life beyond our perceptual world or even carbon-based life as we know it.[52] Here Grosz points toward thinking of Bergson as a precursor to contemporary artificial life scientists and the quest for *potential* forms of life. Indeed, Bergson seems to occupy a key position in the realization that the more primitive forms of life could also be integrated into a novel understanding of what life, artifice, and matter are. In recent years, Grosz has worked to connect Bergson but also Darwin to a neomaterialist understanding of, for example, technology but also feminist cultural analysis. In what follows, I rely much on Grosz's recent writings.

For Bergson, life is a process of overcoming itself, a kind of a sense that is immanent to this process of striving. Bergson read this into a diagram of differentiation in which, first, animal life is differentiated from plant life (immobile) and second, animal life is divided into instinctive and intelligent. The divisions are not exclusive, however. There remains a potential of becoming-plant in animals and of becoming-animal in plants, which suggests the continuously open-ended orientation of the world that defies predetermined mechanistics or thinking in terms of "essences."[53]

As said, in animals, two tendencies reign: instinct and intelligence. Bergson insisted on seeing the mode of instinct not merely as an automated response a primitive animal (such as an insect) gives to a stimulus but in addition as involving "discernment and attunement" to the animal's environment.[54] The insect has, in Bergson's view, "two modes of action on the material world," either creating a direct means via its own organism or constructing an indirect assemblage that acts as an instrument with which to fashion "inorganic matter."[55] The body and structure of an insect can become its natural tools, as Bergson wrote. The main difference from tools as they were understood in early twentieth-century culture is that in the case of insects, the tools are their own bodies and tendencies. In this context, Bergson's ideas of the force of natural instinct as a machine of perfection sound close to those of Darwin:

> Instinct finds the appropriate instrument at hand: this instrument, which makes and repairs itself, which presents, like all works of nature, an infinite complexity of detail combined with a marvelous simplicity of function, does at once, when required, what it is called upon to do, without difficulty and with a perfection that is wonderful.[56]

As Grosz notes, Bergson thought that various forms of life (plants, insects, and vertebrates) are ways of responding to the events and problems that "nature addresses to the living."[57] Here, one way of conceptualizing this would be in terms of technology, which Grosz in another context sees as the "inevitable result of the encounter between life and matter, life and things, the consequence of the living's capacity to utilize the nonliving (and the living) *prosthetically.*"[58] Here, instinct becomes one prosthetical/technological solution to a coupling with an environment and the plane of problems it posits. Curiously, we then find in Bergson an orientation toward instinct–insect–technology in which tools are not separated from the whole of the living organism. Instead, there is a new form of holistic assemblage that acts as a technics in itself beyond a binary setting of natural instincts versus intelligent technics.[59]

In contrast to instinct, intelligence is another form of technology/

orientation, but it is not any "better": "Instinct perfected is a faculty of using and even of constructing organizing instruments; intelligence perfected the faculty of making and using unorganized instruments."[60] Actually, tools constructed by reflexive and intelligent orientation are not organically coupled to the user and remain "imperfect." Paraphrasing Bergson, tools of intelligence might be hard to handle, but because they are molded from "unorganized matter," they can be adjusted to a diverse number of goals and uses, which simultaneously raises the user ("the living being") to a new level of capability in relation to its surroundings, giving it "an unlimited number of powers."[61] This is actually to a certain extent reminiscent of Kapp's ideas of humans as the condensation point of history in the sense that the human as an intelligent tool-maker can transcend his given powers. Bergson continues:

> Whilst [intelligence] is inferior to the natural instrument for the satisfaction of immediate wants, its advantage over it is greater, the less urgent the need. Above all, it reacts on the nature of the being that constructs it; for in calling on him to exercise a new function, it confers on him, so to speak, a richer organization, being an artificial organ by which the natural organism is extended. For every need that it satisfies, it creates a new need; and so, instead of closing, like instinct, the round of action within which the animal tends to move automatically, it lays open to activity an unlimited field into which it is driven further and further, and made more and more free.[62]

Here it is obvious that Bergson appreciated the intelligent design of artificial organs, which he and many of his generation saw as opening new modes of being in the world. It is notable that Bergson saw intelligence as opening up whole new worlds by extending the capacities of the organism. Whereas he saw instinct as something that gives more direct access to the world of things and is perhaps in a more immanent relation to its surroundings, the nature of intelligence allows more room for orientation and hesitation. It implies knowledge of relations instead of the "material knowledge of instinct."[63] This ability of intelligent knowledge and being to "transcend [an animal's] own nature," however, in no way implies a depreciation of instinct. On the contrary, it is underlined as a more perfect form of inventing. Animals are in general inventors, Bergson thought at the turn of the century, but for animals this invention happens mainly through their bodies, which become pragmatic and experimental probes looking for resonating surroundings. For humans, the instruments are something outside of the body, which also affect the whole organization of the body, as Grosz argues in her reading of Bergson's biotechnological thoughts.[64] As John Mullarkey notes, Bergson's idea of instinct was that of a mechanism whose relations are felt rather than thought in an abstraction.[65] Abstraction certainly has been the normal way to think of the coupling of science and technology during modernity. Here, however, the instinct approach points to an understanding of technics as affects, as relations that are concretely felt by the participants in a systematic means of participation. Instinct and intelligence are separated by the objects around which they revolve: instinct taps into the real (but perhaps not always actualized) relations of the world, and intelligence works on abstract relations that are available for conceptualizing thought.[66] Here instincts work as a sign of the continuity of the world instead of the way intelligence works, abstracting, analyzing, and introducing divisions in order to control and reproduce the intensive instinctive processes.

INSTINCT

In several ways, Bergson's notion of instinct can be seen as part of the biological context of his age, and yet gives it a new direction. He was far from unique in his interest in instinct as a specific mode of animal action. Instinct was often seen as the characteristic that differentiates animals such as insects from humans but connects them to machines. For example, the entomologist Jean-Henri Fabre insisted on the mechanistic nature of insects as machines of inner repetition, unchanging in their predetermined nature.[67] The general understanding of the nature of simple, instinctive life often equated it with automated and mechanical reactions in contrast to reflexive intelligent life. In fact, the watershed question related to intelligence versus repeatable actions resided at the core of the age of technology: what actions could be automatized and hence transformed into a machine, and what are unique to the intelligent human being? The emergence of automated machines such as the weaving loom represented the insect in the world of technologies: both were regarded as unintelligent, guided by mechanical patterns.[68]

But life was not only about repetition. Life was often thought to be divisible into three categories: the unconscious and involuntary mechanical processes (respiration, for example), the reflex responses to environmental stimuli, and intelligent activities that follow from perception of objects, their properties, and their relations.[69] *Science* addressed this distinction in 1892 and underlined the key role instinct plays in orientation to the world, as the "schoolmaster of intelligence." For sure, intelligence played a key role in the formation of man as the handy tool-making animal, but instinct proved a curious, automated but still "intelligent" tuning to the world, expressed in the perhaps narrow but effective "tools" insects used:

> Man, in spite of the great breadth of his intellectual range, does occasionally reach something like the inherited clearness of perception and facility of execution of the insect, at special points of the circle; as, for example, in the inherited musical powers of a Mozart and other born composers, who have been capable of composing as automatically as the bee makes its cell; and I assume for both a similar intellectual gratification in the exercise of their powers. Look again at the born arithmeticians and mathematicians; or again, at the achievements of a Siemens. Great results have unquestionably been achieved by enforced attention and patient labor, but the greatest achievements arise by unconscious reflex action of the brain to the stimulus of inherited memories which evolves the idea before it even rises into consciousness. It is precisely this clearness of perception and facility of execution, recognized as genius in man, which characterize the special labors of insects and other of the lower animals in their special narrow fields.[70]

William James was resolute in his quest to dispel the mystical veil of instinct. In "What Is an Instinct" (1887), James proposed that instincts are not abstract schemes an animal might have but instead "functional correlatives of a structure."[71] They are the reflex reactions to certain stimuli and expressions of impulses, as James proposed, drawing on G. H. Schneider's *Der Thierische Wille* (1880) and its classification of sensation-impulses, perception-impulses, and idea-impulses. Moreover, humans are not any different, despite possessing the oft-suggested faculty of reason. Reason is no guardian of impulses or instincts. Only via memory is the human being (and some animals) able to reflect on her habits and use "experience" to her advantage. This is not a lessening of instincts but their channeling into future actions and habits.[72] Despite the fact that several commentators often seemed to regard instincts as closed loops of automatic behavior, it might be useful to also see instincts functioning as intensities—prelinguistic modes of intertwining the body with its surroundings (other bodies), the resonance of bodies in continuity and movement. Intensity marks this readiness for action, a threshold for interactions as affects.[73] In other words, instinct does not have to be taken merely as automated reflex-(re)action, but it can be historicized as a tendency, a potentiality that is not exhausted as a predetermined capacity. Indeed, a number of writers saw instincts as a condensation of habits that became innate through evolution. Repetition was an intensification of certain instinctual reactions.[74] Instincts were at times seen through a processuality and temporality.

This is where the parallel understanding of insects (biology) and machines (technology) starts to move away from the purely mechanical and toward the environmental. Furthermore, this is the point where Bergson stands at the center of the reorientation of both discourses. In this context, a certain Bergsonian reading hints not only at an understanding of the curious immanence that insect life exhibits as part of its surroundings but also at new ideas concerning technics and biopower. The mechanical-machine life of instinct was under continuous analysis in the biologically tuned construction of modern culture, but such figures as Bergson suggested a much more nuanced sense of understanding machines, technics, and animal bodies not as mere repetition mechanisms but as packages of affects and storehouses of inventions.

Such views also question the total separation of intelligence and humans from lower life forms of instincts. Some ideas, such as the one expressed in *Science,* raised the powers of insects to a new level that was no longer reliant on the powers of God to guarantee the fabulous nature of even the minutest expressions of his power. During the nineteenth century, an appreciation of primitive life flourished that took as one of its examples a genealogy of technics based on instinctive life. Bergson was one of the key formulators of this stance, and it fits interestingly with a search for modes of perception (technical and animal) surpassing that of the human. Inhuman and superhuman durations opened up entirely different perceptual worlds.[75] This view resonated with the general "entomological fabulation" of uncanny perceptual worlds that were catalyzed by Darwin's opening up of time to encompass genealogies of weird creatures but also a potential future of novel forms of life. Here the rise of the science fiction genre of weird, often enormously sized insectoid creatures is to be noted, at times also part of popular discourse; for example, a *New York Times* story from 1880 asked what would happen if spiders were the size of sheep and could leap "many miles at each jump" and "in a night traverse incredible distances."[76]

But, as argued earlier, the entomological classic of Kirby and Spence articulated this theme of insect-technics decades before Darwin's *Origins of Species,* offering an early example of where to start the archaeology of insect media. Naturally, a glance at recent decades of media theory shows that for decades Kappian thematics provided the prime model for understanding technologies, organs, and bodies.[77] However, that should not stop us from digging into a countermemory of animal affects that offers a different, and much more curious, image of the emergence of technics. Next I will continue this mapping of early insect "media," with a special view toward insect architecture.

GENESIS OF FORM
Insect Architecture and Swarms

No thinking man ever witnesses the complexness and yet regularity and efficiency of a great establishment, such as the Bank of England or the Post Office without marveling that even human reason can put together, with so little friction and such slight deviations from correctness, machines whose wheels are composed not of wood and iron, but of fickle mortals of a thousand different inclinations, powers, and capacities. But if such establishments be surprising even with reason for their prime mover, how much more so is a hive of bees whose proceedings are guided by their instincts alone!

–William Kirby and William Spence,
An Introduction to Entomology, volume 2

The previous chapter analyzed the notion of the insect machine expressed in early entomology, the capturing of the affects of the animal world, and the logic of the invertebrate in Bergson's philosophy. Bergson acted in the chapter as a pathway between various themes of the entomological discourse and detachment of the technological, or the artifice, from the human body. Similarly, as new media technologies such as telegraphy or various new modes of transportation seemed to deterritorialize the human being into a new assemblage of communication, perception, and thought, the idea of looking for the "origins" of technology in primitive life offered one way of grasping the uncanny affects inherent in technical media. Insects functioned as "carriers of affects," modes of operation and organization from movement and perception to communication, as in the case of ants.[1] Of course, several of the effects of the insect craze of the nineteenth and twentieth centuries have resulted from variations in scales. As Charlotte Sleigh writes, from Maria Sibylla Merian's early eighteenth-century engravings to the 1996 film *Microcosmos,* changes in scale have brought with them astonishment at the living world of the insect.[2]

One should note the changes new techniques and technologies of vision and biological analysis brought about, namely in this case the microscope. Incidentally, during the latter half of the seventeenth century, one of the earliest users and developers of the microscope was the entomologist Jan Swammerdam. Minuscule forms of life were placed under new observation, which dug into their constitutive characteristics. For example, the drawings of Robert Hooke from the seventeenth century were not, then, only aesthetic celebrations but also odes to the new visual techniques of magnification and armchair excavation. Life became a key object of the modern biopower of cultivation, and new techniques of vision and measurement eased the access to worlds before unperceived. In this sense, to be accurate, we should talk about the constitutive take modern techniques of analysis have on life such as that of insects: they are incorporated into modern forms of analysis and knowledge (in biology, technology, etc.) via their coupling with vision and measuring machines. The modern "discoveries" of worlds of viruses and bacteria were results of the new techniques and visions of modern science, and the modern understanding of insects and animal life also followed from a new assemblage of insects + new vision machines + modes of analytical knowledge.[3] A curious further theme of analysis would be how minuscule forms of life were "doubled" in popular cultural takes such as Ladislaw Starewicz's *The Insects' Christmas* (1913) or the George Herriman cartoon *Krazy Kat—The Bugologist* (1916) or a scientific short film by Percy Smith, *The Strength and Agility of Insects* (1911), in which insects demonstrate their relative powers by juggling various objects much beyond their size. In *To Demonstrate How Spiders Fly* (1909), Percy Smith had even constructed an artificial spider to simulate the way spiders construct their webs.[4]

As noted in the previous chapter, with insects the artifice, the "tool," is not distinguished from the body acting, coupling, and affecting within the world. As a medium in itself, the insect differed from the intellectual orientation of the human being. Humans (as a mode of thought and action) are able to reflexively select their tools, which gives them a guaranteed advantage. They are distinguished by certain flexibility, not confined to a certain body form but able to deterritorialize themselves. This deterritorialization of human beings from their "organic bodies" with technology was of course a central point of celebration for various ideas regarding cyborgs, but the idea can be approached as pertaining to earlier co-definitions of humans, animals, and technologies. What Bergson's ideas implicitly enable is a becoming-insect of humans with their tools, a new approach to and appreciation of the distributed affect worlds of social insects. From brains to computer systems, insect worlds to philosophy, distribution and emergence connect various modes of knowledge as keywords that we automatically connect with the more recent network culture.

In this chapter we focus more closely on the social insects and their architectural creations addressed in late nineteenth- and early twentieth-century discourse. The chapter shows that these early discourses saw natural forces as organizing immanently according to certain singularities, often expressed in terms of mathematics. Insects and nature were seen as geometricians and mathematicians, technical designers of a sort, which yielded interesting ideas relevant to our contemporary discussions of the evolution, technologies, and culture of technical media. Whereas the early ways of framing insect organization offered backup for Fordist modes of organizing society into hierarchical relations, the interest in swarms and emergent organization was already part of early twentieth-century fields of research as well. So when we move from mapping insect architecture as a force of nature to swarms and the like, it actually shows how the enthusiasm for such distributed collectivities of recent years stems from a time earlier than that of the present technological culture. It shows how the coupling of nature with the technocapitalism of recent years gains discursive support from a much earlier phase of entomology, and mapping this layer provides a more thorough understanding of the genealogy of current interest in swarms. Consequently, if we see the key political and organizational agenda of contemporary technological culture as one reliant on the insect question, this begs us to look quite closely at how insects have been gradually integrated as part of the creation of media culture, key concepts of body politics, and the diagrammatic capture of "animality" as an affect, an intensity. So the question is, Where, then, lies the potential radicality of swarms and the "insect model" when it has already, from the early days on, been integrated as part of the capitalist and bureaucratic models of creation, connected to Fordist models of labor, disciplinary modes of spatialization and control, and hierarchical political structurations?

In addition to making discursive historical points, the chapter argues for a materialist analysis of animal behavior that challenges the traditional form of hylomorphism that suggests the passivity of material. Instead of mere measuring geometricians, insects were shown to be capable of nonmeasured swarming, a curious form of temporality and individuation. Bergson was keen to underline that whereas intelligence characterizes human functions as an ordering of matter and nature, instinct follows the matter of the environment more intimately; this realization feeds again an understanding of *instinct* as a characteristic of an insect approach to the environment and as a mode of understanding the immanent materialism of the world.

EVOLUTIONARY POWER

In various ways, in recent decades network culture has been eager to adopt the discourse of nineteenth-century evolution and the powers of nature. Swarms, among many other contexts, including those of self-assembling robotics and swarm art, have been seen as optimization machines in a refashioned version of the traveling salesman problem. Various ideas that in one form or another took into account the potentials in uncontrolled behavior were no longer seen as the primary evil of a rational system but as effective forms of computation and organization.[5]

Such "storehouses of invention" embodied by animals were a key theme for various neo-Darwinist writers such as Kevin Kelly, the main proponent of a neobiological turn in the digital culture of the 1990s. Such writers and scientists continued the realizations in the New AI and Alife that the way to understand, and create, complex behavior was through simple living beings—and the power of evolution. Following the enthusiasm for the cyborg, nature and evolution were seen as the key models of innovation:

> The nature of life is to delight in all possible loopholes. It will break any rule it comes up with. Take these biological jaw-droppers: a female fish that is fertilized by her male mate who lives inside her, organisms that

shrink as they grow, plants that never die. Biological life is a curiosity shop whose shelves never empty. Indeed the catalog of natural oddities is almost as long as the list of all creatures; *every* creature is in some way hacking a living by reinterpreting the rules.[6]

For Kelly, drawing here from artificial life scientists of the 1990s such as Thomas Ray, the key to understanding the creative thrust of natural and artificial systems is the force of natural evolution (random variation + selection). Human inventions are seen as merely serving a specific goal and reflecting the imagination of the designer, but nature works toward goals and forms not thought of before. Nature is the ultimate "curiosity shop" and "reality hacker," as Kelly suggests. To anyone familiar with Richard Dawkins's 1986 notion of natural selection, this sounds similar to his notion of the blind watchmaker who "does not see ahead, does not plan consequences, has no purpose in view"[7] but is still able to come up with perfected designs. For Kelly, this force of nature signals an enthusiasm for the various works of genetic algorithms and evolving forms of computation that draw upon the force of infinite variation.

Again, using Kelly as an index of the enthusiasm for biological computation, evolution is seen to be "good for three things":

How to get somewhere you want but can't find the route to.
How to get to somewhere you can't imagine.
How to open up entirely new places to get to.[8]

Evolution is seen as deterritorializing the imaginative powers of conscious design in its nonteleological nature. For such proponents of neobiologism, however, evolution works parallel to the logic of inventive capitalism and the production of novelty. Referring to capitalism as a force of nature is nothing new, but turn-of-the-millennium network capitalism adopted a further new twist in introducing the idea of radical ecologically inspired novelty to its repertoire. In terms of mapping the changing faces of capitalism, we need to understand its special relation to modes of differentiation, evolution, and creativity; in its current form, capitalism works exactly through these creations, imaginations, and accidents incorporated as part of its algorithmic perfection machine.[9] Hence it is no surprise that "swarm logic" was applied to an analysis of the speculative markets of contemporary global monetary flows, where the individual rational models are seen giving way to dynamic socioecological models.[10]

To understand the genealogy of swarms and insect modes of organization, it is important to dig into the early expressions of this kind of belief in the immanent powers of nature to breed "technics of nature" that supersede those of conscious design. However, it is as important to note the potential these ideas offer to be much more than a handmaid to network capitalism. Take Darwin. In his view, nature is a perfection machine that adjusts structures and habits into a resonance. Natural selection works not through a preselected goal but through the potentiality of futures unknown.[11] This weird futurity is at the core of radical evolutionary ideas. To be sure, I am addressing not Darwin's theories in their full complexity (neglecting, for example, the importance of sexual selection, which in itself is a powerful engine of difference of sensations, locomotions, and affects), along with their inconsistencies or deficiencies, but the larger temporal view of evolution and creation that has recently been emphasized by Elizabeth Grosz. For Darwin, the contrast between artificial selection and natural selection was inherent in the fact that "Man can act only on external and visible characters: Nature cares nothing for appearances, except in so far as they may be useful to any being."[12] The internal force of nature is working in a nonhuman manner, which can also be seen as an immanent force. "Every selected character is fully exercized by her."[13] However, for Bergson, the Darwinian idea of adaptation proved inadequate in presuming a certain passivity of the living organisms. Instead of organisms adapting to the environment, both engage in a mutual "negotiation" or becoming. There are no prepared forms or molds in which life should fit, but evolution is exactly this creation of worlds.[14] Life has no ends, wrote Bergson, implying that we can think of life as a striving and differentiation. Despite the seeming harmony, there is a continuous potential for new modes of organization of life and hence for new modes of affection, perception, and locomotion.[15]

Curiously, this immanent force of nature identified by Darwin and Bergson in their respective tones—which in recent years has been elaborated in cultural analysis and philosophy as an agenda of neomaterialism to which I will return later—was connected to the earlier theme of insect technics as well. Even though I seem to put much emphasis on the emergence of ideas of evolution as peculiar kinds of immanent engines of the world that, via continuous probing, look for fitter forms of living, again the origins of primitive forms of life as a self-organizing force is to be found earlier. Thus Kirby and Spence's work also addressed the innovativeness in adjusting to environmental pressures. As they underlined, this instinct was due not to a system of machinery nor to models impressed on the brain, nor was it an expression of deity or reason, as the writers mentioned.[16] Instead, it was for Kirby and Spence a faculty implemented by the Creator that helps to sustain the species and the individual.

To discern this stance from various mechanistic or automated actions, Kirby and Spence placed value on deviations and accommodations to circumstances.[17] They saw "larger animals" as relatively fixed to their habits and bodily orientation, whereas "insects . . . often exhibit the most ingenious resources, their instincts surprisingly accommodating themselves to the new circumstances in which they are placed, in a manner more wonderful and incomprehensible than the existence of the faculties themselves."[18] They saw insects as machines that outperform other excellently built machines (the example used is a loom) in their capability to repair their defects. Variation and accommodation, as an intimate part of the changing environment, they saw as the primary excellence of insects.

NATURAL GEOMETRICIANS

For various writers interested in insects, but also for designers of media and space, insects are natural geometricians. In insects, the mathematical precision of architecture, planning, and adjusting is confined not to a faculty of intelligence imposing form on matter but to primitive life (self-)organizing its milieu into a habitat. Bees are an apt example used by various writers, including Kirby and Spence, in that they seem inherently geometric architects. The foundation of a comb is build at the top of a hive and continues downward, explained Kirby and Spence. The pattern is repetitious to a mathematical degree. The combs are at precisely a certain distance from each other (one-third of an inch). According to seasonal variations, the combs are adjusted:

> On the approach of winter, when their honey-cells are not sufficient in number to contain all the stock, they *elongate* them considerably, and thus increase their capacity. By this extension the intervals between the

combs are unavoidably contracted; but in winter well-stored magazines are essential, while from their state of comparative inactivity spacious communications are less necessary. On the return of spring, however, when the cells are wanted for the reception of eggs, the bees contract the elongated cells to their former dimensions, and thus re-establish the just distances between the combs which the care of their brood requires.[19]

The combs and the building breathe, live with their surroundings and form only a transductive membrane instead of a closed space. The analysis of bee architecture demonstrates how insect life is imagined as one of folding the outside (material elements that are used to build nests or, for example, seasonal variations in temperature, etc.) as part of the architectural inside.

In 1940, summarizing his decades of work, ethologist Jakob von Uexküll came to a similar conclusion when he argued that animals and plants build "living housings" of their bodies that are attached into continuity with their surroundings.[20] Later, in the 1960s, Lewis Mumford reminded us that animals, from insects to birds and mammals, had "made far more radical innovations in the fabrication of containers, with their intricate nests and bowers, their geometric beehives, their urbanoid anthills and termitaries, their beaver lodges, than man's ancestors had achieved in the making of tools until the emergence of *Homo sapiens*."[21] Mumford, however, like Ernst Kapp earlier, did come to the conclusion that *Homo sapiens* was superior in his synthetic capacities to reorganize, use symbols, and abstract himself from his immediate surroundings. However, he was in no way neglecting the powers of creation of the animal world. Technics as biotechnics was seen by Mumford as an experimental opening of the organic capabilities of the human being to new roles and new environmental relations, and even if he did not develop the theme of animal probeheading, it can be seen as a related ethological quest for what the organic body can do, how can it open up toward its surroundings.

For Kirby and Spence, one of the more remarkable characteristics of bee architecture was also its adjustability, its tolerance of anomalies. Drawing from French entomologist François Huber's often-cited research from the early nineteenth century, Kirby and Spence pointed toward the idea that irregularities are perhaps not accidental in the case of bee architecture but a demonstration of this smooth folding of outsides and insides, so to speak. So, "to astonish" some earlier entomologists such as Réaumur and Bonner, the writers suggested a paradoxical move:

> What would have been [Réaumur and Bonner's] astonishment if they had been aware that part of these anomalies are *calculated*; that there exists, as it were, a moveable harmony in the mechanism by which the cells are composed? If in consequence of the imperfection of their organs, or of their instruments, bees occasionally constructed some of their cells unequal, or of parts badly put together, it would still manifest talent to be able to repair these defects, and to compensate one irregularity by another; but it is far more astonishing that they know how to quit their ordinary routine when circumstances require that they should build male cells; that they should be instructed to vary the dimensions and the shape of each piece so as to return to a regular order; and that, after having constructed thirty or forty ranges of male cells, they again leave the regular order on which these were formed, and arrive by successive diminutions at the point from which they set out.[22]

What astonished the writers was this ability to switch between different forms and modes of building. They saw this complex system of bee architecture as constituted of regularities and irregularities, all however woven into a coherent and stable whole. This is the point at which the insects seemed to be more than calculation machines. As Lorraine Daston has argued, calculation was actually not regarded as a sign of intelligence around the early nineteenth century.[23] Instead, it was relegated to the sphere of mechanical actions and hence the regime of automata. Technology, like the new computing machines of Babbage, was calculational, as were instinctual animals such as insects, but the human being was capable of something else beyond mere number crunching. Insects and automata, then, occupied parallel positions in the discourses surrounding technology and life as dumb machines. Yet, as explained earlier, the underlining of the anomalous potentials of animal geometrics was intended to convey a new sense of animal intelligence.[24]

Nonetheless, calculational precision was admired in terms of its problem-solving qualities. Around the mid-nineteenth century, Darwin himself wrote of the awe-inspiring mathematics of bees in *Origin of Species*. Also influenced by Huber's research, Darwin turned to the "exquisite structures" of combs and the refined sense of order. As he explained, even mathematicians have affirmed that the forms bees create in their

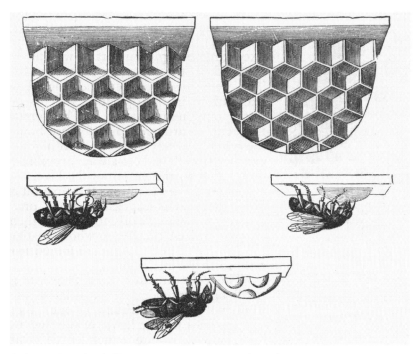

An image from Louis Figuier's *The Insect World* (1868) of bee cell constructions. Figuier referred to the bee architects as intelligent geometricians.

architecture are perfect solutions for the problem of how to optimize the shape of cells to store the maximum amount of honey with minimum construction wax.[25] Darwin addressed the various models of building of different species of bees, noting, however, the continuous precision, expressible in mathematical formulas. Darwin saw this as the work of natural selection as the "perfection machine" guaranteeing the fitness of the living forms:

> Thus, as I believe, the most wonderful of all known instincts, that of the hive bee, can be explained by natural selection having taken advantage of numerous, successive, slight modifications of simpler instincts; natural selection having by slow degrees, more and more perfectly, led the bees to sweep equal spheres at a given distance from each other in a double layer, and to build up and excavate the wax along the planes of intersection.[26]

The motivation for this, notes Darwin, was based on the more economical use of wax, a crucial factor in bee evolution.[27] Wax was the perfect soft molding material for this implicit imagining of how architecture could be in the midst of the emerging rigid steel buildings of modernity.

INSECT CITIES

The perceived perfection of insects ranged across scales. The anatomy of insects such as bees was often introduced as completely perfected for its purpose, a key way of introducing the inventive powers both in the natural theological tradition and in the more materialist Darwinian version. For writers such as James Rennie before the mid-nineteenth century, the bee community seemed to exhibit perfect harmony from social organization to individual parts, such as the structure of the leg of the bee, suitable for carrying propolis and pollen.

Rennie also drew on theological language to explain the instincts of animals. To compare the work of a carpenter bee to a human artisan proved his point regarding the superior, almost miraculous way a bee is able to perfect its habitations without practice or the complex tools of the skilled human being. It is not, however, that the bee is the architect because of its own command; instead the Great Architect up in the heavens has given it a plan to follow and help its mathematically accurate work.[28]

For Rennie, the clean and perfect tunnels of insect dwellings were part of the divine architecture of nature, but urban references also came into play. Bees were seen as living in "miniature cities"[29] of "admirable architecture" that reflected the industrial urbanization of the late nineteenth century. The geometrics of new urbanization had also fascinated larger crowds, for example, in the Great Exhibitions like the one in 1851 that introduced the awe-inspiring Crystal Palace. Besides the materials of steel and glass, the mathematically precise engineering practices demonstrated were seen as indexes of progress. Yet this fascination extended beyond the artifice and to the creations of nature and its mathematical engine of creation. Even St. Peter's Basilica in Rome was seen as remaining second to the colossal insect domes of "precision, audacity, and vastness" that went beyond human structures.[30]

Bee architecture was rather directly translated into material structures via the work of various modernist architects. As Juan Antonio

Ramírez argues in *The Bee Metaphor: From Gaudí to Le Corbusier,* modernist architecture was filled with figures, ornaments, and structural plans that took their influence from apiculture and entomology. Here the mathematicians of nature inspired the use of certain structures that were seen as optimal. The bees did the counting, architects the drawing. In Antonio Gaudí's organic structures, the world, perception, and calculations of the insects were almost parallel to those of angels. As Ramírez noted of the Colònia Güell chapel (on which work started in 1908) and Sagrada Familia, the infinite baroquelike variations expressed Gaudí's disbelief in human intelligence and capabilities to perceive on more than one level of reality. Instead, Gaudí wrote, "the intelligence of an angel operates in three dimensions and acts directly in space. Man cannot act until he has seen the fact: basically he only follows trajectories and lines on one plane."[31] With Gaudí we are dealing with spaces and perceptions that override the restricted capabilities of humans and point to the complexity inherent in angels but also in insect architecture.

In addition to Gaudí, various other architects employed the hexagonal form or other references to honeycombs as key elements of a modern way of rationalized planning. For example, Mies van der Rohe's model for a 1921 Berlin high-rise office building competition was titled Honeycomb and used hexagonal elements in inner space. Submitted for the same project competition, Hans Söder's skyscraper project next to the Friedrichstrasse station presented a "hexagonal vestibule with six polygonal structures radiating from it; another three smaller towers, also of hexagonal cross-section, are situated in the vertices of the triangle,"[32] all presenting an image quite akin to that of a gigantic bee-constructed building, although made of glass. Of a similar nature were, for example, Le Corbusier's early plans for urban settlements developed from 1914 to 1915, with hexagonal ground plans for the building blocks. In a modern version of mathematical regularity, the urban town of Le Corbusier's imagination became functionalized as a perfect social environment for living, which for Le Corbusier was also connected to the new collectivist experiments of Soviet Russia, where he worked as well.[33] In general, the nature of space and architecture was argued to be changing from the Renaissance single-perspective view to incorporate multiple and many-sided cubist spaces, to which we will return in chapter 4.

For architects and others, one crucial feature of optimization was the celebration of the modes of organization of insects. Whereas the urbanization of the human world produced not only glory and progress but also pollution, social problems, and alienation, as several social critics of the nineteenth century underlined, the insect world was a perfect image of coherent, clean organization. Organization of spaces and crowds was a key political and architectural problem and could be addressed in terms of diagrammatics as well: How could the milieus of the modern urban world be organized efficiently, cleanly, and rationally? One option was to turn directly toward animal worlds themselves. Bees, similar to other social insects such as ants, were hardworking, well-organized, and effective. It was as if everything was in tune in this collective of individual insects, which showed highly concentrated social behavior.[34]

A similar image was offered in relation to ants, which seemed to be the perfect animals for diagrammatics of labor and optimization. William Morton Wheeler, who later became famous (and a key thinker on swarms and emergence) for his ant research, wrote early on about ant societies as machines of a kind. Here we see an image like that of an autopoietic machine, postindustrial before its time. The ant machine is flexible in allocation of its tasks instead of exhibiting a rigid caste system as was often found to be the case when analyzing social insects. Polymorphism is the characteristic trait of these flexible animals:

> The soldiers are put to different uses by different species. In the grain-storing species they function as the official seed-crushers of the community. The diminutive workers collect the seeds and store and move them about in the chambers of the nest. They are, however, quite unable to break the hard shells, which yield only to the powerful jaws of the soldiers. In the carnivorous species the workers bring in pieces of insects, while the soldiers act as trenchers and sever the hard, chitinous joints. In the above-mentioned American species with polymorphic workers, I believe that the transitional forms may also be of use to the colony as seed-crushers and trenchers, since the vegetable and animal food is of different degrees of hardness and the work of making it accessible is not thrown on a single caste as it is in the strictly dimorphic forms. In some species the soldiers undoubtedly deserve their name, for they run about with wide-open mandible and attack any intruder with great fury. In other species they are very timid and make for the concealed chambers as soon as the nest is disturbed. They thus manifest an instinct which is

highly developed in the sexual forms, especially in the queens, whom the soldiers also resemble in certain morphological characters more closely than they do the workers.[35]

In Wheeler's analysis, the basis of the insect colony is heterogeneity, which only afterward evolved into a tight collective organism with differentiated tasks. In general, such images transported from the animal and insect worlds were surely closely related to the swarms of workers in factories and at building sites giving a material formation to ideals of progress. Yet in this case, everything was going smoothly, without social tensions. As in the formation of the hive into workers, drones, and the female queen, everything was seen as rationalized. For Victorian society, social insects served as a nice image of a tidy hierarchical structure in which everyone had one's own niche. The community was seen as primary, as one commentator noted concerning the bee: "It appears to know that it is born for society, and not for selfish pursuits; and, therefore, it invariably devotes itself and its labours to the benefit of the community to which it belongs."[36]

BIOPOLITICS OF ORGANIZATION

As cultural historian of entomology Charlotte Sleigh explains, social insects stretched way beyond their entomological boundaries and touched social, political, and even economic issues of organization. Besides the structuring of Victorian domestic order (well illustrated in the 1992 novel *Morpho Eugenia* by A. S. Byatt in the collection *Angels & Insects*), the social division of bees seemed to resonate with Adam Smith's invisible hand. Like nature, the reality of modern technological society was to be structured according to rational management. Everyone was to have one's own duties, and happiness would result from understanding one's place in the whole. Nothing was left to waste, and the study of economy of time and organization was seen as a secular type of religious act.[37] As analyzed in the previous chapter, the measuring and capturing of time and action were key characteristics of the rise of the modern media society. Architecture played a special role, and, according to Ramírez, entomological and apicultural lessons of rationalization had their fair share of influence in the rationalization of human life as well. Much as changes in the designs of artificial beehives resonated in honey production and other "benefits for the beekeeper," the organization of spaces fed directly into the behavior of people inhabiting the spaces[38]—an entomological lesson in rational management (and grassroots-level implementation of Weberian ideas of rationality and modernization). Indeed, in a feedback loop of sorts, notions of division of labor, caste, and the society as a superorganism consolidated power structures with the help of nature coupled with early social theory.[39]

Measurable rationality, duty, and other insect virtues spread from geometry and architecture to other contexts as well. Worth mentioning here are the teachings in the early children's classic *Die Biene Maja und ihre Abenteuer (Maya the Bee)* from 1912. The individualistic little bee discovers a plot the wasps have made against her home hive, and she has to decide whether to escape and save herself or go back to warn the others but at the same time suffer punishment for her individualistic maneuvers. Maya decides to return, a decision that underlines the moral primacy of the social collective.[40] However, in real life collective goals were not restricted to the totalitarian ideologies. Later, in the middle of the twentieth century, John Kieran, in his documentary television series *Kieran's Kaleidoscope,* introduced the harmonious and humanized life of *Ant City* (1949) and *Bee City* (1951). Ant cities are seen corresponding in size to human settlements ("say Minneapolis or Cincinnati or New Orleans, a city of a half a million of inhabitants"), and, like American cities, ant urban zones were mostly composed of workers. Ant cities have main avenues and side streets and various stores. What is painted is an image of a calm but busy, harmonious society in which work is divided among different castes, all contributing their part to the welfare of society. This illustrates how different were the points made by Wheeler, for example, from a more public understanding of the virtues of the hive. Naturally, the casual manner and warm tone of narrator Kieran does not merely describe events inside the insect world but offers an imagined bridge from ant cities to human cities of the post–World War II United States, trying to adjust to new contours of technological life in (sub-)urban reality. In *Bee City,* similar tones are struck:

> Thirty thousand inhabitants of a city are exposed before your eyes, as our camera peers and probes into a community of bees. We witness perhaps

the most ingenious creatures of the insect world—their growth, their myriad activities, their whole society, all of which is an amazing chapter in nature's wonderland.

So the term "busy as a bee" is not an innocent description or a metaphorical translation of bee activities into human world but an order-word—a description of a specific way for power to function beyond the actual context of rationalization and biopower in architecture. Order-words distribute modes of organization across disciplines and the social field. Meaning is secondary; the primary goal is to enact order and work as architectural molds. Order(ing) brings bodies into specific relations in which they are supposed to "carry out implicit obligations or follow a preset direction."[41] Everyone should carry one's own share in the community and contribute to the well-being of the structures (whether physical or mental). In the post–World War II United States, this can easily be seen as connecting to a certain hope for national unity and to the economic and political maneuvering to find a common enemy—with "communism" a floating signifier that came in handy, often depicted in insectlike form, void of individuality, as in the bug movies of the 1950s. In any case, both world wars of the century were massive projects of mobilization, control, and biopolitics of life both on the battlefield and on the home front, where logistics of electricity, technology, and, for example, food production and distribution had to be organized efficiently.

From early entomological observations to popular cultural distributions, the order-words were lessons in rational social organization. This is the obvious political explanation of how insects, and especially social insects, were turned into part of the construction of modern technological and rational society. From the construction of hives to anatomical parts and back to the macro scale of social organization, these were the optimized machines. Of course, the precision of the insect machine fed into dystopic fears of "inhuman technological society" modeled on emotionless insect minds. We can think of E. M. Forster's *The Machine Stops*, a novel from 1909, and Karel Čapek's plays *The Insect Play* (1921) and *R.U.R.* (1921), in which mechanization is a mode of becoming-ant, mechanical, servile, efficient. The film *Metropolis* (1927) produced a similar dystopic view of an "ant city" of a multitude of workers led by a queen at the top.[42] From the first sporadic examples, this theme of insect mechanicality developed into an influential trope that has continued to be recycled in various productions from science fiction to other forms of popular culture. In this sense, insects became an overdetermined, floating signifier for various contradicting ways of referring to and positing bodies and their relations, connecting notions of the concrete animals with much more abstract bodies such as security, individuality (or the loss of it), collective life, and technological dystopias. Insect bodies contract and transduce more abstract social and political concerns; insects mediate. The body politic was filled with animals and insects, but crucially these were also divided into "good insects" and "bad insects." Paradoxically, as we will see later, insects could offer, in addition to the lessons in rationalized management of a Taylorian kind, lessons in agencies without a center, phenomena that during recent years have been raised as the new modes of radical politics through concepts such as multitude, swarms, and smart mobs.

POLITICS OF RATIONALIZATION AND INTENSITIES

Now I want to sum up some of the threads I have been tracking here. There are two things I would like to pick out from the theme of insect architecture and organization, two strands that take us in differing directions. First, insects were captured as part of the politics of rationalization and the birth of a certain "Fordist order" and discipline of spatial institutions. Reflections on the optimized geometrics and social organization of the insect cities were continuously translated into parallels and models for technological human societies as well. So if primitive forms of life seemed to exhibit certain intensities (of movement, perception, and organization), these were turned into models and tools for rationalization ("architectural, economic, and political perfection"[43] to use the words of Maurice Maeterlinck from 1901)—a theme that doubles the previous chapter's focus on biopolitical production based on capturing animal life and affects. Similar themes have been noted by Eugene Thacker, who writes that nineteenth-century studies of insects propounded models of centralized control and "top-down management of task allocation and social function."[44]

Second, it is important to pay attention to the intensive modulations of the affects expressed by the nonhuman modes of organization. We should not reduce the animal, the insect, merely to the position of an index of ideological structures or to a representation of a cultural theme. Instead, or in addition, insects express the complex ecological attachments and contractments of environmental forces in which they function.[45] Seeing insect life as an instinctual folding with its environment hints at interesting subject-object couplings in which the inventive modulation of the living environment on the insects' part proceeds via an immanent engagement. Actually, to be more accurate, we should note that the subjects and objects are secondary to the process of individuation, the projectile nature of their affective relations. If the subject invests in a certain object or a milieu, it is as important to say that the object invests in the subject, affording it a certain potential of affects. Instead of a representational approach to building and technology, insects suggest a mode of inhabiting and creating space by which they seem to track the contours and tendencies of the matter at hand in order to push it toward certain key forms, singularities.[46]

One way to express this tension would be to refer to Deleuze and Guattari's division between royal science and nomad science, something they introduce in *A Thousand Plateaus*. Royal science is the formalizing way of producing hylomorphic ways of thought. It cuts up intensive matter into measurable entities by taking a position outside the matter—a visual observation. Royal science homogenizes matter and imposes laws and universals (for example, the law of gravity, which itself remains invariable). Nomad science proceeds in an alternative manner; instead of reproducing laws and invariables (as grids that can be imposed on matter), it tries to follow intensive singularities. Here variations are posited as primary, and constants are merely secondary views of the variations. A singularity (an accidental feature from the point of view of royal science) is not excluded but expresses a trait and a threshold in the matter.[47] In this context, the focus on insect architecture was characterized by a constant tension between royal and nomad science. Several of the commentators were quite keen on seeing insects as counting architects that seemed to impose invariables on matter. This view underlined the intelligence in this primitive form of life. Yet suggestions toward an understanding of insect building as a tracking of matter and singularities kept popping up as well: insects do not merely "reproduce" ideal models but continuously create them from the grassroots level up, in an emergent manner, so to speak. This is a topological way of tracking the intensive singularities of the habitat and introduces a haptics of space (instead of analyzing optics).

For a long time, many of the emerging ideas of "agencies without central control," swarms, and crowds occupied an anomalous position in the field of culture and knowledge. In a Kuhnian vein, we can see how new temporal phenomena became part of biology, sociology, literature, and philosophy only with the rise of new mathematical ideas and what has been referred to as the temporality of the event of modernist culture.[48] Ideas concerning the intensity of matter and a tolerance of singularities have been proposed in recent decades in the contexts of fluid dynamics, self-organization, and the physics of metastable systems, where interest has been focused on "possibility spaces," "phase spaces," and singularities. As Manuel DeLanda points out, this kind of neomaterialist approach focuses on morphogenesis as an immanent structuration, a probing of matter in search of singular points at which to stabilize for a while. DeLanda's recurring example is the soap bubble:

> The spherical form of a soap bubble, for instance, emerges out of the interactions among its constituent molecules as these are constrained energetically to "seek" the point at which surface tension is minimized. In this case, there is no question of an essence of "soap-bubbleness" somehow imposing itself from the outside, an ideal geometric form (a sphere) shaping an inert collection of molecules. Rather, an endogenous topological form (a point in the space of energetic possibilities for this molecular assemblage) governs the collective behavior of the individual soap molecules, and results in the emergence of a spherical shape.[49]

The point is that we can approach various topological formations as potentialities, tendencies toward certain key points of that specific formation. The soap bubble probes for a solution that would keep it intact, and similarly various physical, technological, biological, and cultural systems could be seen as entwined in diagrams governed by specific singularities. One could object that biological systems are not reducible to physics, which is true. Instead of a reduction, we are dealing with a diagrammatic approach. The solutions found to specific problems are immanent to the functioning of the system, so there is no outside plan governing the action (whether the plan, in our case, would be imposed by genes, instincts, intelligence/rationality, or whatever). Instead, it is a question of bending matter toward certain locally optimized ends.[50] There is no universal law that would be a primary solution to the problem, but the focus is on tracking problems from the intensive matter, where the solutions are found locally from the qualities of the matter—as in the case of an ambulant insect tracking characteristics of building materials found from nature and constructing a nest—not by judging it from outside but by quite concretely following the edges and qualities of matter.

Thus, it is interesting that soap bubbles also pop up in an insect context offered by novelist Maurice Maeterlinck (referring to the research done by the key entomologist Georges-Louis LeClerc Buffon in the eighteenth century). According to Maeterlinck, it is a curious mathematical puzzle that bees form cells as they do. In mathematics, an optimized use of a milieu would use equilateral triangles, squares, or regular hexagons, which is the case with bee cells. This optimization of matter (wax) is proposed as a key problem solved by some mathematicians but on an everyday basis by bees, which, "as if acquainted with these principles of solid geometry, follow them most accurately."[51]

Drawing on Buffon, Maeterlinck, the celebrated author of tales of insect lives but also of new spatial arrangements of non-Euclidian geometrics, proposed that the effects of the collective bee labor producing the optimal hexagons is "precisely what happens to crystals, the scales of certain kinds of fish, soap-bubbles, etc."[52] Yet the reasons for such optimization were various: for some, it seemed to be merely an expression of natural laws and mechanical pushing toward a certain optimal "phase space" (a term that was not used then). For others, like Maeterlinck, this perfection was not a property of matter but seemed to suggest some evidence of the intelligence of the bee. The solutions offered express well the general tendencies regarding an understanding of matter and creation: either they tend toward mechanical solutions in the manner of Newtonian physics or they seem to underline the at times nearly mystical intelligence found in nature, not reducible to mechanics but perhaps closer to some vitalist explanations or natural theology. What I am interested in here is this early sketching of the morphogenesis inherent in matter, and in this case living systems, which soon found their expression in the interest in emergent systems—an interest that started to accumulate in the early twentieth century (e.g., among entomologists) but had its full effects in the sciences and cultural theory in the latter part of the century.

SWARMING: A STRANGE EMOTION

In this historical setting, it is interesting to reflect on the enthusiasm of recent years regarding modes of (insect) organization such as swarms. During the 1980s, swarm optimization became a special technique for understanding and using complex networks. We will return to these in chapter 6. At the same time, swarms forced us to rethink some of the basic metaphysical concepts of the network society. As Thacker suggests, the emergent societies of swarms reside ontologically between the binaries of life and death. Hence, the biophilosophy of the twenty-first century should contextualize itself on such forms of the headless animality of insect societies or the new intensive meaning in states bordering life—the lifelike death of zombies. This biophilosophical moment, which Thacker underlines is not to be reduced to a philosophy of biology, is characterized by a logic alternative to that of the prior approaches to thinking of life, namely the three modes of soul, meat, and pattern.[53] Hence, such a biophilosophy also suggests a new way of understanding materiality not based on a substance or a form but as a temporal variation of affective assemblages.

Swarm intelligence characterizes computer science algorithms, multi-agent systems, and insects. It also presents, according to Thacker, a political paradox between "control and emergence, sovereignty and multiplicity." For Thacker, "insects are the privileged case study" for technological and political ways of organization in which familiar models of the organism are turned upside down. Suddenly, the many preexist the one, animal packs operate without heads (without one specific reason or leader), suggesting such logics of life as would seem uncanny if thought from the traditional subject-object point of view. In Thacker's view, swarms organize the multiple into a relational whole—and one in which the collective is exactly defined by "relationality." This implies, Thacker explains, that swarms are dynamic phenomena and hence different from models such as the network (which stem not from biology but from spatial models in mathematics such as graph theory). Organizationally, swarms are more than the sum of their parts, without an overarching unity principle guiding the actions of the singularities under one umbrella, and hence politically ambiguous.[54] Yet everything is concerted in a fashion that has invited many mystical references and explanations, such as Maeterlinck's concept of the "spirit of the hive," introduced later.

Swarming was early on described as a peculiar group behavior that was of interest to entomologists and researchers of social insects. Even for them, it represented a weird kind of organization that seemed to reside between instinct and intelligence. We can think of this as an alternative lesson on organization, taught by uncanny headless animals and multitudes, horrors of nonindividual groups. They are the same and yet continuously differ, as one eyewitness from 1893 noted, mistaking an insect swarm for an ephemeral smoke cloud at first:

> Near the tower the swarm was narrow and dense, gradually widening and thinning to a distance of about fifty feet, where it seemed to vanish by attenuation. The extent of the swarm varied but little during my observation, but the constant changes within it exactly simulated puffs of smoke driven away by the breeze.[55]

To follow the *Oxford English Dictionary*, *swarming* refers first to bee behavior and the search for a new hive. In other words, it is a concept of distribution. More generally, swarming means "to come together in a swarm or dense crowd; to collect, assemble, or congregate thickly and confusedly; to crowd, throng; also, to go or move along in a crowd" and "to occur or exist in swarms or multitudes; to be densely crowded or congregated; to be very numerous, abound excessively. (Often in reproach or contempt, esp. when said of persons.)" Hence, besides its specific use in the context of bees, *swarming* originally had this double meaning of a multitude of a kind, which, since its attachment to animal contexts, came to mean something akin to an uncontrolled (by a unity) but still concerted organization. This idea, which has inspired a plethora of cultural theorists and writers for years, originally occurred, then, in insect contexts. From insect contexts, the term *swarming* moved to political parlance around the end of the eighteenth century, when the German word *Schwaermen* started to refer to disobedient mobs and raving bee-like behavior adopted by uncontrollable crowds.[56]

Social insects provided, in parallel to the insect technics of the first chapter, a model of social organization that was not present in the official sociological and anthropological studies of the nineteenth and early twentieth centuries but very much integrated into the body politic of emerging media culture. Instead of marking merely a "pre" status, as in pre-rational, pre-management, and pre-cultural biological curiosities, as Donna Haraway notes,[57] animals and insects are a neglected part of the politics of organization.

Social insects provided lessons in strange, unrecognized forms of being social. A good example is found in Maeterlinck's novel *A Life of the Bee* (1901), in which the topic of "the spirit of the hive" is constantly brought up. It could be seen as an expression of mysticism, a natural theology of a kind, but at the same time it connects to the topic of collective intelligence then emerging. Maeterlinck considered this spirit not as a particularly tuned instinct that specifies a task and not as a mechanical habit but as a curious logic that cannot be pinpointed to any specific role, order, or function. The spirit of the hive seems to be responsible for the abrupt but still recurring collective actions that take hold of the bees (as in possessed individuals) and concert their actions as if they were one. The spirit of the hive sees that the individual bees' actions are harmonized to such an extent that they can exist as a collective: from the queen's impregnation to the sudden swarming when the bees leave the old nest (without apparent reason) and find a new one, the spirit of the hive is described by a mix of nomadic intuition that "passes the limits of human morality" to the everyday organization of the hive:

> It regulates the workers' labors, with due regard to their age; it allots their task to the nurses who tend the nymphs and the larvae, the ladies of honor who wait on the queen and never allow her out of their sight; the house-bees who air, refresh and heat the hive by fanning their wings, and hasten the evaporation of the honey that may be too highly charged with water; the architects, masons, wax-workers, and sculptors who form the chain and construct the combs; the foragers who sally forth to the flowers in search of the nectar that turns into honey.[58]

This seemingly automated behavior is described by Maeterlinck as a "strange emotion." Here the emotion acts as a trigger of a kind that points to the way bodies are affectively coordinated in the organizational form. The swarm is a becoming that expresses potentialities that are always situated and yet moving.[59] The affects that trigger the swarming and the birth of the new collective are related to communication in

Maeterlinck's view. This mode of communication happens not on the level of consciousness, human language and concepts, but as affects of murmur, whisper, and a refrain that even the bees might not hear but sense in some uncanny way.[60]

The mysticism surrounding swarming was fueled by the lack of clear explanatory frameworks for such novel phenomena and the ontologies of which they were expressions. Hence, emotions were continuously used to pin down the strangeness in terms of human coordinates. For some, the power of swarms was a frightening one, emerging from the sheer size of the pack. Insect swarms represented economic devastation and disgust, as in the case of locusts.

> Attempts have been made at home and abroad to cipher how many individual locusts there were in a swarm. In 1889, in *Nature,* one of the most reliable of scientific journals, about the following was published: There was a flight of locusts winging their way in November over the Red Sea. The flight covered a space of 2000 square miles in extent, and, calculating the single locust to have weighed one-sixteenth of a grain, the total weight was estimated to be 42.850,000,000 tons.[61]

The swarm was paralleled to a technological superlative: this weight was estimated to exceed that of the total amount of freight carried through

The frightening mass of the swarm is represented in Figuier's *The Insect World.*

the American railroads. The swarm was a frightening force recounted in various popular cultural presentations from the end of the nineteenth century on, usually underlining the vast size of the group. One such gigantic swarm in Kenya in 1928 was estimated to be sixty miles long and three miles wide.[62] It is no wonder that such sights aroused feelings of fright and awe associated with uncontrolled behavior.

EMERGENCE AND RELATEDNESS: A RADICAL EMPIRICISM, TAKE ONE

The interest in swarms was intimately connected to the research on emergence and "superorganisms" that arose during the early years of the twentieth century, especially in the 1920s. Even though the author of the notion of superorganisms was the now somewhat discredited writer Herbert Spencer,[63] who introduced it in 1898, the idea was fed into contemporary discourse surrounding swarms and emergence through myrmecologist William Morton Wheeler. In 1911 Wheeler had published his classic article "The Ant Colony as an Organism" (in *Journal of Morphology*), and similar interests continued to be expressed in his subsequent writings. His ideas became well known in the 1990s in discussions concerning artificial life and holistic swarmlike organization. For writers such as Kevin Kelly, mentioned earlier in this chapter, Wheeler's ideas regarding superorganisms stood as the inspiration for the hype surrounding emergent behavior.[64] Yet the actual context of his paper was a lecture given at the Marine Biological Laboratory at Woods Hole in 1910.[65] As Charlotte Sleigh points out, Wheeler saw himself as continuing the work of holistic philosophers, and later, in the 1910s and 1920s, found affinities with Bergson's philosophy of temporality as well.[66] In 1926, when emergence had already been discussed in terms of, for example, emergent evolution, evolutionary naturalism, creative synthesis, organicism, and emergent vitalism, Wheeler noted that this phenomenon seemed to challenge the basic dualisms of determinism versus freedom, mechanism versus vitalism, and the many versus the one.[67] An animal phenomenon thus presented a crisis for the fundamental philosophical concepts that did not seem to apply to such a transversal mode of organization, or *agencement* to use the term that Wheeler coined. It was a challenge to philosophy and simultaneously to the physical, chemical, psychological, and social sciences, a phenomenon that seemed to cut through these seemingly disconnected spheres of reality.

In addition to Wheeler, one of the key writers on emergence—again also for Kelly in his *Out of Control*[68]—was C. Lloyd Morgan, whose *Emergent Evolution* (1927) proposed to see evolution in terms of emergent "relatedness." Drawing on Bergson and Whitehead, Morgan rejected a mechanistic dissecting view that the interactions of entities—whether physical or mental—always resulted only in "mixings" that could be seen beforehand. Instead he proposed that the continuity of the mechanistic relations were supplemented with sudden changes at times. At times reminiscent of Lucretius's view that there is a basic force, *clinamen,* that is the active differentiating principle of the world, Morgan focused on how qualitative changes in direction could affect the compositions and aggregates. He was interested in the question of the new and how novelty is possible. In his curious modernization of Spinoza, Morgan argued for the primacy of relations—or "relatedness," to be accurate.[69]

Instead of speaking of agencies or activities, which implied a self-enclosed view of interactions, in *Emergent Evolution* Morgan propagated in a way an ethological view of the world. Entities and organisms are characterized by relatedness, the tendency to relate to their environment and, for example, other organisms. So actually, what emerge are relations:

> If it be asked: What is it that you claim to be emergent? the brief reply is: Some new kind of relation. Revert to the atom, the molecule, the thing (e.g. a crystal), the organism, the person. At each ascending step there is a new entity in virtue of some new kind of relation, or set of relations, within it, or, as I phrase it, intrinsic to it. Each exhibits also new ways of acting on, and reacting to, other entities. There are new kinds of extrinsic relatedness.[70]

The evolutionary levels of mind, life, and matter are in this scheme intimately related, with the lower levels continuously affording the emergence of so-called higher functions, like those of humans. Different levels of relatedness might not have any understanding of the relations that define other levels of existence, but still these other levels with their relations affect the other levels. Morgan tried, nonetheless, to steer clear of the idealistic notions of humanism that promoted the human mind as representing a superior stage in emergence. His stance was much closer to a certain monism in which mind and matter are continuously in some kind of intimate correspondence whereby even the simplest expressions of life participate in a wider field of relatedness.

In *Emergent Evolution* Morgan described relations as completely concrete. He emphasized that the issue is not only about relations in terms but as much about terms in relation, with concrete situations, or events, stemming from their relations.[71] In a way, other views on emergence put similar emphasis on the priority of relations, expressing a kind of radical empiricism in the vein of William James. Drawing on E. G. Spaulding's 1918 study *The New Rationalism,* Wheeler noted the unpredictable potentials in connectionism: a connected whole is more than (or at least nor reducible to) its constituent parts, implying the impossibility to find causal determination of aggregates. Whereas existing sciences might be able to recognize and track down certain relationships that they have normalized or standardized, the relations might still produce properties that are beyond those of the initial conditions—and thus also demand a vector of analysis that parts from existing theories—dealing with properties that open up only in relation to themselves (as a "law unto themselves").[72] Instead, a more complicated mode of development was at hand, in which aggregates, or *agencements,* simultaneously involved various levels of reality. This also implied that aggregates, emergent orders, have no one direction but are constituted of relations that extend in various directions:

> We must also remember that most authors artificially isolate the emergent whole and fail to emphasize the fact that its parts have important relations not only with one another but also with the environment and that these external relations may contribute effectively towards producing both the whole and its novelty."[73]

In Wheeler's view, emergence works on and across various levels, from physiological evolution to the social formations in animals and humans. The world is presented as a result of composites and movements of integration, differentiation, accumulation, and so forth, where, despite the common nature of evolution across scales, the products are never categorizable under general notions. Wheeler saw the aggregates as events, but believed that "no two events are identical, every atom, molecule, organism, personality and society is an emergent and, at least to some extent, a novelty."[74] Events consist of series and repetitions, but these repetitions are always repeating a difference. This radically temporal view is in tune with much of the orientation of thought at the turn of the century, from that of Nietzsche to that of Bergson and other theories of difference that were later adopted by Deleuze.

What connected Wheeler to other thinkers of his age (such as Bergson)[75] was also a certain nonhumanist perspective. For Wheeler, the social level is of special interest; he remarked that unfortunately it was left to sociologists of human sociality only.[76] When he called for a comparative sociology, what he wanted was not a functional sociology delineated between different human forms of organization but, in the manner of August Forel and others with a keen interest in the simple things in life, an inspection of animal and insect forms of nonhuman organization. Throughout his career Wheeler transgressed disciplinary boundaries and interacted with philosophers and, for example, sociologists such as William McDougall, the author of *The Group Mind* (1920).[77]

Wheeler thought these primitive forms of organization exhibit the event of emergence, of a superorganism. Here Wheeler distinguished between homogenous social aggregates (individuals of the same species) and heterogeneous aggregates (between species). Furthermore, he pointed out that in the heterogeneous social forms one finds a panorama of forms of interaction, from predatism and parasitism to symbiosis and biocoenosis. These various cases present structural couplings in which a new entity, an event, seems to arise from the specific and very singular interactions taking place on the interface of various individuals and their vectors. Wheeler saw insects as teaching lessons in uncanny organization, whereas he was a firm believer in the validity of translating the observations into human societies, which he suggestively called super-superorganisms due to humans' ability to form bonds beyond the family form. Here Wheeler echoed the scientific work of Peter Kropotkin, the Russian anarchist of the late nineteenth century, who, arguably with a more radical view, proposed lessons from the animal kingdom. For Kropotkin, the sociability of life was not restricted to interfamilial relationships, and he seemed to acknowledge as well a much wider notion of associations in animal life. This "sociability proper" was an expression of a force of coevolution and symbiosis that seemed to differ from natural evolution à la Darwin (whereas Wheeler stuck to ideas of evolution as random probing).[78]

For Wheeler, the organizational event of swarms corresponds to architectural structures. Such architecture is not conceptualized merely as a stable structure of hierarchy that maintains the social organization of, for example, a hive as rigid and nonchanging but as a living organism in itself. Swarms and insect architecture are systems of living not as structures but as events not reducible to an individual programmed (predestined) to an inner model of life or to the pressure of organization from above. The becoming of space is created through haptic probings of the topology of the habitat. Relations do not have to be structural macrorelations but can be lived relations that involve the organisms in common situations, or what Morgan called relatedness. Forms or structures might be perceived as end products of the lived relations but are created from micromovements of intensive kinds and their formation into social and architectural elements. Spatial abstractions, then, are projections formed of intimate relatedness or emergence at the level of the living—a concrete lived "radical empiricism":

> That the social activities may present a very definite emergent pattern is most clearly seen in the nests of bees, wasps, ants and termites. These structures, though the result of the cooperative labor of most of the personnel of the colony, are nevertheless true Gestalten, being no more mere sums of the individual activities than is the diverse architecture of cities built by human hands. Not only does each species have its peculiar type of nest, but the nest of every colony of a species exhibits its own emergent idiosyncrasies.[79]

Here nests and "emergent idiosyncrasies" are tied together in a feedback loop. This also hints at the intimate link between, first, architecture as a modulation of perception (to convey and channel perceptions, bodies, and movements) and, second, its connection to organizational models as politics of bodies and perceptions. The insect modes of building and organization do not merely result in spatial structures that support certain becomings but, more radically, this stance of emergence implies the importance of temporality in the event of swarming. This is the primary mode of transforming inorganic matter into architecture, housings for the body, an art (and a technics) of creation of self, and its primary architecture via a "deterritorialization of the earth and its intensities."[80] Between the one and the many, structure and agency, the swarms and their insect architectures are temporally embodied organisms that are hence open to future becomings as well. Despite expressing certain optimal points or tendencies at which humans have marveled since the early days of entomology, at least since the early twentieth century the greatest interest has been in swarming and emergence tied to temporality in a way that has attracted cultural theory of late modernity as well.

Thacker proposes that swarms and insects suggest new conceptualizations of life. Earlier accounts of life as soul (as in Aristotle's division of vegetative, animate, and rational souls as essences of living beings), meat (as in the cold matter of mechanical thought à la Descartes), or pattern (the coding of life as information entities in the age of cybernetic machines) are contrasted to the lessons of bioart and biophilosophical in "nonanthropomorphic life."[81] Yet, despite the seeming intimate relations of swarming as a biological model to the changes in the body politic of the network society, the translation of biological models into democratic politics is far from clear, warns Thacker. Being connected in networks or in swarms does not imply an emergence of political formation with common goals, and hence addressing swarms as democratic tools in an overly straightforward way should be avoided.[82]

Instead one should engage in a work of translation (this is how I adopt Thacker's points), in which swarms and insect research can imply new shifts in philosophical concepts, technological systems, and even political modes of organization. Yet nothing comes naturally, by its own force (or at least the force is not self-enveloping, a linearly differentiated one), but should be catalyzed in a larger discourse of biophilosophy (and here, a cultural analysis of the media archaeological roots of such concepts). One such key terrain of questioning is the aforementioned temporality of swarms, that is, how insect ethology can hint at temporal ontologies and cultural analysis of affects. I will continue with this theme in the next chapter, which addresses the challenge of temporality inherent in insects and insect research to, for example, Kantian spatial models. In this vein, the key figure of the next chapter is a curious ethologist from the early twentieth century, Jakob von Uexküll, who not only addressed insects and animals in their environmental couplings but produced work that has been discussed in various philosophical and media theory contexts of the twentieth century. The next chapter, then, continues our insect lessons in affects, weird organizations, and the destabilization of a human-centered media technological and philosophical focus.

THREE

TECHNICS OF NATURE AND TEMPORALITY
Uexküll's Ethology

> Science finds in the insect a world that is closed to us. There is no possibility of divining or even suspecting the impressions produced by the clash of the cymbals upon those who inspire it. All that I can say is that their impassive exterior seems to denote complete indifference. Let us not insist too much: the private feelings of animals are an unfathomable mystery.
>
> —J. Henri Fabre, *The Life of the Grasshopper*

This chapter continues some of the ideas introduced previously but with a special eye on Jakob von Uexküll's ethology—and the conceptual "animal" the tick. Through the tick we are able to discuss more in-depth notions of temporality and affect and realize that Uexküll provided important insights into a dynamic notion of nature relevant to wider theoretical applications of media ecologies.

One of Eugene Thacker's key ideas in his take on swarms, networks, and multitudes was to differentiate between effects and affects.[1] Whereas an effect analysis would stabilize the entities involved and regard them as predefined, an affect approach would focus precisely on the micromovement that is formative of the terms involved. In the context of networks, network effect analysis creates a spatial view of a network, an overarching survey of individual entities acting and reacting on a spatial gridlike structure, and an affect view of networks searches for the temporal becomings of the networks. In my take (already elaborated in *Digital Contagions*) such becomings are always multiscalar, and the affects of network culture involve not only technology but also a whole media ecology of politics, economics, and, for example, artistic creation.

In this case, affects are indeed passages among dimensions, contexts, and scales.[2]

Thacker's point relates to larger ontological and philosophical pre-occupations and the need to discover dynamic models of thought that bypass the spatial thematics of ontology of, for example, Immanuel Kant and Leonhard Euler, the developer of graph theory. For Thacker, the problem is what the latter modes of thought owe to their stabilizing spatial ontology, in which networks become spatialized and stabilized in terms of nodes and edges that are primary to the possible relations and movements between them. In Kant's take, time becomes in itself a motionless condition of motion, but radical temporality remains second-ary to this a priori conditioning. Here Thacker turns to Henri Bergson and his overturning of the space-time scheme. For Bergson, time as in-tensive, durational memory is the primary "stuff" of the world, which merely condenses into spatial and stable formations. Many of the prob-lems that Bergson felt existed in evolutionary thought had to do with the danger of thinking in terms of already defined and formed entities (in the case of Herbert Spencer), or traits, which served as the immobile basis for notions of change. Instead, change was to be seen at the core of life, or organization, and change was not restricted to the future; this implies the possibility of approaching the past instances as something other than inevitabilities that necessarily lead us to our current state of being.[3] Bergson notes that it is of course our tendency (as expressed in physiological research on animal capabilities) to dissect duration into phases and such. The actualized perception, however, stems from the virtual forces that are captured by the present and actual concerns. Perception immobilizes the virtual intensity into such modes, where intentional and pragmatic action is possible.[4] This also marks a differ-ence between perception and sensation—the latter being the virtual sphere of potentiality that is never exhausted in the actualized percep-tions of the world. There are continuously elements that are too large, too small, too intensive to fit in the perception but still dovetail with it—enveloping a "multiplicity of potential variations"[5]—what Brian Massumi refers to as the "superempirical." Indeed, as this chapter will show, this superempiricality was developed in the midst of modernity, already at the end of the nineteenth century and in the early twentieth, in various fields from the arts to biological research, but of course also in philosophy, as a way of "opening up" the closed worlds of animals and other nonhuman agencies.

In 1896, in *Matter and Memory,* Bergson offered his solution to the kind of temporalization of the world in which personal, actualized perceptions are actually contractions of nonpersonal durations—an idea that posited becoming and change as the driving force of the world. In Bergson's view, "matter thus resolves into numberless vibrations, all linked together in uninterrupted continuity, all bound up with each other, and travelling in every direction like shivers through an immerse body."[6] Here, despite our tendency to attribute movements to bodies, movement is a much more radical force that precedes the stable positions of the body. Duration is a force that finds solutions in actual forms of life and modes of perception, something that Bergson more concretely analyzed in *Creative Evolution,* which we also discussed in the first chapter. Here it becomes illustrative to see "insect-life" or "human-life" not as substances of a sort but as modes of living and contracting movements into actual entities.[7] As will later be seen, they form tactics in the *technics of nature*—technics that refer not to capacities that are fixed on certain species, categories, or technologies but to tendencies and affects that are concretely embodied in certain assemblages but at the same time are not reducible to repetitions of an essence or to any other prefixed notion. In other words, what is important are the affects and tendencies that nature can express and what can be characterized as technics without being technological.[8] These technics are primarily understood as a temporal becoming, a matter of affects, melodics, and contrapuntal interactions in the ethological and dynamic context proposed by the famous ethologist Jakob von Uexküll in the early years of the twentieth century. In this sense, a biologically tuned philosophy such as Bergson's can offer a much more temporal way of understanding phenomena such as swarms than can the mathematically oriented network analysis.

RADICAL EMPIRICISM, TAKE TWO

Swarms are time. Swarms are not ready-made organizations but are continuously on the verge of becoming one but also dissolving. They are radically heterogeneous but still consistent, local patterns continuously feeding into a dynamic global pattern, so to speak.[9] In the previous chapter we moved from insect architectures and their capacity to attract dynamic but geometrically precise singularities to insect organization and the theme of swarms. Swarms, as articulated in the early twentieth-century theories of insects, animal behavior, and interest in emergence, were conceptualized early on as superorganisms that are not reduced to their constituent parts. Can we think of the superorganism as superempirical—a variationality of molecular kinds, a swarming of potentiality pulling it to various directions? Not a superorganism with a head, as grade-B horror movies often suggest, of an ant and other insect colonies evolving into a consciousness but a relationality of microperceptions that work in concert and unfold in time? Such patterns were much later reanalyzed in the contexts of computer and network science, systems design, and studies of, for example, biocomplexity, where they were deterritorialized from insect bodies into technologies.

Now we depart, momentarily, from Thacker's analysis into the constituents of contemporary concerns over swarms, networks, and multitudes (only to return there later) and continue the grounding of the themes surrounding ideas of relationality and temporality from the 1920s to the 1940s. This also includes a certain shift from Kantian themes of perception and man toward fields of nonhuman temporality. As I said earlier, the framework for understanding Uexküll's ideas and the points about ethology that resonate with a much more recent "wave" of revival of radical empiricism includes not only philosophy but also biological theories and novel post-Cartesian ideas in the arts.

In terms of philosophy, this chapter nods in the direction of Bergson but also A. N. Whitehead and William James. Resonating with several contexts outside philosophy, various new ontological theories promised insights into a nonhuman world. Whitehead's desire to find alternatives to the Western Aristotelian tension of subject-object led him to think in terms of events and process ontology, which has itself found followers in recent decades in Donna Haraway, Bruno Latour, Isabelle Stengers, and Gilles Deleuze, to provide some key examples of writers who have contributed widely to the discourses of posthumanism. Whitehead's philosophy of the organism from the 1920s proposed to allocate everything as a subjectivity and to think through the ways in which these nonhuman subjectivities are fundamentally connected with each other and hence open to changes through their dynamic relationships. Whitehead describes this through the concept of prehension, the process of how an entity "grasps" its environment. Instead of dealing with the world in terms of subjects and objects, this approach allows much more room to maneuver, because prehending subjects are as open to become prehended objects by some other subjectivities.[10] Deleuze adapted this approach in terms of subjectiles and objectiles, where *objectile* describes the new status of the technical object as a continuity of variation, a dynamic serialism of the automated production machinery. Subjectiles are the corresponding way of seeing the subject as a contraction of variations. This is a version of perspectivism that, however, states not a relativist position to knowledge but the truth in relations—that all of reality is a contraction of variation in which the subject is an apprehension of variation—or metamorphosis.[11]

Whitehead's idea, stated in his *Process and Reality* (1929), of thinking in terms of prehensions and superjects instead of subjects and intentions, gives us tools to understand how subjectivity can be contracted beyond the human form. It is the world of experience that *gives* the subject-superject, instead of the subject having an intentional relationship with the object-world.[12] Whitehead sees his "philosophy of organism" as an overturning of Kant. Consider Whitehead's words:

> For Kant, the world emerges from the subject; for the philosophy of organism, the subject emerges from the world—a "superject" rather than a "subject." The word "object" thus means an entity which is a potentiality for being a component in feeling; and the word "subject" means the entity constituted by the process of feeling, and including this process. The feeler is the unity emergent from its own feelings; and feelings are the details of the process intermediary between this unity and its many data.[13]

This also could be understood as the perspective of the metamorphotic subject—a subjectile that occupies points of view in variation, is a product of the real relations of the world instead of just a prefixed universal subject. We are being individuated by the objects as much as we individuate them, and perception becomes an event instead of a grid imposed on the world. Objects and subjects emerge through such concrete events, which always have a stronghold in the virtual defined as a potentiality of future and past actualizations.[14]

Without the assumption of perception in general, writes Claire Colebrook when mapping Deleuze's notion of affect, perception is deterritorialized, and the reterritorialization on man is not the only possibility for a transcendental philosophy.[15] Although we are not going to fully engage with Whitehead, it is important to point out the connection to the wider agenda of recent years. In a manner that resonates with Whitehead's metaphysics, the realizations relating to New AI and the design of swarming and evolutionary systems (whether software or physically embodied) exhibit a similar approach that underlines the importance of the coupling of the agency with its environment. The perturbations stemming both from the milieu and from the agent are what provides, or affords, the functionality of any agency, any assemblage. Here perturbations, variations, and "bugs" are not the elements that need to be excluded from a functional system but what provide it with a lived relationship and "life," so to speak.[16]

Radical empiricism also provides perspectives from which to understand nonhuman agency. William James shared with Whitehead a valuation of the virtual experiences of the world—that is, the potentiality of radical experiences beyond the confines of our actual experiences. Relations are not actual but have the potentiality for actualization.[17] Indeed, in his radical empiricism James tested primarily the limits of human fields of experience, underlining that there is always more in the world that we actually experience at one moment.[18] Yet, in addition, the speculative nature of such an enterprise implies radically nonhuman forms of being. Perception contracts the world, and there is a potential infinity of ways of folding the milieu and an organism. In this endeavor, Jamesian radical empiricism moves in another direction from that of the phenomenological enterprise from Brentano to Husserl, which had the disadvantage of not being interested in the existence of things beyond our human perception. For Husserl's refashioning of Cartesian philosophy (in his 1931 *Cartesian Meditations*), philosophy turned inward and the psychological and objective realities of the world were bracketed in advantage of the viewpoint of the transcendental-phenomenological ego. Here, the objective world (as experienced by this ego) also derives from the transcendental plane of the phenomenological subject.[19] However, *things* can also be seen as in themselves active interventions and "provocations for action," as Grosz explains based on James and Bergson. Things, including technology, matter, and living things such as animals as inventors of bodily creation, are to be regarded as continuous experimentations, a "certain carving out of the real."[20] Beyond our phenomenological perspective, there is a whole plane of immanence on which *things* (including animal agencies) are interacting, as will be discussed later in this chapter.

It is worth noting that it was exactly these thinkers of temporality who were continuously popping up in the 1920s discussions concerning emergence and evolution, such as C. Lloyd Morgan's *Emergent Evolution* from 1923, in which he referred not only to Bergson, Whitehead, and James but also to Spinoza, Poincaré, and Einstein, among others.[21] This well represents how modes of experience, perception, and thought beyond the standardized human (male) model were continuously sought after in various fields, from different philosophical theories to the arts and biological research, for example.

But the main character of this chapter is not a great philosopher but a conceptual person (a contraction of the forces of the cosmos under a figure of a persona), perhaps, or a conceptual animal: the tick. It is curious how this tiny insect became one of the key philosophical conceptual entities of twentieth-century thought, an insect that was commented on by Martin Heidegger, Gilles Deleuze, Giorgio Agamben, and others. In this chapter I mostly follow Deleuze's ideas in which he connected the ethology of ticks with the concept of assemblages.

The tick and its cultural status are perfect examples of the work of translation and mediation, of how an insect and studies of insects can be transformed into a whole other discourse or a territory of thought, deterritorialized from its strict confines as exemplary of animal behavior to a mode of thought. But this mode of thought can also do things—and act as a vector from one mode of experience and perception to another scale and layer.[22] Perhaps the tick does not do much thinking, but it does, however, reside at the center of a whole discourse on philosophy, affects, and, as we will see, media theory as well. In addition to the tick, and the ideas of the life-world of animals and other entities proposed by Uexküll, we will track the ideas of "post-Kantian" experience in relation to some notions relating to insect worlds. Here, again, philosophical ideas such as those of James and others are "put to work" with the help of these little animals.

ETHOLOGICAL MAPPING OF MILIEUS OF PERCEPTION

Jakob von Uexküll was already enjoying high prestige during the 1920s and 1930s after having published works such as *Umwelt und Innenwelt der Tiere* (1909, 2nd edition 1921) and *Theoretische Biologie* (1920, 2nd edition 1928). Both introduced his ideas that the Kantian constitutive spheres of space and time, *Raum und Zeit,* were not so much absolutes but rather special conditions of variation found in all animals and entities that sense. As he wrote at the end of the 1930s, "Kant had already shaken the complacent position of the universe by exposing it as being merely a human form of perception. From there on it was a short step to reinstall the Umwelt space of the individual human being in its proper position."[23] Johannes Müller, despite his appreciation of Kant, had inaugurated a certain crumbling of Kantian apperception. In a similar manner, Uexküll wanted to continue the Kantian project into the life-worlds of animals as well but to push it further. In his mix of the physiological psychology of Hermann von Helmholz (where he saw the founding principle for a perception of things in the intensive qualities of sense organs) and Kant, Uexküll wanted to emphasize the role of the body (and alternative organizations of bodies) in perception as well as in the feedback loop between perception and action. As Jonathan Crary notes, this Kantian unity was shown to be exposed to various kinds of manipulations via the physiological system, and in a similar vein Uexküll, who appreciated Müller as well as Kant, can be thought to show the crumbling of the human apperception via the potentially infinite number of perceptual worlds existing in animals—with the world of perceptions too small or too large to comprehend from the human perspective.[24]

For Uexküll, what defined the objective world was not a single reality disclosed similarly to all its inhabitants but the way we perceive and act in the world. Put the other way round, the way we perceive, valorize, and act in a world defines its objectivity to us. From this perspective, there was no objective time or space but a reality consisting of various differing ways of *contracting* time and space.[25] Needless to say, Uexküll was here repeating the same realizations introduced in physics, modern art (e.g., cubism), and philosophy. He was not the only writer rethinking time and space through the nonhuman, and actually these ideas resonated with many of the emerging ideas in philosophy as well. Indeed, through various philosophies of process and radical empiricism, the world of experience was opened up much beyond the human being. Kantian transcendental philosophy of experience was extended to the world of animals and things as well.[26]

Hence, ethological mapping of the perception beyond the human being can be connected to a broader philosophical task of understanding the human being as one singular way of contracting the world and as a specific capacity to signify, exchange, and communicate.[27] What can be seen as early phases of animal ethology were, however, according to Georges Canguilhem, much less focused on temporality and dynamics. Jacques Loeb's and John B. Watson's research into animal behavior was still more akin to the mechanistic (and later behavioralist) understanding of the relationship of bodies and milieus. Here the milieu is seen as determining the organism's pose as part of the milieu, a physical continuation (expressed in the centrality of "reflex" responses) of its surroundings.[28] Entomologists such as William M. Wheeler had grown dissatisfied with the morphological view in studies of animal life and proposed to move toward dynamics of bodies. This stance had something more in common with an ecological or ethological analysis, as Wheeler proposed in 1902.[29]

Uexküll also wanted to distance himself from a physiological and structural understanding of the bodies of animals. Such a mechanistic way of understanding interactions of the bodies and lives of animals did not capture the active, individuating ways of *living* in the world. So instead of seeing animals as mechanistic structures and machines, Uexküll adopted the idea that the simpler animals are, the more potential there is for undifferentiated openness in them. Hence, for Uexküll amoebas were less machines than horses, as the latter are more structurated animals in terms of their development.[30] He understood technology in terms of automation of functions and predetermination, but thought structural openness implied something else. Yet, because Uexküll did not want to succumb to an idealist or vitalist position, he continuously maintained his interest in the idea that the perception and action systems of animals are material and physiologically real.

What an animal perceives *(Merkwelt)* becomes structurally integrated into its action-world *(Wirkwelt)*. Hence, the world of an animal is characterized by this functional circle, which integrates an entity into its

environment (or a milieu to other milieus). A tick is in this sense characterized by three modes, three ways of perception/action: it (1) smells a
mammal with its olfactory tendency and then drops down from a straw;
then it (2) perceives the temperature of the animal and (3) finds a hair-
less spot where it can stick its nose and draw some blood.[31] According
to Uexküll, a physiologist would be content to regard this as a simple
machinelike reaction-action pattern that expresses the functional connections between perception organs and the central nervous system.
Animal-machines are mechanical entities that interact without the need
to add any agencies into the picture. However, Uexküll's account provided
a much more dynamic image of nature than that.

What Uexküll implied was that we are dealing not with predetermined
objects of nature but with subject-object relations that are defined by the
potentiality opened in their encounters. Entities of the world, such as the
tick, are only in these relationships of significance and there is no world
beyond these relations. As Agamben underlines, adopting Uexküll's example, a laboratory experiment in Rostock where a tick was kept alive for
eighteen years in isolation without food demonstrated this. The tick sunk
into a dreamlike state of waiting but, without time, a suspended moment.
Uexküll's conclusion: no relationships, no world, no time. The world is
fundamentally a dynamic one; where relations are temporal and without
defining relationships, the world seems to stop.[32] In other words, there
is no time "in general," but time is always folded through temporal relations that can be both actual and virtual. The temporality and reality of
the world are then enacted through lived relations in a Jamesian manner.

Dynamics afford the structuration. Even though highly structured,
a living form is continuously potentially open to its environment, with
which it forms a functional circle (what cyberneticians would later call a
feedback circle.) Life is a dynamic enterprise that forms through the relations of entities with each other. In a radical posthumanist way, Uexküll
never got tired of accentuating that so far we have approached the world
through our human, oh-so-human lenses but that there is a panorama
of perceptions and ways of approaching the world that are closed to us
humans but continuously lived by other life forms:

> Among the animals, with their smaller Umwelt horizons, the celestial
> bodies are essentially different. When mosquitoes dance in the sunset,

they do not see our big human sun, setting six kilometres away, but small mosquito suns that set about half a meter away. The moon and stars are absent from the sky of the mosquito.[33]

SPYHOLES INTO THE WORLD

As I explained in chapter 1, animals offered lessons of "nonhuman perception" due to their capabilities to sense, move, and mold the world. The new animal worlds in physiological research and beyond (such as *Alice in Wonderland*–type ideas of Victorian England or the emerging science-fiction genre with its hyperbolic insects from the end of the nineteenth century) presented peepholes or vehicles that transported the human experience to worlds otherwise unperceived. The idea was that we do not know what a potential future mode of life is able to do. This was a very Darwinian idea, expressed in the *Origin of Species,* but was also used by such critics of Darwin as Samuel Butler, who in 1865 speculated on "mechanical creation," writing that "we see no a priori objection to the gradual development of a mechanical life, though that life shall be so different from ours that it is only by a severe discipline that we can think of it as life at all."[34] Exploration was not only part of the geographical travel of the scientists, but a more general mode of tapping into novel worlds of experience and perception.

Hence, in a fitting fashion, the popular and perhaps most celebrated entomologist, Jean Henri Fabre, in 1922 was pronounced the prototypical explorer, "Homer of the Insect World," excavating new environments as had Alice. As one newspaperman wrote of Fabre : "The insect—this 'little animated clay, capable of pleasure and pain'—is to him, as it were, a tiny spyhole through which he looks behind the scenes of the terrible, mysterious universe. His knowledge merely serves to deepen his sense of wonder and awe."[35] Just as the quests of the early entomologists created a new mapping of the superempirical (or subempirical to humans) worlds of insects, the novelists of the imaginary were able to invent worlds not seen, heard, or thought before, as in the case of Alice's plunge into Wonderland.

In the 1920s context, these new perceptual worlds, "spyholes," curiously resonate with the discourses of film and media technological deterritorialization of human perception.[36] New technological apparatuses, as noted in the first chapter, were able to capture even wavelengths of sensation that would otherwise elude the human senses.[37] As Agamben explains, Uexküll's work is closely related to quantum physics and the artistic avant-garde movement in its valuation of the primacy of variation, an "unreserved abandonment of every anthropocentric perspective in the life sciences and the radical dehumanisation of the image of nature,"[38] and thus a continuous interest in an infinite possibility of parallel worlds.

But Uexküll was not keen on parallels between animals and machines. The animal was at best an imperfect machine.[39] For Uexküll, (media) technologies were still very much mechanistic machines. In a Fordist manner, he thought that machines meant clocks, factories, and blindly repeated processes whose physiological equivalents were the reaction-time experiments from the nineteenth century on.[40] Against this spatializing understanding of technology and physiology (something that, for example, Bergson also criticized), Uexküll proposed a more temporal take, a so-called musical approach to natural technics: animals were not mechanical machines, but they seemed to express technics understood as an art of perception and orientation, as do the bees who are able to coordinate on a field toward certain key forms of openness and closedness found in flowers.[41] In other words, instead of imposing external meters and measurements on the intensive capacities of animals, we should approach them as creating the measurements by their unfolding with the world. Animals create worlds as an unfolding not unlike the temporality of music, whereas physiological understanding of technology seems to be a mere tracing of this creation. This resonated strongly with Bergson's view in *Creative Evolution,* where he noted that even though matter was seen to express an order that was "approximately mathematical," the intensive forces of nature were not reducible to such a tracking. Instead, nature was a creative evolution without finality, a radically non-human-centered becoming.[42]

Curiously, Martin Heidegger picked up on Uexküll's points in his meditations on instruments, animals, and humans. To a certain extent, Heidegger was following ideas similar to those of Uexküll and even Bergson. The animal is different from machines in its dynamic nature, its temporal unfolding. The organs of an animal are not instruments in the sense of a machine because the latter are "ready-made pieces of equipment" and always subject to preregulated forms of action. In addition, as Heidegger said in his 1929 lectures on metaphysics, the machine always needs a creator and an operator.[43] Organisms are radically contrasted to such an inert technology, which shows that Heidegger's idea of technology was very much stuck with the rationalized Taylor-Fordist paradigm of his age. Only organisms are seen as self-reproductive, self-regulating, and self-renewing. Even though there was a radical difference between his view and the Deleuzian and Bergsonian "machinics of nature," when Heidegger wanted to differentiate the animal from the human (the animal is poor in the world, it lacks history and self-consciousness and is not able to exist beyond its factual environment in the way *Da-sein* is able to be in the world), his view of the temporality and processuality of nature stayed in touch with Uexküll. The world is filled with events such as seeing, hearing, grasping, digesting, and so forth, all of which are "processes of nature."[44] Where animals differ from inert matter (such as stones) is in their nature as unfolding events, a behavioral relationship they have with their environment. Insect perception is localized not in the structure of the eye, for example, but in the continuous tension between the capacities of the insect that have formed the physiological eye and the environment as its needed partner in unraveling the perception event. The organs of an animal are not just instruments that follow the prescriptive paths but are bound to the animal's lifespan (to use Heidegger's words) and also to the temporal span of its environment: "Rather the organs are bound into and are bound up with the temporal span which the animal is capable of sustaining as a living being."[45]

Uexküll for his part used the idea of "emergence" to differentiate between the mechanical understanding of structures and the inert forces of physical nature. The Estonia-born ethologist thought an animal is to be considered a dynamic and living entity; it is always more than its bodily mechanism, which is built from the constitutive parts of cells and "formation building orders" *(Formbildungsbefehl).*[46] Instead, life is music and melody, a curious kind of understanding of material forces that we should now turn to. This resonates with a broader ethological project as well, defined as an analysis of "patterns in time," some of which might elude the human senses and demonstrate alternative perceptions of time and bodily patterns.[47]

MACHINIC ASSEMBLAGES OF NATURE

A key part of Uexküll's "technics of nature" consists of the idea that compositions or aggregates of nature are centrifugal. Although such mechanical machines as watches are always turning only toward their inner principles, which are predetermined and rely on those components (i.e., are centripetal), the "building" of an animal works as a project that always orients away from a center to the world.[48] In *Bedeutungslehre,* a short and lucid explanation of his key ideas from 1940, Uexküll referred to this kind of understanding of technics as a melodic one; in other words, musical ideas of composition act here as the needed "lesson," showing that harmonies are always produced of at least two notes. Notes, punctuation, and patterns form, only together, a contrapuntal relationship both in music and in matter (nature).[49]

Uexküll thought that such melodics can conjoin various kinds of phenomena across scales, as his examples show. The leaves of an oak form a coupling of melodics with raindrops, the leaves themselves acting as a channeling and a distribution machine while the raindrops engage in a compositional becoming with the "living machine" of the oak and its cells. In the animal kingdom, an apt example is the living machine formed by an octopus and seawater, with the water becoming a "carrier of significance" *(Bedeutungsträger)* for the animal, which uses it for its movements.[50] Furthermore, in the world of insects, such couplings, or foldings with the world, are constantly taking place.

The perfect example is the coupling of the spider and its web with the fly. The spider is here referred to as a tailor but one that does not measure the fly with a measuring stick but somehow contains an image *(Abbild)* of the fly of an a priori nature *(Urbild).* A certain perfectness that parallels the previous chapter's focus on insect geometrics is evident here as well. The threads are in optimized composition regarding the size and perceptive capacities of the fly. Weaving the radial threads stronger than the circular threads allows the spider to capture the fly in the web, and the fly with its rough eyesight is not able to perceive the finely constructed threads.[51] As Agamben notes, the "two perceptual worlds of the fly and the spider are absolutely non-communicating, and yet so perfectly in tune that we might say that the original score of the fly, which we also call its original image or archetype, acts on that of the spider in such a way that the web the spider weaves can be described as 'fly-like.'"[52] In the melodics of nature, entities possess a certain score that defines their affect-worlds, the potential affordances, potentials, or affects they have with the world, and in which the score of the spider and the fly are interlocked at least on a virtual level. One can find the same rhythmics and contrapuntal levels on various scales, from primitive levels of life such as that of amoebas and insects to social life, as Uexküll seemed to hint in his collection of biographical texts originally from 1936, *Niegeschaute Welten* (Unseen worlds): like ants and mosquitoes, counts, barons, and, for example, Neapolitans have their own closed worlds, a pattern that is multiscalar and defining.[53]

Such an idea of technics characterizing the whole of creation can be understood well with the emphasis Deleuze and Guattari placed on Uexküll's ideas. This is what Deleuze and Guattari refer to as a concept of machinic assemblages, the machinics of the world. There is a primary artificiality and technics that characterizes not merely the human historical world but creation in general, a sphere that precedes the division to nature and culture. What Uexküll constantly underlined was the need to see nature and its actors not as structures and predefined categories (species or genus) but as becomings that are dynamically intertwined with their surroundings (not static). In other words, "machines, devices, and technologies of animal and human life, such as spectacles, telescopes, lathes and so on, are to be viewed as 'perceptual tools' and 'effector tools' that are a constitutive feature of the 'worlds' of living things,"[54] as Ansell-Pearson clarifies. In this context Deleuze and Guattari use the idea of associated milieu as a structuration going on across various scales of living entities. Associated milieu works through the dynamics of capturing energy sources, sensing and perceiving relevant materials nearby, and fabrication of compounds based on the perceptions and captures—a responsive gesture toward environment, that is.[55] Drawing directly from Uexküll, the structuration of an animal milieu is seen as a morphogenetic feature that parallels the importance of the form of the animal. That is, even though Uexküll noted the importance of the physiology of an animal in a materialist vein, the structures are active only in their associated milieus:

> Since the form depends on an autonomous code, it can only be constituted in an associated milieu that interlaces active, perceptive and

energetic characteristics in a complex fashion, in conformity with the code's requirements; and the form can develop only through intermediary milieus that regulate the speeds and rates of its substances.[56]

IMMANENCE AND THE ARTIFICE

The technics of nature relate to the idea of positing a plane of immanence on which the issue of categorical differences between animals and humans, nature and technology is bracketed and the view of affects, movements, and relations among parts is posited as primary. Deleuze (and Guattari) think Uexküll is best read here together with Spinoza in order to create a synthesis of ethological ethics: there is only one nature as a plane of immanence on which variations and interactions take place. In this framework of assemblages, bodies are primarily relations of speeds and slowness, motion and rest and defined by their capabilities to affect and be affected by other bodies. There is a plane of nature on which bodies are articulated as affects (passages between bodies) and change. Living things are singularities composed of relations and intensities, an approach that tries to think of life beyond structure, substance, or constitutive subject-object relationships.[57] Here the primary temporality and metastability of living entities is what characterizes individuals across scales, from the coupling of the tick with mammals to the emerging swarm or the spider and the fly conjoining in a common rhythm. This kind of ontological technics seems to have been, then, already in its emerging context in the early twentieth century, grounded in a new understanding of the primacy of temporality as a structuring force.

It is also worth noting the difference to phenomenological accounts of experience, something that Uexküll's research could also easily be seen to address. Whereas in phenomenology the experience of something is always conceptualized as a relationship between a subject and an object, the Deleuzian idea of a plane of immanence sidesteps this Kantian-Husserlian understanding and looks for the events of experience as constitutive of its participants. This is a field of experience designed for no one in particular, even though actualizing and resulting in actual bodies. This also implies that experience is not limited to one transcendental form of experiencing, such as the human being. This radical variation, or radical empiricism, was already proposed by William James and can be seen as well illustrating how to move beyond the epistemological problem of how we can know or experience anything beyond our own human form.[58] A multiplicity of real relations are neglected by our perceptions, raising the question of on what level or scale those superempirical relations are experienced.

This was naturally the inspiration and the problem of research into unknown worlds in entomology, the arts, and philosophy, as well as the new technologies: how to grasp (or "prehend") fields of experience that would reach beyond our particular worlds. As one entomologist of the Indian tropic wrote in 1909, the problem was one of translation and transposition:

> The senses, the instincts, the modes of expression of insects are so totally diverse from our own that there is scarcely any point of contact. In the case of mammals, of birds and to some extent of reptiles, we have in the eyes, in the feathers and in the movements, a clue to their feelings, to the emotions that sway them, to the motives that guide their actions; in insects we have none, and the great index of insect feeling, the antenna, has no counterpart in higher animals, and conveys nothing to our uninformed brains.[59]

Heidegger tackled a similar issue as the primarily human faculty of being always beyond oneself (although not denying that animals could not transpose themselves).[60] On a broader diagrammatic level, biology and sciences of physiology tried to construct such planes of inspection on which they could try to track down the intensive qualities of animals and map them as media technologically determined functions. Such experimentation can be seen as in a way trying to construct subjectless spaces of experience, but still remained under a very functional logic of slowing down the uncanny experiences of alien nature.[61] As an alternative to such processes of slowing down, or phenomenological enterprises, one should also keep an eye on the radical difference at the heart of the world. Instead of a relativity of perceptions (phenomenology), we have a continuous reality of relations, as Deleuze underlines, backed up by James. The question is, How can one tune oneself so that a part of that radical difference, the experiences that overwhelm us, would be able to enter our registers of experience? How can one enter a plane of immanence and open oneself up to durations of animals, insects, stones, matter, technology, etc.?[62] Or, in other words, how can one move toward the horizon of the unliveable and the inhuman forces and nonhuman material intensities and rhythms in contrast to the phenomenological enterprise of what can be experienced as human beings? This means, as Elizabeth Grosz notes, that we must replace Husserl with Nietzsche[63]— and humans with insects, we can add.

In resonance with Uexküll's ideas, Deleuze extends this plane of immanence to a technics of nature, in which "artifice is fully a part of Nature, since each thing, on the immanent plane of nature, is defined by the arrangements of motions and affects into which it enters, whether these arrangements are artificial or natural."[64] This means that we must focus on the affective potentials of animals, human beings, or any other interactional entities, a defining factor of existence as becoming: what affects is one capable of, what can they do, with whom, when, and with what results?

The answers to all of these questions, as Deleuze ceaselessly underlines, are not known a priori but only through experimentation. Hence, he also mentions Uexküll as a great experimenter, one who looked for the potential melodics in nature, from the scale of local interactions to harmonies of nature. The animal (or, if we want to talk on a more general level of becoming, the living entity) is continuously coupled with its environment, stretched through counterpoints such as the plant and the rain, the spider and the fly. It is not a question of a body representing drives, forces, or even ideologies but of intermingling with the world.[65] There is a material connection (beyond consciousness or representations) that the body folds with itself. Bodies always exist via their limits and membranes, points of connection with other bodies across scales. For Deleuze and Guattari as readers of Uexküll, the interior and exterior are intermingled and selected as well as projected through each other, which already echoes the theme of folding as constituent of subjectivity, something that Deleuze elaborates in his book on Foucault written a couple of years later (1986). An individuality is always constituted as a tension or a machination between elements. So even if, as Bergson notes, the technics of animals and insects are immanent to their bodily formations in contrast to the intelligent externalization we find in humans, these technics are in constant tension with an outside, a folding, instead of a self-enclosed system.[66]

EREWHON: TECHNICS OUT OF BOUNDS

Interestingly, Uexküll's ideas of technics of nature that move beyond a Fordist and mechanist understandings of technology have early precursors in the ideas of a critic of Darwinism, Samuel Butler. Having traveled to New Zealand in 1859 to become a sheep farmer, Butler published during the following decades numerous articles and books that were critical of Darwin (propagating, for example, Lamarckian ideas)[67] but that, in a funny way, continued Darwinian ideas of radical evolution. Hence, nowadays one connects Butler more closely to ideas of machines as dynamic, evolving creatures than to sheep breeding.

It is interesting, then, to read Butler's early writings as relevant to the development of the notion of ecologies of media as well. In Butler's 1872 novel *Erewhon,* set in an idyllic, isolated place reminiscent of New Zealand, technology is seen as capable of evolving and reproducing. More specifically, Butler proposed a kind of symbiotic relationship between humans and technology, something akin to the relationship of an insect and a flower:

> Surely if a machine is able to reproduce another machine systematically, we may say that it has a reproductive system. What is a reproductive system, if it be not a system for reproduction? And how few of the machines are there by other machines? But it is man that makes them do so. Yes; but is it not insects that make many of the plants reproductive, and would not whole families of plants die out if their fertilisation was not effected by a class of agents utterly foreign to themselves? Does any one say that the red clover has no reproductive system because the humble bee (and the humble bee only) must aid and abet it before it can reproduce? No one. The humble bee is a part of the reproductive system of the clover. Each one of ourselves has sprung from minute animalcules whose entity was entirely distinct from our own, and which acted after their kind with no thought or heed of what we might think about it. These little creatures are part of our own reproductive system; then why not we part of that of the machines?[68]

Humans and machines were interlocked in Butler's vision in a mutual agency that is actualized in event-assemblages. In a Darwinian (after) wake, Butler satirically questioned the idea of men as the innovative motors of evolution and technics and suggested in this quoted passage a more complex view on the machinology of the living world. Machines were no organ-projection of the human form but exhibited a curious logic of their own. This view distinguishes Butler from the anthropological view on technics of Kapp and others and connects him to a more hidden history of seeing technology as *machinic connectionism*. This, I would suggest, is something that can be intimately connected to later ideas of Uexküll and the view of primary artificiality and natural technics. Uexküll thought the melodic partners in contrapuntal relationships form what could be called in Deleuze and Guattari's vocabulary machinic entities, and this idea already resonated strongly with Butler.

As Luciana Parisi explains, in a machinic view on cultural reproduction, there cannot be any privileged terms or origins, as Kapp- or McLuhan-inspired views might imply. Instead of seeing technological extensions as stemming from the body and moving outward, on a plane of immanence technical machines are always relative to a larger social machine. The technical machines are inseparable from their relations with biochemical, biosocial, and bioeconomical assemblages.[69] Butler contributed to such a view in which the human body or technology as a specific substance is not specified beforehand, a priori, but becomes selected in complex assemblages. In such a synthetic view, almost anything can become technological, a platform for intensification of certain potentials that can be called technical after the fact. For example, reproduction is not a matter of a specific center designed for the task (whether a biological form or a specific center in the human body).[70] In a much more cosmic take on sexuality, bees and clovers (and spiders and flies) are interconnected in a system of mutual becoming, and similar ideas of multirelationality can be seen working in spheres of culture and technology as well. In other words, nature is the perfect crystalization of technics as a potential for intensification and variation; media technologies are good runners-up. In a nature–culture continuum, the relations define and self-organize without an external principle or point of view in a process that was later incorporated into theories of autopoiesis by Maturana and Varela. Yet this kind of an autopoiesis does not recognize the existence of a harmonious state of balance but rather works with the realization of a continuous excess and overcoding. There is something that is always beyond the coupling, a potentiality of the new (deterritorialization). Multirelationality implies potentiality as virtuality: the ecological principle of "there is always much more where it came from."[71] Thus it is not only the human body that affords technology ways of modulating movements, perception, and affection but bodies of animals and other intensities. In an assemblage, anything can be captured as an instrument and technology and can act as a project, prosthesis, or tool. With Butler, and various other examples that frame animal life as active and differentiating, the question of technology becomes deterritorialized from (1) a specific material form and (2) the human body as the primal locus of technological organization.

Ansell-Pearson explains that this mode of understanding evolution as a machinic engineering of desire echoes later Deleuze-Guattarian themes of machinic ontology. Butler saw this not as a vitalist stand (there is no unity before the machinic connections, a stance perhaps similar to that of Uexküll), nor is it a mechanist position (there is no fixed determination, again something that Uexküll wanted to underline with the dynamics of nature).[72] Invention and innovation are not characteristics of the human being creating machines but part of the essence of nature as art(ificiality).[73] This realization concerns not only the fact that insects have been treated as machines of a kind but, in addition, the idea that nature is itself a technics of radical invention, a virtual force of creation, also capable of mutations and accidents. In one sense, this could be connected to ideas raised by Darwin about the radical posthuman temporality of the world (expressed in variations and natural selection), which exceeds the teleological utility-oriented view of breeding artifices only for human purposes and as "images of man," so to speak. Instead, a radically temporal technicity/creation of evolution marks a technical time beyond the technics of humans.[74] Here perhaps Nietzsche can be seen as one of the continuers of Darwin's project,[75] but in a similar way all those other voices speaking of the technics of nature, from Bergson to Uexküll, entomology to Deleuze, have contributed to a machinology of matter and nature.

The machinology is also an expression of the aforementioned Spinozism, ethics-ethology underlining a fresh perspective of the dynamics of matter. What is interesting, and what I will return to in later chapters, is how these ideas of the dynamics of matter have also been incorporated as part of media theory and contemporary media design and biotechnology, for example, in robots and their dynamic coupling with their surroundings or in artificial life projects of self-organization and "perception" of environment in software. The 1980s interest in distributed and embodied structurations of organisms in environments took advantage of this kind of low-level intelligence, an entwining of local bodies and a costructuration of environments and perceptions.[76] Already in 1929, Whitehead proposed the idea that a key lesson insects can teach us is that we do not need hierarchical unifying control to operate as bodies. We are, in any case, distributed systems with "millions of centers of life in each animal body."[77] Centralized control might characterize the cerebral existence of humans, but life has come up with various other ways of coordinating the living body with its environment—a crucial understanding in the artificial life paradigm of recent decades. Such kinds of a media archaeological rewirings, from the insect research of the late nineteenth and early twentieth centuries to contemporary media production, highlight a nonlinear understanding of media and its history.[78]

ETHOLOGY AS NOMAD, MINORITARIAN KNOWLEDGE

To conclude this chapter, we note that a creative, relationally unfolding temporality characterized the early twentieth-century ideas of the technics of nature. This connects with the notion argued by Thacker that in order to come up with a satisfyingly dynamic notion of networks and media technologies we have to find radically temporal approaches. Of course Thacker was writing mainly about network organization patterns, and we have been dealing with perception in a dynamic world of animals. However, these things are intimately related. "Being organized means *being capable,*"[79] Heidegger reminded us, saying that a form of organization is an articulation of the potential, of a potential dynamic unfolding. This implies, then, not an unchanging structure but a thinking through of organisms with their constant potentiality for a deterritorialization, a margin of excess. As it is, temporality stands at the core of the post-Kantian ideas concerning animal perception, coupling with environments and the idea of life as a becoming pertaining not to a universal time-space a priori but instead to a continuous variation. Themes raised in philosophy were doubled in biology and insect research, where animal perception spurred later notions of the dynamics of primitive life, from Heidegger to Deleuze. Whereas Heidegger was keen on clearly marking the differences among inanimate matter, living animals, and conscious, self-reflective human beings, Deleuze (and Guattari) promoted the idea of ontogenesis or an artifice-approach that is characteristic of nature and beyond. They wanted to present an ontological view that would not differentiate between various "classes" of being but that would keep an eye on the potentials of affect: what is X capable of? In Whitehead's terminology, this amounts to a task similar to those of creative abstractions, which served as "lures" that philosophy can use to vectorize experiences, capacities, and tendencies to bypass false problems and false abstractions.[80]

The wiring of biological themes concerning coupling, affects, and temporality can also help us to understand the biopolitics of network culture, where technology is in a way using an increasingly biological mode of organization and logic. This does not imply that technological cultures would be "natural" in the categorical sense of following a predetermined plan beyond a politics of choice, framing, and valorization. Biology—or, more accurately, ethology as a mapping of complex interactions and temporality—can help us to understand how affects are captured as part of a capitalist creation of value and how new modes of organization are developing as dynamic, temporally tuned networks. Quite concretely, I refer to the historical modes of mapping and transposing biology not only on the level of politics, as writers from Michel Foucault to Roberto Esposito have argued, but also on the level of media technologies, where ethology gains new currency as a way of understanding the relational affording capacities of objects, processes, and agencies.[81]

In fact, ethology can be differentiated from the transcendental organization of biology as it emerged during the nineteenth century with its focus on organisms, functions, and norms. These are regulatory categories that designate bodies, what they can do (physiologically, socially, culturally), and how they should do it (norms as the way to stabilize variations). In ethological mapping bodies are not defined as organisms but are seen as dynamic systems "of non-subjectified affects and powers."[82] Ethology is more akin to experimentation and construction of a plane of immanence than to building a plane of organization that is a reactive mode of knowledge—a knowledge of definitions, classifications, functions, and spatialization. The sense of this ontoethologics, to use a term from Eric Alliez, flows from the dynamism that moves further from phenomenologies where (human) flesh and the organism is posited as the starting ground of sensation and thought, and it also moves away from an understanding of ethology (presented by Konrad Lorenz) in which phylogenetic evolution explains the expressive becomings of entities in their environments. The internal "drive" does not explain how an animal occupies a territory, but there is the continuous tension and in-between of milieus of the inside and the outside. Here, exactly, ethology turns to an experimental probing, a superior ethology: "to think in terms of becoming rather than evolution, of expressive qualities rather than functions, of assemblages rather than behaviours."[83] Instead of a poorness in the world, animals can be seen expressing various modes of becoming, color-becomings and sound-becomings, which are expressions not of any inner drive or physiological structure nor of a simple environmental pressure but of the rhythms and counterpoints "set into a refrain by the animal in the movement of territorialization,"[84] as Alliez continues. This is where I see Uexküll distancing his position from that of Kant and moving closer to an experimental mode of transcendental empiricism, or radical empiricism. It moves from a Kantian and a phenomenological focus on the life-world and its conditions of possibility to the potentials of life beyond recognized forms.[85]

It is easy to overestimate the impact and ideas of Uexküll; ethological mappings also work toward fixing capabilities of bodies to species that are then understood as transcendental conditions. Especially in his earlier work, the 1920s *Theoretische Biologie,* Uexküll was prone to think of the environmental relation in very geometric terms as a gridding of the spatial surroundings. Furthermore, he was at times outspoken in his debt to Kant and at times far from the radical thinker of open-ended becomings he has later been filtered to be via Deleuze and Guattari. The melodics of nature in Uexküll are exactly melodics as strict predetermined structures whose first note determines the rest of the scale of possibilities. Hence, at times it seems that he was much more interested in transcendental laws of experience than merely in variation.[86] It is important to note the possible different ways of reading him and giving a bit more emphasis to different aspects. As is clear from what I have written here, I follow a reading that places emphasis on temporality and becoming in his work while paying attention to the specific contexts in which Uexküll's ethological theories emerged as well as their potential links to a rethinking of ecologies of media as well. A historical and contextualized understanding of the role of ethological research can highlight, despite the difficulties, how Uexküll worked at the same time toward weird perceptual worlds in his process of tracking animal affects. He differed from Darwin in his insistence on the plan of nature but still offered a microtemporal view of the interactions in the world that can perhaps be well characterized as a temporality of breathing—of milieus in interaction and folding.[87] In this sense, a Deleuzo-Guattarian reading is able to take the ethological analysis into a mode of analysis that emphasizes experimentality, probing, and speculating as distinctive modes of animal bodies—and cultural analysis.

Here ethology becomes a mode of nomad knowledge, or science, in which variation is primary and becoming is rewired at the heart of an understanding of the world based on nonhuman events.[88] Instead of seeking universal laws to be reproduced (in the manner of structures, behavioral laws, or, as has later been the case, the determination of genetic programs), a nomadic interest in knowledge wants to look at the singularities and their movements and constitute an understanding of what "matter can do." This is a fundamentally and radically temporal way of looking at the world. It avoids the spatializing grids of royal science by paying attention to the "smallest deviation," where another step and another look will add something to the whole so as to constitute a change. Naturally Deleuze and Guattari have had their fair share of critique, or "correction," for example, from Mark Hansen. According to Hansen, Deleuze and Guattari's biophilosophy has neglected a thorough analysis of the organism, which has been too hastily discarded as being part of the "molar sphere" of rigid organization. Although Deleuze and Guattari do offer a consistent reading of and contribution to biophilosophy, with their work resonating with various holistic models of research into the interrelations of the body, the brain, and the world (Andy Clark); agency as an ecological event (Maturana and Varela, Bateson); and cognitive science that has opened up to adaptive behavior and dynamic models of cognition as part of the world (Rodney Brooks, Clark), they are still, according to Hansen, much too focused on the plane of immanence as the virtual, uninhibited force of becoming. Again according to Hansen, this is an abandonment of the organism as a restriction (but a creative one) that leads Deleuze and Guattari much too close to posthumanist ideals of the body as a programmable, completely fluid entity.[89]

This flags an important issue, even though I am not convinced that Hansen's critique of Deleuze and Guattari is accurate. In this model the body is not purely a restriction but a potentiality through which non-human virtuality might function. By insisting on a double-faced reality with the other face toward virtuality as a force not exhausted by actualizations and actualizations as the folding of organisms with the world, we are able to think the ecology of bodies as a dynamic but continuously material, animal enterprise, a kind of abstract materialism in which bodies are defined by self-variation.[90] Even if we accept Hansen's criticism of Deleuze-Guattarian biophilosophy that draws heavily on Uexküll's ethology, I would insist on the value of temporality it offers. Its focus on relationality and becoming through an unfolding in time is something that transports Uexküll from his own perception of machines as only mechanical to an appreciation of machines that are not reducible to the already defined. Deleuze and Guattari write their ethology in the age of temporal machines, soft machines of variation, metamorphosis.

Although rewiring a bit of ethology into existing understandings of media and culture might help us to summon a more dynamic approach, it also offers tools to grasp a politics of organization, perception, and coupling that takes place on metaphysical layers that bypass rigid distinctions between biology and technology, man and animal (or even man and insect). Following the "insect paradigm" of modern media culture seems to be continuously hinting at the importance of the animal not as a transcendent figure but as a continuous deterritorializing factor, a movement of sensations and perceptions that presents variables into thought. In this sense, insects act as art (creation) and media. They suggest new percepts and affects but also movements that can be taken up by philosophy and cultural analysis, which are keen on finding a more temporal, machinic, and ethological way of approaching the world as one of immanent becomings and territorializations.[91]

Next we turn to another mode of temporality and another theme of noncognitive modulation while continuing themes surrounding art and perception. It is no wonder that the curious metamorphosing animals from entomology to Franz Kafka also inspired the world of avant-garde artists. In this chapter I briefly mentioned that the discourse on cinematic and technological perception can be seen as forming an alliance with philosophy and biology, but similarly, between the two world wars the surrealist movement in particular was busy coupling new modes of perception with a fascination for morphing insects—a biomorphing of sensory capabilities. In the next chapter I will turn to surrealists and avant-garde art, especially the work of Roger Caillois, who, most actively among the French, was interested in the zone between worlds of animality and worlds of artifice. Relatively recently, Caillois's work on games has been incorporated as part of the emerging field of digital game studies, but this link between his interest in animals and the research on games and artifice has not yet been excavated. What we need to focus on are the implications for understanding space and temporality that Caillois is suggesting and that the theme of animality in the work of Caillois and other surrealists is not a mere metaphor but a vector that can be used to more thoroughly understand the affect life of modern subjectivity.

FOUR

METAMORPHOSIS, INTENSITY, AND DEVOURING SPACE
Elements for an Insect Game Theory

Ultimately, from whatever angle one may approach things, the fundamental question proves to be that of *distinction:* distinctions between what is real and imaginary, between wakefulness and sleep, between ignorance and knowledge, and so on. These are all distinctions, in short, that any acceptable project must seek to chart very precisely and, at the same time, insist on resolving. Certainly, no distinction is more pronounced than the one demarcating an organism from its environment; at least, none involves a more acutely perceptible sense of separation. We should pay particular attention to this phenomenon, and more specifically to what we must still call, given our limited information, its pathology (although the term has a purely statistical meaning): namely, the set of phenomena referred to as mimicry.

—Roger Caillois, "Mimicry and Legendary Psychasthenia"

Even though the previous chapter addressed temporality as a key theme of insect media and the ethological analysis of affects, we neglected the theme of metamorphosis. However, metamorphosis marks for the majority of us a defining feature of the image of "insect life": transformation, development, and change. Hence, it is a concept of temporality par excellence in which variation becomes a defining and primary feature of "identity." This proneness to change was evident in the caterpillar's arrogant response to Alice in Wonderland, and it has been a constant source of research for both entomologists and also as a much broader cultural concept. With roots in metaphysical and spiritual thought,

metamorphotic processes served as a key tool for understanding metaphoric and metonymic transformations of language, as well as mythical, abrupt crossings between men and animals, for example, when they
could suddenly, by metamorphosis, start to speak. As the *Oxford English
Dictionary* explains, the passage from metamorphoses in language and
metaphysics to biology happened around the mid-seventeenth century,
when the first biological analyses of insect transformations as part of
their growth emerged.

Frequently the radical transformations were described in the genre
of gothic horror stories that raised the events to metaphysical dimensions. A good example of an earlier frightening temporal change was
the fin-de-siècle novel *The Beetle* by Richard Marsh, in which a mystical
beetle-figure terrorizes Victorian London. Man–beetle–woman transformation is uncanny not only because of the entities or the molar forms
it connects into a continuum (reminding us of the nature–culture continuum). It is uncanny as much because of the speed and abrupt nature
of the change: "If that transformation was not a bewildering one, then
two and two make five. The most level-headed scientist would temporar-
ily have lost his mental equipoise on witnessing such a quick change as
that within a span or two of his own nose."[1] The horror was evident in the
weird temporality of the change, condensed into one figure that exhibited a strange internal differentiation in its form. From myth to biology,
fiction to science, metamorphosis marked the thresholds of change from
one stage to another in animal development, a transformation from im-
mature state to adult, or the imago, as in the case of insects. As Sanford
Kwinter explains, biological development was surpassed by a modernist
interest in radical, nonlinear changes. Rational and organic development
are challenged by new geometries and laws of change expressed both in
emerging physics and in the avant-garde arts.[2]

STAGES OF METAMORPHOSIS

In 1864 Fritz Müller proposed an idea for a division of labor pertaining to the metamorphotic stages. The idea was influential for a long time
and in 1909 was promoted by a P. Deegener in his *Die Metamorphose
der Insekten*. In the three developmental forms of insects, the first stage,

larva, takes care of alimentation and growth; the second phase, pupa, is one of transformation into the third stage, imago, whose priorities are reproduction and dissemination of the species.[3] The idea includes a certain teleological framework, whereas the fact that the larva is always more than its actualized end result, the imago, is interesting. Growth as actualization is actually becoming less than in the earlier stage of intensity, of potentiality, which fades off in terms of organs that the larva might have but the full-grown insect does not.

Of course modern research into metamorphosis has had to deal with a whole Western history of intrigue surrounding the phenomena of revolutionary change, starting with Ovid. This is also the reason that James Rennie, in his 1830 *Insect Transformations,* refused to use the term *metamorphosis*—because it was too loaded with fabulations.[4]

In *Insect Transformations* Rennie listed a number of false conceptions of metamorphosis, like the one of James Harvey, who came up with the notion of circulation of blood. No matter how false it may seem from a biological point of view, Harvey did, however, draw interesting parallels between art and nature, comparing the parallel modes of creating that a carpenter might use with those of insects:

> There are two ways in which we observe one thing to be made out of another (as out of matter), both in art and nature, especially in the generation of animals: one is, when a thing is made out of another already in being, as a bed out of wood, and a statue out of a stone; when, for example, all the materials of the workmanship exist before the workman begins the work or attempts to give it any form. The other way is, when the stuff receives both being and form at the same time. As, therefore, the works of art are performed two ways; the one by the workman's dividing, cutting, and paring away the matter prepared for those operations, so as to leave behind, like a statuary, the figure of the thing he intends to make: the other, by the workman's adding and moulding, as well as paring away, the materials, and at the same time tempering the matter itself, so as to produce, like a potter, the figure; which, for this reason, may be said to be made, rather than formed; in the same manner it happens in the generation of animals; some of which are formed and transfigured out of matter already digested and increased for this purpose, all the parts springing out together distinctly by a kind of metamorphosis, and thus forming a perfect animal, while other animals are made piece by piece.[5]

It is not our concern here to follow the development of accurate accounts of metamorphosis as a physiological stage. Instead I want to focus on the exchange between fabulation and scientific or ethnologic accounts of insects at the first half of the twentieth century, especially with the help of the surrealist thinker Roger Caillois (1913–1978). Here the theme of metamorphosis becomes deterritorialized from the biological images of evolution and predetermined development. As Kwinter notes, such an image of metamorphosis can also be seen working in Franz Kafka's writing from approximately the same era. In the new narratives of modernism, linear growth and naturalized changes give way to a realm of intensive movement.[6]

Animality turns into a vector of becoming and is less a biological figure than an image by which to think of the distribution of affects between animal bodies and their milieus. Biology became one new crucial "image of thought" that acted as the plane on which several other cultural assemblages such as technology were articulated. Through notions such as metamorphosis and mimicry, entomologically inspired accounts of life and culture also explained new ways of understanding intensities of space and time. In addition, various artists, from Jean Painlevé to Franz Kafka and on to writers such as Lewis Mumford, embraced the importance of animal life for their creations, which I argue are both emblematic to key modernist discourses but also good vectors by which to understand more recent media cultural developments.

TRANSDISCIPLINARY SCIENCE

Caillois was an interesting figure who moved to the fuzzy zone between being an academic writer interested in anthropology, literature, and the mythical structures of society, including the importance of the notion of the sacred, and, at the same time, an experimentalist interested in the modes of knowledge created through activities of art and games and, for example, insects. These spheres, and the interzone between traditional institutions of knowledge he developed, could perhaps be seen as connected by his interest in a "subversive, revolutionary New Science" that was to bypass the narrow rationality of the classical sciences and incorporate art and experimentality as valid, consistent ways of producing knowledge.[7] Even though I seem to suggest that Caillois should be put under the banner of the French surrealist movement, he was never neatly and unproblematically part of this movement. In the 1930s his relations to various key surrealist artists and writers were close while he remained critical of a certain mysticism inherent in much of surrealism. As Caillois pointed out in a letter to André Breton in 1934, he was more interested than Breton in unraveling things to see how they work, how the inside of any entity (part of the so-called Mexican jumping bean question) is a mechanism that can be deciphered through rational means.[8]

In this chapter the figure of Caillois acts as the node and the point of transformation connecting heterogeneous spheres: through Caillois we can understand some of the enthusiasm for primitive life interfaced with surrealist considerations concerning space, time, and the human experience. In addition, Caillois transports these considerations as part of a much more recent media technological discussion concerning games, media, and the shift toward the play elements of our culture. In the field of insects, so much seems to be about metamorphoses and vectors of translation, from natural theology to scientific entomology and Darwin's work, all of which fed into an emerging interest in insect technics. Insects gradually became a key topic throughout popular culture and popular science that both inspired and awed. Figures such as J. H. Fabre were among the key conduits that helped a further translation from entomology to philosophy (for example, in Bergson's work) but also to avant-garde arts, such as that of the surrealists with their enthusiasm for novel ways of representation and perception but also for such figures as the praying mantis, seen as a devouring, half-human half-animal *vagina dentata*.[9]

In a completely different context, Caillois's considerations regarding mimicry as a form of play but also a characteristic of the time–space world of the praying mantis were being adopted into the emerging field of digital game studies. Caillois's book on games and play from 1958 was an early inspiration for a nondigital view of the culture of games, alongside Johan Huizinga's *Homo Ludens* (1938). However, what I argue is that game studies have not addressed the importance of Caillois's broader interests in metamorphotic modes of engaging with the surroundings, and consequently what have been neglected are the radical steps beyond phenomenology and classification of forms of games. Tracking those steps might also lead us to realize the importance of Caillois's transdisciplinary studies for media cultural topics.

GEOMETRICS OF PERCEPTION

As argued by various researchers, foremost among them Linda Dalrymple Henderson in her extensive studies of modern non-Euclidean geometry and the early idea of the fourth dimension, avant-garde art was largely defined by the practices and discourses of and the general interest in alternative perceptual worlds. As Henderson points out, both Poincaré's geometry and the ideas of the fourth, spiritual dimension offered artists what she calls "liberation"—liberation from the confines of the one-point perspective system and the whole field of knowledge that pertained to that humanist system. The fourth dimension interested artists such as Frantisek Kupka, Kasimir Malevich, the cubists, and the futurists, whereas later non-Euclidean geometry offered a new material reality to, for example, Tristan Tzara and the surrealists.[10] For instance, the previously mentioned "insect novelist" Maurice Maeterlinck had expressed an interest in new configurations of space in his book *La Vie de l'espace* (1928), which possibly found readers in the avant-garde circles as well. The fourth space, and new geometries in general, proposed new beings of hyperspace that were, to paraphrase Maeterlinck, something between the nightmare of an engineer and the family of Alfred Jarry's literary figure King Ubu—a world of weird monsters and insects that were nonrepresentable in the old geometric rules.[11]

For writers such as Siegfried Giedion, the dissolving multiple points of view of modern architecture and art produced a shift from the perspectival position of man. This break with Renaissance perspective was producing a new view on objects and architectures of modernity that trained the eye and the body into what would be now called post-human relations.[12] Also Jean Epstein, already mentioned in the previous chapter, saw the reconfigurations of vision and thought via technological means as intimately connected not only to the new spheres of perception probed by cubists and simultaneist painters but also to the "thousand-faceted eyes of the insect,"[13] which codeveloped a new understanding of geometry. Instead of the single gazing eye outside space, space was split and entered by the painter/insect/shot and the perspective was multiplied into a variation. Epstein is a good example of the early interest in the nonhuman characteristics of media and the "intelligence of the machine," which is framed, however, through concepts that come from nature. The machine is an animating machine that works through movement and variation.[14] Variation acts as the force transversal to the technological, animal, and creative worlds, where insects proved not only the "others" of human beings but, more accurately, variations in perception, movement, and duration. They are not only symbols of variation but through their bodies live variations in embodied environmental relations.

However, although direct links between animal worlds and the clear influence of geometrics on avant-garde modern art cannot always be deciphered, I think it is justifiable to claim that the animal worlds summoned and touched in various art pieces expressed a much-related aspiration to perceptions beyond the conventional geometrics and human-centered vision. In surrealism and other avant-garde expressions, a certain decentralization of perception and a new understanding of other sensations could be figured through animal worlds as well, from Kafka's literary zoology to the surrealists' words and images. This interest can be seen as turning toward the imperceptible and the experimental analysis of the thresholds of visible and rational via artistic means, as expressed by Gabrielle Buffet-Picabia in her essay reflecting the earlier years of Dada and the avant-garde.[15] In this sense, it might be worthwhile to continue from where Henderson concluded her book *The Fourth Dimension*—a quote from the painter Tony Robbin from the 1970s that, despite the later time period, seemed to sum up much of the earlier interest in worlds so far imperceptible:

> Artists who are interested in four dimensional space are not motivated by a desire to illustrate new physical theories, nor by a desire to solve mathematical problems. We are motivated by *a desire to complete our subjective experience by inventing new aesthetic and conceptual capabilities.*[16]

I will shortly introduce the surrealist interest in animal worlds in the context of modernity, followed by a short excursion into Jean Painlevé's documentaries. After that section, I elaborate on Caillois in the same context, paying particular attention to his writings on insects in the 1930s. Finally, I conclude with an eye toward Caillois's writings on games and play, recent digital game studies, and how these distinct fields could provide new ways to approach the diagrammatics of modern media culture.

ANIMAL MODERNITY

The surrealists, and many other avant-garde artists, stood at a curious crossroads. Already Sigmund Freud had contributed widely to an analysis of the unconscious as populated by animals, a whole multiplicity of animal forces of which the human body consisted. Animality remained an archival trace of an earlier phase in the history of the human species. Manifested through senses and sensations, it also functioned as a faint memory of abandoned sexual zones, as Akira Mizuta Lippit reads Freud. Here animality as part of emerging modernity is a perversion in its reintroduction of the lost world of senses and sensations (especially the olfactory sense), long-lost alien media in ourselves. In a letter to Wilhelm Fliess in the 1890s, Freud wrote:

> Perversions regularly lead to zoophilia and have an animal character. They are explained not by the functioning of erogenous zones that later have been abandoned, but by the effect of the erogenous *sensations* that later lose their force. In this connection one recalls that the principal sense in animals (for sexuality as well) is that of smell, which has been reduced in human beings. As long as smell (or taste) is dominant, urine, feces, and the whole surface of the body, also blood, have a sexually exciting effect. *The heightened sense of smell in hysteria presumably is connected with this.*[17]

The human being in itself, because of its unconscious archive of past animality, was a topology of alien perceptions and uncanny, even perverted, sensations that psychoanalysis translated as part of the biopolitics of body and psyche of modernity. Naturally, as Deleuze and Guattari later pointed out, Freud's mistake was to neglect the intensive affect forces of animality and see them as representations and symbols of the Oedipal complex. Instead of interpreting dream elements as phantasies that refer back to the family relations among father, mother, and child, the assemblages examined, for example, in the case of little Hans ("Analysis of a Phobia in a Five-Year-Old Boy," 1909) are intensities, affects, and constitute a plane for animal becomings. Animals do not represent but work as carriers of intensities that circulate affects: "There are always apparatuses, tools, engines involved, there are always artifices and constraints used in taking Nature to the fullest."[18]

Lippit argues that animals had disappeared from the midst of technological modernity. Nonetheless, they remained as shadows, phantasmatic echos that transposed their intensive capacities as part of media technological modes of communication. Borrowing Derrida's idea, animals are the conditioning and establishing framings of nature in modernity but at the same time lack a voice.[19]

Surrealists participated in this translation of animals as part of human society and unconscious with their images and work, which questioned the boundaries of language as rational communication. If we approach some surrealist themes as excursions into "imaginary media," we can perhaps more fully understand the interest in animals and insects, which were often used as figures and symbols but could signal asignifying approaches to bestiality.

As Caillois himself perceived in a short meditation on surrealism as "a world of signs," for surrealists, animals and insects were everywhere: Max Ernst had his "ferocious birds," Chirico the "prancing horses"; Magritte was occupied both with birds and metamorphoses, for example, one in which a "girl becomes an antimermaid with the bust and the head of a fish"; Dali expressed a fascination and obsession with insects but also with lobsters, Tanguy with "a population of giant amoebas," and so on.[20]

To this end, we could easily add Caillois himself with his fascination with ants, praying mantises, and the popular entomological work of Jean-Henri Fabre (who was by then widely read both in France and abroad) and William Morton Wheeler, who died in 1937, just a couple of years after Caillois's key writings on insects. The wonder of animal worlds was not a theme restricted to artists only but demonstrated how biology and other modes of analysis of animal worlds such as ethology inspired engineers and designers as well. Thus, it is important to mention Karl Blossfeldt's work in Germany at the end of the 1920s and in the early 1930s: his return to the idea of nature as the perfected artist but now in a modernist setting and a new technological framework tuned to a quasi-teological belief in the supreme functionality of nature.[21]

SURREALIST CINEMATICS: PAINLEVÉ

Photography and cinematography were able to cut into this miraculous world with something that seemed not much short of scientific accuracy. The new realism brought about by new technologies of vision cutting into the intimate, unseen layers of material reality, as Walter Benjamin spoke of the new vision machines, was succinctly producing an intimate relation between art and science. In other words, Caillois was not alone in his animal interests. A good example of the surrealist motifs around animals was the cinematographic capturing of animal life by Jean Painlevé. Known for his wonderful poetic animal documentaries, Painlevé actually studied biology in the Laboratoire d'Anatomie et d'Histologie Comparée at the Sorbonne at the beginning of the 1920s, working on vital characteristics at the cellular level.[22]

Painlevé's poetic documents dug into the lives of seahorses, bats, weird underwater creatures such as *hyas* and *stenorhynchus,* but also opened up the habitats of well-known animals such as shrimps and jellyfish. His dips into the lives of aquatic creatures were made possible by new technologies of underwater shooting, which allowed him to turn the "medium" of those animals into a screen. Water as a milieu affording different movements and forms than the solid land and air of gravitational fields inspired Painlevé to turn the form and movement of aquatic animals into a ballet.

Continously making references to the human world and receiving accusations of anthropomorphism, he experimented with such themes, which were close to the avant-garde filmmakers. For Painlevé, as he recounted at the start of his perhaps best-known film, *The Vampire* (1945), the world of animals is filled with strange and terrifying forms and movements, gestures both frightening and graceful, things that Painlevé described as "living sculptures" with a reference to seahorses, his balletic take on those half-horse, half-caterpillar inhabitants of the seas. The vampire itself, a South American bat *Desmodus rotondus,* is described in terms of its refined mechanisms for sucking blood. In this example, the victim was a guinea pig. Sharing the enthusiasm for the winged animal of Caillois—whose interest in praying mantises had emerged from a chapter on bats in A. Toussenel's book *L'esprit des bêtes, zoologie passionelle* from 1855[23]—Painlevé was able to turn natural images into surrealist art of a kind, whether as abstract movements, as in the case of several of his sea films, or through meticulous images arising from his fascination with the vampire-life of the bat, which seemed to offer an animal approach to the myth of the Nosferatu. Images from the 1922 Murnau film of that name turn into a natural documentary, providing a transformation and translation not only in scale but in the images themselves. As Tom

Gunning notes, the Murnau film already offered a way to understand the intertwining of the new aesthetics of knowledge that the moving image provided in the context of animals and insects. Gunning flags the importance of the cinematic translation from the Nosferatu figure to the world of animals inspected through microcinematographic capturing of "a polyp with tentacles," the animal equivalent of the vampire. Murnau framed the vampire and the animal world as parallel enterprises—and hence emphasized the centrality of the new optical devices in opening up this world of ethereal beings.[24]

In Painlevé's subsequent translation, Nosferatu is further metamorphosed back into an animal. The vampire figure acts as an ephemeral point of transfer, a body of mediation between the natural world beyond morality and the cultural world in which the Nosferatu is a threat to the veins of society.[25] What connects this manlike figure and the bat are certain affects: "A Kiss of the Vampire," as the bite is called in Painlevé's documentary, consists of the bat's selecting a spot on the guinea pig, pulling out the flesh from behind the fur, and using its saliva as an anticoagulant and its concave tongue to effectively suck out the amount of blood that can be drained out a guinea pig in one session. What is the vampire but a becoming-animal of a sort, tracking affects and intensities of a bat—a metamorphosis in itself?

Painlevé's project can be characterized as driven by a becoming-animal that allows the cinematic enterprise to enter into such assemblages, which give us a glimpse of what it feels like to sense, move, and live in the world of a mollusc, seahorse, bat, or sea urchin. It is less a matter of representation or imitation than of establishing relations on a plane of immanence. It is a focus on impersonal movements and rests in a Spinozan ethological fashion. This endeavor breaks from an organized, functional viewpoint and looks for thresholds of affects through which to understand the relations that compose entities.[26]

Painlevé's way of intertwining animal life with moving images and sounds intensified the screen into a natural habitat of its own. Interested in J. H. Fabre's insect fabulations, Painlevé can be seen as putting his camera to such use as might have appealed to Epstein and Benjamin as well; his work, performing a sort of cinematographic psychoanalysis, opened up the hidden layers of reality, something that Benjamin called the "deepening of apperception."[27] Turning the commonplace into a new regime, by means of close-ups and other techniques, the film camera, according to Benjamin, expanded space but also extended movement (through slow motion). Here slow motion reveals "entirely unknown" movements, "a different nature" that opens up between things.[28] With similar ideas, Epstein had signaled in 1926 that the cinematographic mode of reality is by definition animism, where the living machine is also a nonhuman eye of such heights, depths, durations, and transmutations as are found through the coupling of nature-cinematography (new media) only.[29] Indeed, the motion capture inherent in surrealist works such as Painlevé's does not only register what was there but is ontogenetic as a technical milieu. It creates a new second-order reality that experiments with its own limits and potentials.[30] The creative potentiality of the animal in a milieu is doubled by the experimental technicality of the milieu in which it is reinvented through the registering.

Here animal life as the probehead of movements—a multiplicity of movements—proved a key inspiration to both scientists and artists. The theme thus sets some of the surrealist experiments such as Painlevé's as part of the diagrammatic capture of animal intensity analyzed in earlier chapters. As we approach the relation between experimental sciences of life and the media technology of moving images—both of which emerged in the same period as intimately connected—we can see how later experimental takes on cinema continued a related theme. As Pasi Väliaho argues, cinema can be approached as a "technology of this form of life." It provides the frame of reference for experimentation on life that was translated as part of the politics of life that sought new control of the human as an animal body whose higher functions such as language are analyzed and reproduced as material tendencies.

Elaborating Friedrich Kittler's ideas, Väliaho argues that, for example, chronophotography is a technique of slowing down bodies, making them quantifiable and predictable, and hence produces a new knowledge of the object of control of biopolitics.[31] This is something we addressed briefly in the first chapter through Marey. In such a scheme, the diagrammatic dividing line between the human being and the animal becomes fuzzy, which explains the simultaneous interest in such simple forms of life as insects. In other words, simple forms of life provide elements for new ontologies of life, as in the case of Xavier Bichat's research in the early nineteenth century. As most clearly demonstrated through recent years of biotechnological modulation of life, the social control and production of Life is not restricted to human beings but takes shape through a wider agenda of *zoe* as animal life. Here the sharp microscopic "eye" of the movie camera functioned as an early tool of biopower. The discursive and political regimes of *bios* are a tracking of the intensive, imaginative potential of *zoe*—and technical media are participating in this intensive creation.[32]

MIMICRY AND TOPOLOGIES OF AGENCY

An interest in new technologies, science, and the animal world was something that Painlevé and Caillois shared. What is interesting is that for both this amounted to a rethinking of the nature of spatiality as well. With the cinematic analysis and synthesis of movements that Painlevé introduced, the nature of space and temporality were under scrutiny as well. Caillois can be seen as interested in this agenda in his early work on the praying mantis ("La mante religieuse," published in 1934 in *Minotaure*) and on mimicry and psychastenia ("Mimétisme et psychasthénie legendaire," published in 1935 in *Minotaure* as well). In both papers Caillois addressed the function of mimicry not as a representation of figures or space but as a spatial assemblage that bordered on disorder. In Caillois's aesthetic-entomology, which was to inspire Lacan in his development of the concept of the mirror stage, what is crucial is the demarcation of the organism from its environment. Focusing on the expression of mimicry in butterfly wings, fish, octopuses, and mantises *(mantidae),* Caillois tried to track elements of spatiality and temporality from this visual phenomenon. The morphological functions of the imitating insects were for Caillois modes of "new media" as well—a form of teleplastic sculptural reproduction of spatiality in the manner of photography:

> Morphological mimicry would then be genuine photography, in the manner of chromatic mimicry, but photography of shape and relief, on the order of objects and not of images: a three-dimensional reproduction with volume and depth: sculpture-photography, or better yet *teleplasty,* if the word is shorn of all psychic content.[33]

We see how Caillois deterritorialized mimicry from the animal sphere but also from the sphere of images as purely visual phenomena to that of bodies in interaction (affects). Space and vision became haptic. Caillois objected to the interpretation that mimicry is purely a biological function in service of utilitarian goals. Offensive mimicry is used to surprise prey, and defensive mimicry helps an animal in hiding from a hunter, or even terrifying it. Caillois picked up these notions from Maurice Girard's 1888 paper "Sur le mimétisme et la ressemblance protectrice," though he remained reluctant to see mimicry only as an instinctual tool for survival. In an almost amusingly meticulous fashion, Caillois recounted why mimicry is actually a dangerous luxury for an insect; one example he used was the "geometer moth caterpillars [that] so perfectly simulate shrub shoots that horticulturists prune them with shears,"[34] leading Caillois to conclude that here we are perhaps dealing with "collective masochism."

In order to complexify its function as Bataillean excess, Caillois suggests that mimicry is more akin to a psychic disorder than to a straightforward evolutionary method or a tool that an animal (or human) could control. As a disorder, it can be used to understand the spatial modulations and environmental relations of entities, from perception of space to inhabiting it. Again we are dealing with an articulation of the eye and the body or, more precisely, of perception and action. Beyond the "psychic content" of images, visual phenomenon are material, tied to embodied forms whose boundaries are porous. This is a "lure of space" that may function in the same manner as Bergson thought insect technics based on instinct do. As Caillois wrote: "*Mayfly* larvae craft themselves a sheath case from twigs and gravel, and the *Chrysomelid* larvae use their own excrement in the same way. The *Oxyrhinchi* crabs or sea spiders randomly pick seaweed and polyps from their habitats and plant them on their shells."[35]

The materiality of vision underlines a fundamental shift in the understanding of matter in general. Caillois's realization of the new constellations of space, which were reminiscent of the early avant-garde interest in geometrics and new topologies, was a connection point among "Finsler's spaces, Riemann-Christoffel's hyperspace, abstract spaces, generalized spaces, open, closed, dense, sparse, and so on"[36] and the perceptual worlds in the midst of twentieth-century perception—here approached through the vehicle of insect life and psychic disorder. What Caillois offered in a very dense passage of his text was a translation among the entomological worlds of insects, the new physics that emerged as part of technological modernity, and the psychological work of Pierre Janet and the schizophrenic perception of everyday urban life under the name of psychastenia: *"I know where I am, but I don't feel that I am where I am."*[37] The cognitive experience of the space in which the body moves is detached from the actual movement of the body in that space. It relates to mapping the potentially confusing transformations of a body in non-Euclidean topologies that are not as predictable as stable architectures are supposed to be. What Caillois referred to here was some kind of "technology of movement"[38] different from that of Euclidean space.

Caillois's reference to Saint Anthony reveals that the "I" is dispersed into a depersonalized matter "whatsoever."[39] As Denier Hollier noted regarding Caillois's two early insect texts from the 1930s, in that period in French psychiatric parlance, *psychastenia* referred to an exhaustion of personal energy, a becoming (inanimate) of the energetic ego. According to Hollier, this reveals the implicit thermodynamism in the concept of mimicry and also in relation to the mantis example Caillois used. Like the male mantis, which is assimilated during the sexual act by the female, the thermodynamic mixing of cold and warm sources is one of assimilation of energies that can be seen as a devouring contagion by the other. Besides pointing toward the surrealist fascination with the "vagina dentata," this was to be read as a theme of physics. Carnot's second principle of thermodynamics from 1824 stated that entropy is a general law of the world signing how the continuous increase of disorder is inherent in Caillois's biophysical conception of art, insects, and human societies. However, Caillois wanted to go further than the human mind in his refashioning of the psychoanalytic ethos and to take into account the biological layers of the orders and disorders of the human world. In a way he wanted to reach toward the animal life that nineteenth-century physiologists and biologists such as Bichat had worked toward—the life of the organisms beyond that of language.[40] Freud's ideas of the pleasure principle as intimately linked to the death drive, and also Fechner's constancy law, which suggested that an organism tries to minimize the waste of energy, are related intellectual streams that preceded Caillois. Both were related to the thermodynamic worldview that had emerged since the nineteenth century, which signaled the physical version of the "tending toward death" theme of the early twentieth century.[41]

Through insects' mimicry and adaptation of elements of their environment as parts of their bodies (in a body–milieu continuum, a distribution of the body), Caillois was able to underline an argument about space as depersonalized. However, his references to Christian and Western metaphysical notions of matter were in a way in contrast with an idea of the activity of matter that was also present in his appreciation of modern physics. Matter differs, and not just in contrast to the animal "life" of the soul: "Matters become critical with represented space because the living creature, the organism, is no longer located at the origin of the coordinate system but is simply one point among many. Dispossessed of its privilege, it quite literally *no longer knows what to do with itself.*"[42] Caillois was sketching a post-grid-geometric view of matter and agency in which the center of the coordinate system, the perceiving I, is replaced with space, becoming devouring, intensive, active. Space becomes topological, and instead of merely trustworthily guiding and providing reassurance of the coordinates, it infects and seduces. The reflective mind is forced to follow the noncognitive knowledge and motility of the body. The nonrepresentational mode of navigating the body through various attraction points is the mode of the affective relationality in which the body suddenly finds itself. This is a nonphenomenological mode of understanding the lived topology of the event, to follow Massumi's ideas; the body and its perceptional movement are not intentional, not personal, and not reflective.[43] The space itself is swarming with flows of energy and matter, which not only attracts and seduces the subjects but also poses a frightening threat. Whether Caillois himself actually thought that this is a danger to true individuality or whether he was excited by the depersonalizing mattering unconscious is beyond the confines of my argument or interest here.[44] What are interesting are the directions these notions allow and the way we can read them as catalysts of relations among animals, technology, and modernity. Bestiality and insects become figures through which to question the notions of space, intensity, and affect and also the distribution of the body across a space that is intensive, a participatory space of affects. Space and time are not general independent backgrounds or functions in which agency is at the center of the coordinate system; rather, the whole system is in continuous flux in a fashion reminiscent of the early twentieth-century interest in exceeding Euclidean and Cartesian geometrics. Space and time afford agency by forming assemblages based on the heterogeneous conjoining of capacities. Here James J. Gibson's term "affordance," used in ecological theory, offers a way to understand the interactions between relations of entities. A temporalized space is tuned to specific kinds of agencies, and this tuning is based less on intrinsic properties than on real relations.[45]

Interestingly, Callois's attempt to incorporate new topologies into an understanding of space presents a haptic version of the space–agency coupling. By using the concept of dihedron, Caillois referred to how space continuously changes "its size and location."[46] The person who inhabits the spaces is pulled between action-space and representation-space and is a force in his own right as well, always pulling, shaping the space via his position. Criticality of matter presents itself through this horizontal and vertical crossing of planes, which instead of adhering to Cartesian coordinates becomes part of the body of the perceiver/user. In a way, Caillois seems to have suggested a conception of active space closer to that of a computer game topology than that of a visual representation even though his explanation of the ideas of the dihedron nature of space remained a bit undeveloped. I will return to the point about games at the end of the chapter.

A SHORT NOTE ON TOPOLOGIES OF TRANSFORMATION

According to Sanford Kwinter, the intensity of space was a wider rubric in modernist architecture and literature of the early twentieth century. Instead of positing a stable ground or a substratum (whether the Cartesian notion of space as the coordinated background or even the Maxwellian notion of ether as the "material seat" of forces), the notion of field and the plastic structures "found" by Riemann and Einstein gave us new tools with which to approach space/matter, "susceptible both to partaking in physical events and to being influenced by them."[47] The field has become an intensive, temporal space that distributes functions, vectors, and speeds. Here spatiality and temporality are not passive material backgrounds for events but are the very participating conditions for what takes place through "local relations of differences."[48] These themes, analyzed in physics, resonate with Bergson, who similarly focused on the affording nature of the environment, with a body always surrounded by aggregates of other images (image being the basic ontological entity in

Bergson's philosophy). Any perception is part of the surrounding world, and there is no material image "which does not owe its qualities, its determinations, in short its existence, to the place which it occupies in the totality of the universe."[49]

In addition to the works of architects and writers on the new forms of space-time, such as Giedion, one example of intensity, movement, and metamorphosis can be found in Franz Kafka's work that Kwinter addresses. Naturally, reading Kafka's famous short story *Metamorphosis* (*Die Verwandlung*, 1915) would be the easiest way to understand the importance of intensive transformations not only in body structures but in relations of bodies with their environments.

In Kafka's story, the poor Gregor Samsa, turned into an insect, a type of vermin, finds that his strange metamorphosis has turned his family home space into a weird and hostile environment. Gregor's environment forces a new orientation on the body transformed from one having two legs, two eyes, and a human voice to an insect body making animal noises and walking on multiple legs. Gregor's voice catches a new "squeaking" undertone, which signals an infiltration of his body by foreign forces (Whose voice is that? Where does it come from if not from the lungs of Gregor?). At first his body is out of control:

> Disposing of the bed-quilt was quite simple, he had only to inflate himself a little and it fell off automatically. But after that things became difficult, especially since he was so uncommonly broad. He would have needed arms and hands to raise himself to a sitting position; but instead he only had the numerous legs, which were constantly executing the most varied movements and which moreover he was unable to control.[50]

The metamorphosis is not a predetermined animal change, and it becomes a much more thorough event in the sense that Kwinter explains is exemplary of the turn-of-the-century modernist culture. The transformations that characterize Kafka's works—not only *The Metamorphosis*—should be understood in terms of "intensive and not extensive movements."[51] Beyond naturalistic or geometric developmental laws, the intensive movements constitute singularities, changes in the intensive temporal topologies of entities. Kwinter's point is to emphasize the concrete (but not necessarily actual) nature of such intensive changes, which occur through the intimate link of the perceptual apparatus with the network that sustains it.[52]

Kafka's work, then, is a lesson in the temporal metamorphoses that characterize modernity, where the insect-figure becomes an emblem for the radical temporality and network nature of the body. Just as in Caillois, the body is depersonalized, becoming detached and displaced from being a personal event to being a more general, intensive relay among political, social, and communicative bodies.[53] Kafka's bodies and passages between bodies are insectlike not in their concrete figure only but in the affects that trigger a becoming, an intensive change, a relay that can be also considered relevant in the biopolitical regime that has emerged with technical modernity. Here *biopolitics* refers both to the question of the distribution of bodies in the intensive, temporal, metamorphotic spaces of modernity and technical media and to the integration of knowledge from animal bodies as part of regimes of control; I use *control* to refer to the various overlapping fields, from biosciences to media design, in a context of capitalist production. In these animal contexts we find the rationale of researching animal transformations, environments, and perceptions from early insect research to surrealist animals, Kafka's metamorphosis, and, for example, Uexküll's way of explaining the nature of the action-sensation-environment triangle. In fact, the claims addressed earlier could all be opened up in the context of *Umwelt* theories as well, as Kwinter argues. The intertwinings of the material body and the schematized object of perception are tied together in the function-circles that define animals' relation to the world. In his take (what Kwinter calls "a biology of events"), Uexküll topologizes the relation of subject and object into a continuous milieu of "pure exteriority": functions are not reducible to the organs that participate in the event or to the actual material forms, but they become a new body of exterior relations.[54]

RECONNECTING GAME STUDIES WITH INSECTS; OR, THE INTENSITY OF DEVOURING SPACE

Despite being neglected for a long time by researchers, especially in France, Caillois has been addressed in recent years in at least two eminent contexts. In digital game studies, as mentioned, Caillois's later work on games and culture has attracted attention. The focus, however, has been mostly on the classifications of games that Caillois suggested. In an alternative fashion, the feminist philosopher Elizabeth Grosz has underlined the importance of the nature of space in Caillois's early writings on insects, psychasthenia, and the previously analyzed notions of depersonalization. According to Grosz, the notions of space presented by Caillois in the 1930s can give us important cues for understanding subjectivity, corporeality, and space. As Grosz writes, "The primacy of the subject's own perspective is replaced by the gaze of another for whom the subject is merely *a* point in space, not *the* focal point organizing space."[55] The subject becomes dislodged from its position and captured as part of the gaze of the other—a clear indication of why Jacques Lacan adopted crucial ideas from Caillois for his theories of the mirror stage.

As Grosz argues, the insect/psychotic becomes part of an affording space, which presents another way to see this coupling of organism and environment. In what is almost a continuation of Uexküll's theories of *Umwelt* and the function-circles that make the animal part of its milieu, Caillois offered a way to understand the porous nature of the barrier between outside and inside. Such a barrier is to be understood more as a topological field and a surface than as a discontinuous border.[56] In this sense, one could continue and elaborate Grosz's notions toward highlighting Caillois as part of the diagrammatic mapping of the surfaces and distributions of the animal body in the age of technical media. Just as psychoanalysis as a theory of subjectification and media[57] insisted on this crucial role of capture of the individual by the environment (although under the banner of signification and the Oedipal complex), the history of modern media and biopower is one of capturing the intensive capacities of the human animal body or, as is argued throughout this book, the affective, intensive capacities of other animal bodies as well. As is implied in an interview with Grosz, perhaps the insect's psychotic, anomalous qualities of immersion into surrounding space are characteristic of the modern sphere of media culture.[58] Similarly, while psychasthenia can be seen as a "lure posed by space for subjectivity,"[59] modern media function by means of a lure, or desire, that affixes bodies in media through various regimes of signification but, most important, asignification.[60] Here I would not want to emphasize the role of the visual and the gaze as much as does psychoanalysis and Grosz but would rather look at the distributed, multimodal nature of this coordinated analysis and theorization of the animal and the creation of the modern media sphere. A similar critique of Grosz has been voiced by Hansen, who has tried to steer clear of both Caillois's Heidegger-influenced technopessimism and Grosz's emphasis on visuality.[61] As noted earlier, Caillois's notes on the topologies of space and the event of the body as affective and impersonal dissolution of the cognitive/reflective function suggest a different, non-Euclidean mode of inhabiting spatiality and architecture than that of the eye.

In recent cultural studies of digital gaming, Caillois's ideas have been picked up in a different mode. Whereas Grosz does not address Caillois's later ideas relating to games, the take adopted in game studies is almost exclusively focused on his book *Les jeux et les hommes* (translated as *Man, Play, and Games*), originally from 1958. I want to conclude this chapter with an excursion into game studies and try to flag one potential transversal connection that has been neglected between insects and media technologies, games to be exact. Indeed, it is striking how these two themes, which are related in Caillois, have been detached in subsequent uses and elaborations of his ideas even though, as I see it, exactly this link among media, technology, and animality in Caillois is the most interesting thing one can extract from his writings. Basically the problem is that Grosz does not adequately develop Caillois's themes of insect space and affects in media theoretical contexts, and game studies neglects the broader agenda of Caillois relating to biopower and the underlying affect-life of immersion—a certain generalized psychasthenia that characterizes media technological modernity. My choice to focus on games here is a result of the direct link between animals and games via Caillois. Otherwise it would have been as relevant to refer to, for example, the use of new technologies in such reconfigurations of lived space as those of Rafael Lozano-Hemmer and his *Body Movies* (2001), which is emblematic of the contemporary way of redistributing perception and layering bodies in space.

As hinted, game studies has adopted Caillois as a theorist of game classifications. This often formalist approach has argued that games can be divided into four general categories. To quote the entry on "Caillois' classifications" in Jesper Juul's dictionary of video game theory:

> Caillois (1961) posits four categories of games: Agon (contest), alea (chance), ilinx (vertigo), and mimicry (make-believe). Additionally, Caillois describes games as being placed on a scale from ludus (rule-based)

to paidea (free-form). It is unclear to what extent Caillois' categories ultimately include or exclude each other, and some of the general claims made about their possible combination are at odds with most contemporary games: Caillois claims that "... games are not ruled and make-believe. Rather, they are ruled or make-believe" (1961, 8–9). This claim is contradicted by most commercial board games, almost all video games, and generally all rule-based games that include a fictional element.[62]

Similar accounts are plenty and represent the general understanding of Caillois's significance for cultural studies of contemporary media culture. Caillois has been approached as a theorist of classifications who argued that there are four ideal types of games and two key modes of game: *ludus* and *paidea*. In another recent take on digital games by Lauwaert, Wachelder, and Van de Walle, Caillois's ideas are taken as tools with which to unravel the cultural anthropological basis of the contemporary culture of gaming.[63] Between *paidia,* which refers to the uncontrolled, nearly anarchic enjoyment of playing, and *ludus,* the rule-bound, "civilized" mode of playing games that we find in most organized sports and games, the media culture of contemporary capitalist game production is proposed to be a mix of various tendencies. Not claiming that Caillois's ideas should be seen as directly applicable models, the text by Lauwaert and associates does imply that the media culture of games is to be approached as one of classifications, genres, and formal characteristics. This critical perspective claims that Caillois's classifications are unable to account for certain key characteristics of contemporary digital games, and hence the authors offer two new categories to take into account this lack. *Repens* and *repositio* are the terms suggested to provide a more comprehensive understanding of the temporal dynamics of the back-and-forth nature that characterizes digital gaming. A tension of unexpected events (described as the surprise element) and the potential for repetitious time looping is what should be emphasized, according to the writers, in the context of new technologies of gaming. It is the new nonlinear time economy that attracts and captures the attention of players.

Undeniably, Caillois devoted a huge amount of his game book to classifications, and the aforementioned four play the key roles. *Agon* refers to what we often take as the key form of games: rule-bound competitions such as football or chess. And of course *alea,* in which luck plays the crucial role, is also something we see as an elemental part of a game. Quite understandably, Caillois, who wrote the book in the midst of the emerging organized business of casinos, national lotteries, and the like was emphasizing the centrality of this form of gaming. But in addition, Caillois listed *ilinx* as a characteristic of games of "dizziness" and voluntary confusion of the senses, as well as the fourth class on his list, mimicry. In mimicry, the relation to animals is perhaps most obvious, as Caillois himself admitted, making references to his earlier research. Because all games include a certain voluntary acceptance of a new world the game imposes, on the user/player, mimicry is an apt image to use to illustrate this more general function of games. Games are in this sense milieus that act as vectors for transformation. Instead of seeing insects as an inferior form of life compared to civilized game-playing, nonfunctional humans, Caillois insisted on their commonalities. Insect life is not any less complex or elaborated than human life, he wrote, underlining that the desire for masking, depersonalization, becoming-other is expressed on a continuum from animals (especially insects) to human societies.[64] Certain games and play patterns can be seen as engines of metamorphosis that transform the participants and the spaces of action. Such activities have for a long time been part of various religious rituals and, for example, shamanism, which can be seen as a process of becoming, of summoning inhuman voices, sounds, and affects. For example, masks can function as a force of transformation and reception of a certain "drunkenness" of the senses.[65]

This interest in bridging nature, animals, and human culture was of course not restricted to Caillois. It was an emerging current, connected with the interest in games and play as part of culture that was articulated in the works of Johan Huizinga and Lewis Mumford in addition to those of Caillois. In his peculiar anthropology of technics, Mumford was willing to admit the common roots humans and animals share in the history of technology. In addition to the utilitarian tool-nature of the hand, Mumford kept underlining the excess nature of tool-technics, always much more than a clearly delineated function. Instead of seeing the creation of the modern human being as a linear rationalization process, Mumford argued that we were dealing with a much more complex intertwining of technics and the human body—a "biotechnics" that consisted of the excess element in every tool or bodily habit.[66] In a similar fashion, play became integrated as a defining feature of both man and animal in Huizinga's classic *Homo Ludens* (The playing man, 1938). Complementing my point about the primacy of biopolitics and biopower for understanding the modern significance of affects, games, and spatiotemporal relations, Huizinga also wanted to underline the significance of nonutilitarian actions and habits. The essential quality from animal habits to those of human beings consists of the voluntary, disinterested, out-of-the ordinary nature of games and playing in their temporal nature, tuned as "movement, change, alternation, succession, association, separation."[67]

In contemporary discussions, the origins of the biopolitics of the post-Fordist era have been continuously pinpointed to Karl Marx's writings in the *Grundrisse* on the "general intellect." For example, Paolo Virno, as part of the broader post-Fordist wave of theory including Michael Hardt, Antonio Negri, and Maurizio Lazzarato, argues that our contemporary capitalist society functions through the generic capacities of the human being. Drawing on Marx but also on Gilbert Simondon, Michel Foucault, and others, Virno explains that biopolitics should be understood as the capitalist power of tapping into the general capacities for producing knowledge and affects. In the human being, this refers to the dynamic powers of abstract thinking, communication, memory, motility, and so on.[68] Virno specifies his interest in the biopolitics of the work force, which naturally emphasizes the need to focus on the generic human potential. However, when he argues that post-Fordism "takes advantage of abilities learned before and independently of entrance into the workplace"[69] and refers to human capacities fine tuned in modernity like technologies of video games, he implicitly steps into the area of physiological measuring and modulation of the human being not as social but as material, animal life.[70]

Without wanting to dispute Virno's reading, which has its merits, I wish to flag the importance of another, more surprising context for consideration of the immersion of bodies in contemporary capitalist media culture. I would argue that we find just as interesting a starting point in the early theories of games and play that work themselves from the animal world of play to the human sphere of games. As part of the emerging interest in the nonutilitarian aspect of "play" for culture, Caillois and others introduced the idea that play and games constitute crucial aspects of the ethnological formation of civilization. This already echoes the interest that emerged decades later of tapping into the productive powers of the human being in its dynamic capacity. However, what these authors insisted was that we must take into account the continuities of this account with animality. For example, in this respect it would be valuable to discuss Huizinga and his ideas of the temporal, intensive nature of playing. Huizinga refers to the oppositional nature of games' relations to work, which would be interesting to analyze in the light of current notions that activities of a playlike nature are at the heart of capitalist biopower.[71] However, I have chosen to use Caillois's ideas on games and the connections he makes with insect lives to merely point to the possibility of approaching our culture of play and gaming through the earlier points he made regarding insect worlds, mimicry, and the immersive powers of spatiotemporality in modernity. This also establishes a link from the early avant-garde concerns with space, temporality, and perception to those of recent years with high-tech media. I argue that by insisting on the connections between Caillois's earlier writings on animals and the later theories of games and play we are supplied with media archaeological tools with which to understand some of the mechanisms of capture used by digital media such as video games.

Digital gaming is based on capturing the attention, perception, and sensation of the human body, and holding that attention is a crucial feature of modernity.[72] It can be seen connected to the long *durée* of the physiological understanding of the intensive capacities of the human body in its temporality, already measured and reproduced by the nineteenth-century experimental scientists. This point was addressed in the first chapter in the context of Marey and the tracking of the flight capacities of insect bodies. In this chapter we can argue that Caillois's surrealist and peculiar scientific notions regarding the relations between human cultures and animal worlds suggests a minoritarian view of the physiological nature of space and time in modernity.

What was defined as a psychic disorder by Pierre Janet, then recapitulated by Caillois as a mode of animal behavior, is something that could be seen as characteristic of the way we engage with the action-perception patterns demanded by games and, more widely, digital computer interfaces (from keyboards to mice and more recent developments such as the Wii gaming system and Kinect). Caillois already hinted at this haptic dimension of dihedron-space and perception–action coupling in his

1930s article "Mimicry and the Legendary Psychasthenia."[73] Reading this together with Uexküll's theories of perception–action coupling provides us with an ethological way of understanding the nonpersonal affect world of environments both technical and natural. Of course it is clear that technological spaces are designed and created, which marks a difference from nature, as critics continuously note. However, this does not deny that both of these worlds engage with the human being on a very primordial level that spans much more of her affect world than just intentions, symbols, or discourses. The framing of the human sensorium in relation to the designed spaces, rhythms, and intensities of technical media is not far from how Uexküll described the framing of the life-worlds of the animal. His theory offers a way to understand how the fragmented worlds that do not preexist the relations they enter into with animals are constituted through the process of synthesis. As Kwinter explains, the fragments are "built into chains and gathered and made whole under a function."[74] Here signs offered by the environment are not so much signifying as signaling potential for agglomerations or assemblages. Similarly, technical media can be better deciphered as technical signals and their capacities to capture the perceptive worlds of human-animals than through their semantics or signifying discourses. Just as Caillois saw contagion by mimicry as a concrete physical event,[75] by continuously framing ethology in physiological research, Uexküll was saying that we should focus much more on *nerves* than on *minds*. In this sense, while writing *Theoretische Biologie* in the 1920s Uexküll still considered machines as outside of this framework interested in life. For him, machines did not perceive the signalings of their environment but remained dumb repetitive function-performers.[76]

As noted earlier, it is a physiological and ethological prerequisite to allow the topological continuity with space and time to encapture the agency as part of their territorial refrains. This ecological view of subjectivity,[77] furthermore, takes into account that the networks, relays, or topologies in which agencies are formed in technical media culture are never defined by technology only; in addition, the abstract capitalist relations are as real as the concrete environments in which the perception-action functions, or the depersonalized psychasthenias of people playing *Counterstrike, World of Warcraft,* or *Second Life,* occur. Indeed, the technical media products that so effectively frame everyday life in our current culture are intimately linked to globalized agendas of biopower. However, what I have proposed in this chapter is that we can use a very surprising example to point toward a new way of approaching technical media, biopower, and the body, namely, that of insects, as seen through Roger Caillois's work. Again, research on the biopower capture of human potential proves to be not the only relevant way of understanding the nature of contemporary capitalism. In addition, there is a whole world of insect affects that extends further from the actual insect bodies and touches the spaces, politics, and media of modernity and late modernity.

Intermezzo

What, however, if human labor power turns out to be only part of the story of lively capital?

—Donna J. Haraway, *When Species Meet*

The nineteenth century brought a curious crystallization of the early interest in capturing animal affects. On the one hand, the scientific and technological mechanisms for measuring, defining, and reproducing animal affects were for the first time designed in a rigorous manner and as the basis of the future media culture of reproducing animal sensations but outside animal bodies. On the other hand, radical ideas of nonteleological evolution, the activity of animal matter and instinct, and noncentralized modes of action and communication emerged, which already represented themes crucial for the contemporary consideration of what kinds of modes of organization the network society might promote, how such bodies are formed, and what the future folds and modes of the human being might be.

The interconnections of animal life and technologies were of utmost importance to the state since the nineteenth century in Prussia but also in France, England, and various other countries. Technology was not always necessarily seen as a conscious, self-reflective result of human development, even though the human body was constantly used as a model of successful and coherent technological systems. For social theorists such as Karl Marx, it was the human mind and imagination that secured the possibility of insightful planning.[1]

In addition to the connections seen between architecture and animal structurings, Laura Otis has shown that imagining telegraph networks and human nerves was a parallel venture from the 1840s in the theories of Hermann von Helmholz and Emile Du Bois-Reymond, to name two examples of physiologists of the nineteenth century. Telecommunication physics and physiological laws of biological bodies were closely paralleled in a manner that was not removed from political and national interests, as a quote from a speech by Du Bois-Reymond from 1868 illustrates:

> Now, do you see the soul in the brain as the only sensitive, conscious region of the body, and the whole rest of the body as an inanimate machine in its hand? Just so the life of the great nation of France, otherwise centralized to the point of desolation, pulses only in Paris. But France is not the right analog; France is still waiting for a Werner Siemens to cover [überspinnen] it with a telegraph net. For just as the central station of the electric telegraph in the Post Office of Königsstrasse is in communication with the outermost borders of the monarchy through its gigantic web of copper wire, just so the soul in its office, the brain, endlessly receives dispatches from the outermost limits of its empire through its telegraph wires, the nerves, and sends out its orders in all directions to its civil servants, the muscles.[2]

In this vein, several of the key researchers of the human body, such as Wilhelm Wundt and the father of modern pathology, Rudolf Virchow, embraced the idea of nerves corresponding to telegraph systems. Ernst Kapp was grounding his own analysis of the correspondence between the new technologies and the human body in the statements of such esteemed researchers.[3] Moreover, Kapp saw the state as the ultimate form of organization for the human form, a social equivalent of the totality of the organ projection. Here the *res interna* of human nature becomes the *res publica* of the state, and the state forms into a self-referring system, an organic being-for-itself.[4] By the twentieth century, the idea of seeing the state as a living organism and governed by biopolitics was becoming consolidated. Not only metaphorical in the sense of parallels between the state and the body, the new rationalization of life referred to how the forms of organization could take nature as their object and "incorporate and reproduce nature's original characteristics,"[5] as Roberto Esposito argues. Of course nature and insect societies provided seeming legitimation for a widespread political and cultural distribution of racist, sexist, and classist ideologies that branded nineteenth- and early twentieth-century societies. This is what Diane Rodgers has called a work of naturalization of the hierarchical modes of sociality through discursive practices such as entomology.[6]

As part of the structuration of modern societies and their hierarchies, the media sphere of nineteenth-century technological systems was characterized by centripetal forces. This resonated with the rise of the bureaucratic systems of the nation-states. Networks of nerves and telegraphs flowed and were connected at the center of the brain/mind. Networks of communication such as the telegraph were of such crucial interest for business and national security that access to wires was restricted to the "head," the key nodes.[7] The spider's web of communication and swarming of bees needed in the last instance the central dispatcher to keep the system intact. Such a view had already been illustrated in an eighteenth-century story by Denis Diderot. In *Le rêve de D'Alembert* (*D'Alembert's Dream*, 1769), Diderot engaged in a speculation concerning what has been referred to as a dynamic materialism and also introduced a philosophical delirium about self-organizing swarms.[8] Interestingly, this delirious philosophizing introduced the idea of emergent systems way before their time. D'Alembert (here paraphrased by Mademoiselle de L'Espinasse) imagines the world as a huge decentralized hive:

> "Have you ever seen a swarm of bees leaving their hive? . . . The world, or the general mass of matter, is the great hive. . . . Have you seen them fly away and form at the tip of a branch a long cluster of little winged animals, all clinging to each other by their feet? This cluster is a being, an individual, a kind of living creature. . . . But these clusters should be all alike. . . . Yes, if he admitted the existence of only one homogenous substance. . . . Have you seen them?" "Yes, I have." "You have?" "Yes, dear, I am telling you so." "If one of those bees decides to pinch in some way the bee it is hanging on to, what do you think will happen? Tell me." "I've no idea." "Tell me all the same. . . . So you don't know, but the Philosopher does. . . . If ever you see him, and you are bound to see him sooner or later, for he has promised you will, he will tell you that this second bee will pinch its neighbour, and that throughout the cluster as many individual sensations will be provoked as there are little creatures, and that the whole cluster will stir, move, change position and shape, that a noise will be heard, the

sound of their little cries, and that a person who had never seen such a cluster form would be tempted to take it for a single creature with five or six hundred heads and a thousand or twelve hundred wings."[9]

However, his delirious views are corrected by the sanity of Monsieur Bourdeu and replaced with an idea of human (animal) nerves as spider's webs but subjugated to the control of the consciousness (the spider). Nerves are the ministers or slaves of the brain.[10] There is no communication *between* the minuscule invisible threads that connect/govern the animal system. In other words, this "delirium" of swarms demonstrates that it was still too early to come up with radically distributed systems outside a madman's thoughts. Clearly this also related to fears of the uncontrollability of an organism and the traditional need for sovereignty that controls the individuated bits and parts of an organism. Around the mid-eighteenth century, only through the voice of someone insane was it reasonable to approach ideas of radically distributed intelligence and control in which the spider's web was not reducible to the control of the spider or the hive of bees was not controlled by a single sovereignty. This was naturally a problem that touched the fields of material ontology and biology, but even more so politics. What form of control could such a seemingly chaotic system have?

Such mind-centered views dominated the coupling of biology and technology. To a large extent, technological systems were articulated in relation to the capabilities of the human as a cognizant, intelligent, and centrally led autonomous being. In addition to the human-centered anthropological views, one variation insisted on the "intelligent design" of the world mechanism that also persisted after Darwin made his remarks concerning the radical temporality and evolution of the world. The world was still often seen not as a result of the evolution of anonymous forces but as a machine designed by a supernatural mind.[11]

Raving delirious philosophers were in the minority in relation to dominating ideas of centrally led sovereignty in technological systems and politics. In this sense, references to insect sensations and modes of organization occupied a place of a kind of minoritarian knowledge. One of the dividing questions had to do with the evolution from instinct to intelligence and a reflexive relationship with the world. Were the origins of technology in intelligent reflexive creations of artifice, or should the anthropological interest in knowledge be expanded to animal "technics" as well, such as insects? This agenda was not addressed in such explicit terms, yet the questions were popping up every now and then in different contexts.

However, approaching the new millennium, the ideas that were considered insane in Diderot's story were much more feasible and were integrated as part of various fields of knowledge and practice in science and the arts. For instance, the Hungarian-born network scientist Albert-László Barabási explained as part of his ideas relating to scale-free networks that there is not a central node in a spider's web—and thus no one privileged place of surveillance and control, which separates it from the earlier models of societies of discipline that required a hierarchical positioning of power:

> In the absence of a spider, there is no meticulous design behind these networks either. Real networks are self-organized. They offer a vivid example of how the independent actions of millions of nodes and links lead to spectacular emergent behavior. Their spiderless scale-free topology is an unavoidable consequence of their evolution. Each time nature is ready to spin a new web, unable to escape its own laws, it creates a network whose fundamental structural features are those of dozens of other webs spun before.[12]

Alex Galloway and Eugene Thacker elaborate Barabási's ideas in terms of the biopolitics of distributed networks. It is the changing body politic that this is a sign of, not just a shift in, scientific understanding of networks. An observation of networks is inherently and always a political one, they claim, and they address the shift as one relating to the new forms of control that characterize the network society. Instead of spatial architectures of human phenomenology, we are dealing with techniques of control that rely on the logic of biology interfaced with informatics. However, as Galloway and Thacker note, the medicalization, or biologization, of politics is not a new phenomenon but already characterized Plato's take on the body politic as well as Hobbes's model of sovereignty of the Leviathan. An artificial man was the image of the politics of hierarchical power, already criticized by Foucault. However, beyond the model of man, the biopolitics of living networks, as Galloway and Thacker coin it, is reliant on altogether alternative biological ideas.[13]

The second half of this book turns toward digital technologies and the era of cybernetics. Now we focus on technology and media as insects. We look at the era that roughly began at the end of the Second World War and the continuing integration of biology with informatics. This is an era of high-technological culture but also of bugs swarming around popular culture in graphic novels, films, science fiction, and so on. Overgrown Japanese nuclear insects meet the creeping nightmares of William S. Burroughs and David Cronenberg and also the masculine dreams of wars against insects in the novel *The Forgotten Planet* (1954) as well as the manga horror of *The Bug Boy* (2004), which tells of a bullied boy metamorphosing into a vengeful bug after an insect bite. This is the age of insecticides and chemicals such as DDT but also of the emergence of a new phase of insects in information sciences and software.

This is an era branded by cybernetics but in broader terms than just the official field inaugurated at the Macy conferences. Now the earlier interest in alternative modes of perception and movement and in entity–environment relationships acquires a new, more gratuitously (but nonetheless state-) funded context with research into computers, communication, and the relationships between animals (including humans) and machines. What the following chapters focus on are the ideas in nonrepresentational perception, new informational objects and their environmental network environments, and the experimental work done that has hinted at posthuman and, perhaps more radically, also nonhuman ways of understanding the ontology of technical media culture. As argued at the beginning of the book, the posthuman era should not be only about what comes after the Man, but about replacing the agenda more radically.[14] It is about the fundamentally nonhuman forces of which the world consists in any case—an ontology of becoming-animal, as I suggest in this particular context.

Animal or *insect* does not just mark a specific biological entity. In fact, we are dealing not only with specific physiological bodies of insects but, in the process, with how knowledge of and interest in those small actants was deterritorialized and subsequently reterritorialized as part of media technological systems, design, and theory. In various ways, the animal and insect worlds that fascinated people throughout the nineteenth century, for example, Marey, were parallel to the emerging fields of new technologies beyond the human phenomenology. Both included forces that were imperceptible in themselves, for example, electricity or insects' wing movements, but whose effects could be traced and brought as part of the human sensorium and regimes of knowledge.[15] Similarly, current technologies of digitality and networks deal with forces imperceptible to human understanding but glimpsed through their effects only—the logic of algorithms, calculations, and voltages unreachable in itself, yet continuously mediated and affecting the bodies of humans. The nonhuman nature of technology can be easily connected to the nonhuman worlds of animals, as has been explicitly done in such endeavors as those of the new cognitive sciences. "Bugs" are not, then, only instances of a breakdown or of unwanted elements in computer systems. They relate to a wider reevaluation of the "intelligence" of simple life and nonorganic life as well, as evidenced in this meditation by Michel Serres that escorts us to the second part of the book:

> If winds, currents, glaciers, volcanoes, etc., carry subtle messages that are so difficult to read that it takes us absolutely ages to decipher them, wouldn't it be appropriate to call them intelligent? How would it be if it turned out that we were only the slowest and least intelligent beings in the world?[16]

ANIMAL ENSEMBLES, ROBOTIC AFFECTS
Bees, Milieus, and Individuation

That they are able to fly by an indirect route and yet reconstruct the true direction without the aid of ruler, protractor, or drawing-board is one of the most wonderful accomplishments in the life of the bee and indeed in all creation.

—Karl von Frisch, *The Dancing Bees*

Quite often the Second World War is represented as the dividing line between two worlds: the industrial era of modernization and the postindustrial era of computers, network technologies, and "postmodernization." The concerted planning, funding, and building of intelligent information systems from signal engineering to computing and social systems took off during that postwar period branded by the Macy Conferences in Cybernetics (1946–1953), officially titled Cybernetics: Circular Causal and Feedback Mechanisms in Biological and Social Systems. The conferences synthesized much of the interest in research into animal worlds, affects, and technological systems and represented a peculiar social institution in themselves—something that has not escaped the interest of cultural theorists and historians. John Johnston offers, to my mind, the best and most refined analysis of the significance of that cybernetic period as a rethinking of the various complex ties among actual machinery such as computers, information and control sciences, and the refashioning of living systems as information entities instead of heat engines.[1] The coinvestigation into computing and how life is fundamentally conceived is defined by "the regulation of passage of information," which incidentally pointed out for writers such as Norbert Wiener not only the importance of Gibbsian statistical mechanics but also the crucial context of "Bergsonian time," which both living organisms and modern automata shared.

However, most often the critical focus has been on the theoretical and practical discourses surrounding human–machine interaction. The talk about "giant brains" and "thinking machines" was only the popular cultural tip of the iceberg in a much more complex field of translations among informatics, psychology, sciences of the brain, and other disciplines in which work on formalizing the functions of thought was taking place. The research surrounding computers was focused on the specific faculty of thinking, and the human being was seen as the ultimate behavioral and architectural model. Physiology fed into design of computer systems that remediated organs and memory as if in the human "system."[2] Popular representations of science embraced these references to similarities in machine and human brains,[3] and indeed the scientific discourse used a lot of biological metaphors as well: John von Neumann's pioneer research relied much on such metaphoric uses, in which the radically nonhuman wirings of computer architecture were made familiar with the help of ideas relating to the human measure and phenomenology. Quite strikingly, technical media that had not much to do with the human dimensions were mapped onto the human body plan that had structured politics and models of thought for centuries. For example, the McCulloch-Pitts model of the brain neuron provided a bridge between fleshy embodied brains and logical patterning that could be used to build computer "brains." Despite attempts of this type, using the human being as a model of intelligence to cover the material reality of the world, the problem was far from resolved, as N. Katherine Hayles has remarked. Continuously haunting the scientists was the task of "how to move from this stripped-down neural model to such complex issues as universals in thought, gestalts in perception, and representations of what a system cannot represent."[4] No matter how well thought, there always remained a fringe of unrepresentable stuff in/of the body.

As Hayles notes, Warren McCulloch was continuously interested in the importance of embodiment for calculations. The drive was toward seeing how human beings and computers could share a similar ontological background in flows of binary codes. This could be seen as part of a very pragmatic "management task" of controlling the temporality of animal bodies in terms of informational events. Hayles continues that McCulloch was continuously interested in signal processing, where the signal is always a very material one. What interests Hayles is how concepts such as the McCulloch–Pitts neuron stood as "liminal object(s)"[5] that helped to translate between interests in mathematics and concrete embodied constructions. To paraphrase Hayles, the embodied constructions provided an effective way to value cybernetics "in-action." Indeed, a whole cybernetic zoo emerged after the Second World War, ranging from William Grey Walter's robot tortoises to Norbert Wiener's moth automata that reacted to light (the moth working toward light, the bug running away from light) and from Claude Shannon's maze-solving rat devices to the interest in ant and bee communication that emerged in the midst of the Macy conferences.[6] Animals were at the core of the cybernetic interest and the turn toward the informatic biopower of network society. As Johnston has recently demonstrated, the postwar period can be characterized as one of a systematic rethinking of the relations between physical processes (life) and information (computers as the symptomatic machine). Such transactions between discourses provided a new ontology for rethinking "computational organisms," as in the case of cybernetist W. Ross Ashby's suggestion that any system that is sufficiently complex and dynamic will produce a group of organisms specific to it.[7]

This chapter focuses on the zoology of communication and cybernetics. Embodied forms of life became of crucial interest for the emerging technologies and discourses of control. Dealing not only with disembodied logics and a Platonist dualism of body versus matter, they more closely suggested translations between different spheres in terms of pragmatics: what works, what does not. Experiments along these lines emphasized the contrast to the post-1956 artificial intelligence research that focused more on disembodied logic and cognitive psychology; cybernetic zoology relied on the embodied and contextual animality of both machines and nature.[8] This insistence on embodiment inherent in the new regimes of cybernetics, informatics, and their machines and robots can be further connected to the themes and arguments I have suggested concerning biopower and the capturing of animal affects in the culture of technical modernity. In addition, in this latter context we see the theme of technology or media emerging as an animal or even an insect. Naturally insects were not the only animals discussed, but they represent one particular example that was of interest in terms of their less brainy but complex modes of action, behavior, perception, and, not least, communication.

Communication was of special interest in the postwar situation. As Charlotte Sleigh argues, the communication was well recognized in terms of the funding and attention it received in the United States. Animals provided examples of "effective orientation and meaningful communication"[9] in a manner that was to be directly translated into military and social tools. From ants to bees, fish to various other examples that could be turned into cybernetic circuits, communication was seen not only in technological terms. Or, to be more accurate, the technological interest in communication and perception was broadened to also encompass living entities such as insects.[10] If the nineteenth-century era of early technical media was intimately tied to experimental psychology and the measuring of the reaction times and perception thresholds of the body, the post–World War II rise of the digital media culture was embedded in a new valorization of experimental biology. As Warren Weaver has noted, experimental biology was seen as a priority research area that could feed solutions to social registers as well.[11]

From Karl von Frisch's communicating bees to William Grey Walter's tortoise robotics, the question of the perception of the environment and orientation in space and time became key themes for the development of sensing technologies. These can be framed in the theoretical innovations of Gilbert Simondon, writing around the 1960s, on notions of information that tried to evade the age-old hylomorphic schemes of "matter-form." Hylomorphism can be seen as characterizing the cybernetic models of communication as well. Instead, with Simondon, information came to be understood as intensive relations with the environment, something that was pragmatically understood in research on matters from problem-solving robotics to bees' food excavation trips. With Simondon and his ideas on "individuation," we gained a strong theory that the relation between an entity and its environment is not to be understood in terms of structure, a priori forms, or stability. Instead the individuating entity is a temporal becoming that works by creating topological solutions (instead of "having" geometrical presolutions) to problems encountered. Instabilities are organized into metastabilities.[12] This is where a link with the temporal dynamics of the ethological relations of animals, analyzed in earlier chapters, connects with the cybernetic discourses of 1950s and 1960s and where Simondon offered a materially situated way of evaluating and appreciating information—not as a pattern that is beyond or outside its material expressions but as an intervention between entities and milieus to be understood through notions such as individuation and transduction. We will return to these complex notions later.

The adoption of ants and bees as problem-solving machines has been a key theme in information sciences since the early analysis of ant trails and bee hives around the 1950s. Researchers such as Adrian Wenner suggested approaching the hive as a Markov process that was to be analyzed according to population-level probabilities.[13] In recent years research into social insects (especially ants) as "optimization machines" has risen to be a whole research field of its own.[14] Ant colony optimization algorithms have been used to find ideal ways of managing networks and other distributed systems. The idea is basically to adopt an ant way of solving the food problem by randomly scanning the environment and enhancing the good solutions found. The positive feedback patterns then reinforce certain solutions over others and prove, it is claimed, nature's way of solving complex mathematical problems.

Random evolution of solutions through environmental perceptivity is related to other informational solutions that seem to take their cue from the effective calculative processes of nature. For example, take genetic algorithms that were hailed in the new millennium's popular science literature as a key innovation in harnessing nature's powers. The early experimenter John Holland's idea was to let solutions to algorithmic problems rise from a predefined "genetic pool" that worked as if according to a Darwinian principle of evolution.[15] Different solutions were tried, but only the "strongest" survived. As we saw in the second chapter, this is where the early insect discourse on the innate mathematics of nature and bees seemed to be of interest to the network-minded scientists and enthusiasts of the turn of the millennium. However, another question will be whether this neo-Darwinian model is the most accurate and interesting in terms of understanding the insect turn in media design and theory. Is addressing insect colonies, emergence, and self-organization as a form of random selection the most accurate description? Or is the suggested environmental relation of ants and bees, as already argued during the early research, a more complex description that involves instinctual systems that extract much of the information needed from the intensive encounter with the insects' milieus? This would lead us to another way of understanding the harnessing of nature and toward a nature–culture continuum[16] instead of just another version of a hylomorphic scheme (ideal genotypes vs. material phenotypes). Next, through bees and milieu-bound robots, we are going to address this question concerning relations, intensity, and individuation as a key theme of the early interfacing of animals and technological entities.

BEE WAGGLING: LESSONS IN COMMUNICATION STUDIES

It is rarely mentioned that Norbert Wiener's first published paper was on ants. As Sleigh explains, this suggests that the history of cybernetics was not "only engineering and neurophysiology but also natural historical," involving the study of other animals and their ecological relations.[17] After the Second World War, communication was seen as a crucial catalyst of social and technological relations, from the micro levels of dealing with computers in human–machine environments to the macro levels of cold war and social development.[18] This was the period when bees were analyzed as communication animals, as in the much-hailed Karl von Frisch's studies on bee language. Von Frisch himself could not hear without being wired. The Graz, Austria–based professor's 1940s trip to the United States was shadowed by his being half-deaf and dependent on machines (a hearing aid and a personal assistant) that amplified the noise of the world into something significant for him.[19] He responded by wiring bees into a perspective of knowledge that introduced them as communicating through dance.

The animals of Von Frisch's 1953 book *Aus dem Leben der Bienen,* translated a year later into English as *The Dancing Bees,* were much more perceptive. The book was based on research that Von Frisch had performed since the 1910s, and already in the 1940s it had earned him an international reputation, with theorists far outside the biological sciences, such Jacques Lacan, drawing on his findings.[20] The book covered a wide range of bee behavior in a reader-friendly fashion, continuing the popular literature of the insect genre that had been successful since the nineteenth century. As we learned from earlier chapters on insects, bee life was filled with their astonishing capacities to build, live, and sense the world. One of the curiosities that Von Frisch emphasized was the bees' ability to express complex navigational instructions through dancing.

The discovery that bees have a language was a spin-off from Von Frisch's other experiments. Already around 1917–1919 his observations regarding bees' sense of color led him to the activity of the bee dance, which seemed to communicate information about nearby food resources.[21] Later his emphasis changed, but in any case Von Frisch was looking into the perceptive qualities of bees with the help of different tests that provided surprising results on how single bees attracted to honey treasures were later followed by several others from the same hive. This involved meticulous tracking of the bee in ethnographical fieldwork fashion: constructing an observation hive, painting the visitors for differentiation purposes, and then following the interactions with other bees. What followed for the scientific spectators was the "round dance": "On the part of the comb where she is sitting, she starts whirling around in a narrow circle, constantly changing her direction, turning now right, now left, dancing clockwise and anti-clockwise in quick succession, describing between one and two circles in each direction."[22] As a form of crowd behavior that was a key issue for modern sociologists and city planners, the dance "infects" the other bees, which start to follow the first bee's movements. This train of dancers continues for some seconds or even half a minute to disgorge honey she has brought with her.

Not too surprisingly, using the word *dance* made Von Frisch susceptible to accusations of anthropomorphism. His work was debated from the 1930s with constant accusations that he was conflating human superiority with the more affective animal communication.[23] In fact, as Eileen Crist argues, the use of the word *dance* was a much more figural way of addressing the interest of the reader, whereas the idea of this bee movement as a "language" was to be taken literally.[24] What Von Frisch suggested was that the movements were related to the source of food and that the dance communicated both the direction and the distance of the find. With shorter turns in the dance, the bees signal a distance of a hundred yards, but longer intervals signal a greater distance, something that Von Frisch was able to demonstrate with a stopwatch and a mathematical graph. The bees' movement is directly related to distances, which led Von Frisch to suggest that the bees "must possess a very acute

sense of time, enabling the dancer to move in the rhythm appropriate
to the occasion, and her companions to comprehend and interpret her
movements"—even more astonishing to the observers because the bees
"do not carry watches."[25]

Here we discover again the theme of insect bodies as relational entities whose technics are inseparable from the bodies themselves. As
Henri Bergson claimed approximately fifty years earlier, the way insects
solve the problems of life is intimately tied to the technics of their bodies
immanent to their surroundings. The spatializing forms of knowledge
that enable the projections into the future that characterize intelligent
humans differ from the lived relations of insects, for example. Bergson
reminded us that instinct does not have to be resolved either as a form
of pre-intelligence or a mechanism, but it can be seen as a potentiality of
relations that does not reside outside the terms. Caterpillars are not just
systems of spatially definable nerves and nervous centers but modes of
relating. Consider Bergson: "The Ammophila, no doubt, discerns but a
very little of that force, just what concerns itself; but at least it discerns
it from within, quite otherwise than by a process of knowledge—by an
intuition (lived rather than represented)."[26]

This relates to the idea of technology as machinology addressed in
chapter 3. In the machinological context, Samuel Butler's nineteenth-
century fabulations of the machinology of technology sidesteps the general understanding of the origins of technology à la Kapp or McLuhan.
More recently Luciana Parisi has taken up this machinic ontology and
argued, with the help of Deleuze, Guattari, and Simondon, that it helps
us to bypass the dualist division of the given and the constructed, nature
and culture, and see creation in terms of an ontogenesis of machinic relations.[27] Machines are mixtures of heterogeneous components (from biological to social), and machinic assemblages are the processes through
which organizations of the body are constructed by cutting from flows
of intensive elements of the world.[28] Such a perspective assumes that
technologies are also machinic in the sense of relational enterprises that
organize bodies. As part of a certain Spinozan ontology, the focus is on
bodies concerting with other bodies and the powers to connect and dis-
connect. This intensive layer of machinics is then an analysis of the continuous orders of couplings from which stratified organizations emerge
and are spatialized, for example, through scientific analysis.[29] Instead of

the focus being on single elements interacting (such bees and flowers), it is on the systematic relationality of the elements where the relations are primary. As elements of relatedness (as Morgan named it), the terms connected emerge only as part of a wider system of environmental referentiality, which is to be judged in terms not of passive adaptation but of active becoming. This is of course a peculiar and perhaps a stretched way of looking at nature in terms of technics or machinology. However, it provides a way out of the impasse of seeing nature as oppositional to cultural terms, which is reflected, for example, in the difficulty of understanding what Von Frisch meant when he referred to bee communication as language. What I would like to argue is that the bees he is referring to are not representational entities but machinological becomings, to be contextualized in terms of their capabilities of perceiving and grasping the environmental fluctuations as part of their organizational structures. The hive, then, extends itself as part of the environment through the social probings that individual bees enact where the intelligence of the interaction is not located in any one bee, or even a collective of bees as a stable unit, but in the "in-between" space of becoming: bees relating to the mattering milieu, which becomes articulated as a continuum to the social behavior of the insect community. This community is not based on representational content, then, but on distributed organization of the society of nonhuman actors.

What is curious is that this environing extends as a parallel to the early trends in robotics and the crucial recognition that perhaps an effective technological system works not through intelligence input into the machine but through creating various affective modes of relating and responding to the fluctuations of the environment as a "naturing nature" in process. The way research on bee communication worked toward intensive environmental relations can in fact be connected to the way pioneering work on responsive systems had to come up with ways of maneuvering in concrete space. Despite the epistemological distance, these movements are parallel in constituting the emerging interest in context-sensitive ways of understanding nonhuman actors and how this knowledge stretches from "intelligent" perception–action sequences into dumb but interconnected emergent "intelligence"—or what would have been called an instinctual approach some fifty years ago. This tracking distances itself from approaches that stick to the ontology and epistemology of cybernetics and their view concerning language and informatics. Instead, as we will see later, the alternative notions concerning information, entities, and environments developed by the French philosopher Gilbert Simondon around the same time provide a much more fruitful way to think of bodies in action. With Simondon, concepts of individuation, transduction, and intensive environmental relations are more accurate and complex ways to understand natural or technical processes. First, however, we turn to another example of a zoology of cybernetics, W. Grey Walter's robotic tortoises.

MACHINE ANIMALS

Technological zoology is not only a recent trend. During the earlier phases of modernity, automata introduced slightly different but no less revolutionary ideas concerning the nature of (technological) life. Then an artificial duck was a celebrity. The Vaucanson creation demonstrated, as Jessica Riskin argues, a threshold machine in the simulation of natural beings.[30] It not only resembled a duck in appearance and habits but simulated the internal workings of the animal as well. Living processes were incorporated into the experimental creations that produced knowledge about the animal world but also about the interfaces of humans, nature, and technology. Here two phenomena acted as watersheds for the distinction, explains Riskin: movement and speech. What can move itself is, according to the much-embraced Aristotelian idea, a living being, and what can respond in terms of speech is an *intelligent* living being. Of course speaking machines existed, and they seemed to question this division. Julien Offray de la Mettrie believed in speaking machines, and in 1791 Wolfgang von Kempelen from Hungary explained the workings of such a machine. In this kind of machine, speech was the physical result of the movement of air through the imitations of lungs and other human organs. Nevertheless, it provided important lessons on the question of what is reproducible and what seems to be unique to the intelligent human being. Such an interest in mechanical ducks and the like fed into very pragmatic goals in terms of the emerging factory system and the redistribution of labor from humans to machines. Animals and machines could do several types of repetitious and nonintelligent work, such as weaving, and hence could amplify the production of all those goods needed for the emergence of the modern world.

Is it a bee, then, instead of a duck that stands at the beginning of the postmodern era of communication and cybernetics? For some, like Steven Shaviro, it is the insect that is the "totem animal" of postmodernity owing to its refashioning of the inside and the outside, its radical becomings evident in the transmutations that its goes through.[31] Certainly the 1950s were filled with gigantic bugs that threatened the organized society of the United States—hence it was a figure overladen with fears of communism, disorder, and environmental pollution. The film *Them!* introduced gigantic nuclear ants in 1954, and only a year later *Tarantula* applied a similar logic to spiders. There were plenty of similar examples for years to come.[32] However, in terms of communication and the optimization of efficiency, movement and language were marked as threshold questions in new technologies that were to brand the emerging network world. Much as in the case of the automata of the eighteenth century, the fields of knowledge concerning nature and experimental engineering of technological objects guided the analysis by reproducing examples of life. Paraphrasing Riskin's argument, such experiments simultaneously functioned as the organizing division of what remains beyond artificial reproduction in life and hence drew or reinforced differences between artificiality and nature. However, in the field we address in this chapter we encounter various fabrications of artificial objects, and the natural talking bees are also "artificial constructions," as I will argue.

W. Grey Walter's cybernetic tortoises are a good example of more concrete robot animals of the 1950s. Walter was a pioneer of different physiological measurements of the human body and one of the early developers of the electroencephalograph machine that mapped the electrical activity of the brain. Brains were his primary interest not only as organs but as transmission and crossroad points of living organisms. Nerve-knots define life from its simple forms such as ants and bees on, which fascinated Walter: "Who would call brainless a creature which can return from a long flight and report to its community, to within a few yards, where it has discovered honey supplies?"[33] Indeed, Walter seemed to be aware of the research into bee communication, which he saw in terms of nerving with the world: "Appraised by results, the bee is a highly developed mobile unit of a sedentary brain."[34] Bees were an early form of mobile communication in this 1950s influential take on the centrality of the brain.

Walter thought that evolution is to be read in terms of brain development, which itself is a function of nerve complexity. The brain is conceptualized as a communication system in its own terms, a mediation point between external and internal communications. Nervous systems are networks for receiving, correlating, storing, and generating signals,[35] which emphasizes their status as media systems but ones grounded in living bodies.

In order to tap into the complexity of the brain, Walter built experimental objects, cybernetic tortoises, that were designed to illustrate what complex wiring even a simple orientation in space demands. Of course the Vaucanson duck was already a cybernetic unit of a kind based on feedback mechanisms, but the cybernetic tortoises were designed to take into account environmental variations. The "Machina Speculatrix," as explained in the book *The Living Brain* in 1953, was to practically investigate the question of whether brainpower works through the number of units in the brain or through the *"richness of their interconnection."*[36] Thus it worked as an experimental object that implicitly maneuvered between the nature–technology division and looked into the brain as a complex network that interacted with its outside. Walter's idea was to build a very simple machine equipped with goal-seeking and scanning abilities together with movement. The electronically wired "animal" was speculative in its push toward exploration of its environment instead of waiting for impulses.[37] It was not only a reactionary entity but was equipped with a certain spontaneity bound, however, by "positive" and "negative" tropism. In other words, it was tightly coupled to certain environmental attractions, as Walter called them, through simple sensors. Positive tropism referred to its push toward light, negative tropism to a pull away from "very bright lights, material obstacles, and steep gradients."[38]

The tortoises (which looked more like toasters on wheels than actual animals) were hence ecological units of a kind equipped with a simulation of a nervous system of a very simple animal. Yet the obstacle to a complex environmental relationship was that the machines could not be taught to learn. Learning to learn was still the stumbling block for the tortoises, which did not have extensive memories that could help them to summate their experiences.[39]

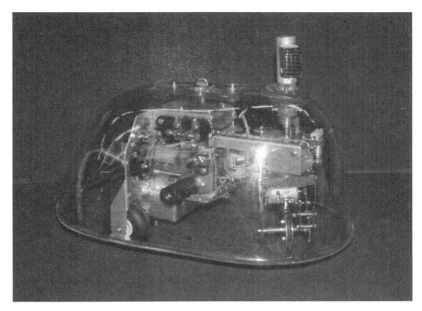

A replica of the Walter tortoise. Courtesy of University of the West of England, Bristol.

What was remarkable according to Walter was the tortoises' recognition of their surroundings, which seemed to present unforeseen results. The machines worked through specific but simple thresholds of perception of their surroundings, maneuvering past objects and toward lights. In addition, they showed traits of "self-recognition" in front of a mirror surface, where responsive photo cells responded to their own headlamps. This led Walter to claim that this behavior was signaling their similarity to some higher animals that were able to understand that a mirror image was an image of themselves instead of other animals. Furthermore, two machines could be seen exhibiting mutual recognition that according to Walter was a form of community building of sorts; the stimulus to community and communication was recognition of the light from the other machine. However, this banality of community, reducible to response to a bright light from another Machina Speculatrix, resulted in surprising behavior:

Some of these patterns of performance were calculable, though only as types of behaviour, in advance; some were quite unforeseen. The faculties of self-recognition and mutual recognition were obtained accidentally, since the pilot-light was inserted originally simply to indicate when the steering-servo was in operation. It may be objected that they are only "tricks," but the behaviour in these modes is such that, were the models real animals, a biologist could quite legitimately claim it as evidence of true recognition of self and others as a class. The important feature of the effect is the establishment of a feedback loop in which the environment is a component. This again illustrates an important general principle in the study of animal behaviour—that any psychological or ecological situation in which such a reflexive mechanism exists, may result in behaviour which will seem, at least, to suggest self-consciousness or social consciousness.[40]

Hence, looping the environment into a component of the emerging system or a community of machines was the early phase of "intelligence building," so to speak. Here the banal mode of communication was far from communication of content in terms of abstracted symbols; it was rather a mode of embodied interaction in a shared space. This stance implies that communication is actually based in perception, and perception is furthermore conceptualized as an environmental being and a perceptiveness that Walter tried to hardwire into the speculating machines. Building machines included a simultaneous building of milieus for the machines. Environments were to be incorporated as part of the plans of any circuit, animal or machine, as Uexküll had already argued.[41] A contemporary example of such "machine species" might be the robotic spiders of Ken Rinaldo, which resemble the tortoises to a slight degree but are more chimeratic robots that interact in real time with their viewers: "The Auto telematic Spider Bots installation is an artificial life chimera; a robotic spider, eating and finding its food like an ant, seeing like a bat with the voice of an electronic twittering bird."[42]

The ethological task of the speculating machines was to provide the needed links among notions of the environment, perception, and communication, all key themes in the context of cybernetics, which was working toward more embodied models of automata and communication. This is also the context in which the research agenda started to move from classical artificial intelligence (AI), with intelligence as the information processing of an intelligent machine, to intelligence as a *result* of numerous simple parts' interacting. Emergence was no longer an event of the insects but a mathematical way of understanding how several simple bits can produce complex, heterogeneous wholes. This was an engineering problem because the older models of AI were not able to produce efficient robots or embodied intelligences. Instead, models such as the perceptron, a form of artificial neural network designed by Frank Rosenblatt, introduced ways to conceptualize more brainlike actants. The perceptron idea could be seen working in a certain radical empiricist tradition in which the potential novelty of connections should be accounted for. Instead of spatialized models of memory and nerve systems, Rosenblatt suggested the primacy of connections and associations. Information is never only a passive recording in the brain matter of a living being or a machine but rather works as a "preference for a particular response" and hence lives in the connections that are not modeled as recognitions or representations.[43] In other words, the perceptron machines lived through temporal relations in which networked nerve relations were continuously renewed.

Walter's machines fit into that concept of networked actors, as well as Herbert Simon's realization, also from the 1960s: an agent such as an ant is only as intelligent as its environment. The ant is intimately coupled with its outside much as any artifact can be understood as an interfacing of its inner environment and its outer surroundings. Simon sees it as a meeting place, a relay, and through this intensive environmental relation its capacities for living and functioning are determined through an unfolding in time.[44] Environmental variation is temporal unfolding. Simon thinks that the ant works as a "machine" similar to Walter's creations. An ant is an adaptation machine, a speculatory vector that "deals with each obstacle as he comes to it; he probes for ways around or over it, without much thought for future obstacles."[45] Here the turtle can be transformed into an ant, a supposition Simon makes, suggesting that we turn the turtle's dimensions into those of an ant as well as the means of locomotion and "comparable sensory acuity."[46] Simon thinks that the electromechanical turtle is parallel to the adaptive ant; both entities owe their complexity of behavior to the interfacing of the machine/insect/turtle with the environment. Far from reflexive communicators, the agents are more akin to the Bergsonian instinctual machines/insects that extend their bodies as part of the intensive, varying milieu that opens up only through time.

PERCEPTION AS COMMUNICATION: BEE LESSONS IN DEALING WITH THE ENVIRONMENT

Turning back to the 1950s context, the so-called bee language can also be understood through similar considerations of environmental relations. Here communication becomes less a matter of abstract conveyance of symbols and more a matter of embodied interactions in intensive spatial environments. However, this is where Lacan, and following him Friedrich Kittler, pointed out the difference between Von Frisch's dancing bees and the cybernetic zoo (including computers). They think that animal codes are not language because their signs have a fixed correlation with reality. Symbolic language and subjectivity are in contrast, defined by the discourse of the other, which leads Kittler to state in his idiomatic style: "Bees are projectiles, and humans, cruise missiles."[47] This refers to how the natural communication of bees and the like consists of "objective data on angles and distances," whereas both humans and computers are more tuned to the if/then modulation that takes account of environmental factors. This is the point at which, according to Kittler, computers can become subjects but not bees: "IF a preprogrammed condition is missing, data processing continues according to the conventions of numbered commands, but IF somewhere an intermediate result fulfills the condition, THEN the program itself determines successive commands, that is, its future."[48] In other words, animals do not have a (sense of) future, but machines do. However, as we will see later, this dualism gains its momentum from a Heideggerian tradition that fails to understand the animal environments as dynamic and works toward a continuous analytics of why humans, animals, and machines *differ* from each other.

Von Frisch and his bees stand in an interesting interzone in which different interpretations try to fix him and the communicating bees as part of different traditions and possibilities of agency. The focus on bee language as an abstract processing of symbols is one that remains in the classical model of AI and in notions of language as disembodied symbol processing. The other path, opened around the 1950s and 1960s, started to emphasize the embodied environmental relations of any cybernetic relation. Hence, communication could also be seen as moving from being a mere informational pattern to a more nonrepresentational account of capabilities of agents, whether we are talking about perception or communication.[49] In a way, the language was not about "containing" information, an idea that was used around the 1960s when discussing the patterns. In contrast, language enacted perceptions, movement, and actions in which the division between "intelligent" self-guiding users of language and instinctual, passive, mechanistic followers of signals was bridged.

In fact, revisiting Von Frisch's text clarifies the ties between bee language and bee modes of perception. Throughout his scholarly career, Von Frisch was interested in sensory physiology; he was also a student of his uncle, the experimental physiologist Sigmund Exner.[50] As explained earlier, Von Frisch's research in itself was carefully framed for scientific observation, involving the setting up of an observation hive that transformed the insect habitat into a theater for the scientists. This disclosed visibility of the hive, then, led to an understanding of the sense organs and capacities of bees that was the crucial prerequisite for any discourse concerning bee language. The sections on communication were contextualized in a much wider discussion regarding the bee eye and its workings. Von Frisch argued that the bee eye is especially well tuned to perception of movement. The panoramic visual perception of the insect is composed of "eight to ten thousand little eyes" coordinated to take in rapidly changing impressions.[51] In addition, the bee eye is capable of perceiving polarized light that remains imperceptible to humans. In fact, insects can even "distinguish the direction of [the light's] vibrations, which they use to help them in their orientation."[52] The bee as a coordination device is tuned to such frequencies and phenomena of its milieu, which it can contract to help in its placement and individuation. In this context, the physiological nature of the compound eye proved to be an "ideal kind of analyzer"[53] and hence a focal point for the perception of polarized light. Thus the eye stood for Von Frisch at the center of this intensive environmental relation as a relay of a kind that could be artificially modeled by six units of Polaroid glass.[54]

Furthermore, Von Frisch reminded us that the bee language that is visual for us is in fact sensed by other bees through feeling and smell due to the normally dark hive. Hence, we move from the abstracting capacities of vision to the murkier regimes of tactility and olfactory senses. Of course the major criticism targeted at Von Frisch since the 1960s was actually that he had neglected the world of smells. Adrian Wenner's argument was that bee communication happened not on the level of bodies but in terms of sounds and smells (i.e., chemicals).[55]

In the book *The Dancing Bees,* the section on bee language frames the movement of the dancing bee in terms of distances and directions, which actually correspond more closely to a coordinate system than to a symbolic language. A dance works through indicating the spatial and temporal relations among the body of the dancing bee, the food source, the other bees, and the hive, enveloping them all into a machinic assemblage of language as an ordering of reality into a very functional entity. This is underlined by the fact that the bee dance works differently depending on whether it takes place "inside the hive on the vertical comb or outside on the horizontal platform."[56] In case the bees can see the sky, according to Von Frisch, the sun can act as their compass, which the bees can use to tune the dancing body to a right angle: "The bees who follow after the dancer notice their own position with respect to the sun while following the wagging dance; by maintaining the same position on their flight, they obtain the direction of the feeding-source."[57]

Inside the comb, things are different due to the lack of visibility and the different positioning of the upright-standing comb surfaces. Here, explained Von Frisch, the bees use a different mode of getting the message through:

> Instead of using the horizontal angle with the sun, which they followed during their flight to the feeding place, they indicate direction by means of gravity, in the following way: upward wagging runs mean that the feeding-place lies towards the sun; downward wagging runs indicate the opposite direction; upward wagging runs 60° to the left of the vertical point to a source of food 60° to the left of the direction of the sun ... and so on.[58]

Von Frisch argued that a process of transference takes place: the bees' "delicate sense of feeling for gravity is transferred to a bearing on the sun."[59] In fact, I would extend this notion of transference and suggest that this is the much more interesting aspect Von Frisch is trying to elucidate. A process of transference between bodies and environments is the key force of this dance language that acts as an embodied tool or an indicator, not a patterning that could be extrapolated outside the topological surroundings and bodies of the bees. In other words, perhaps Von Frisch could be read in the context of a whole different mode of understanding language and information than the hegemonic cybernetic view of patterns.

This context draws from nonrepresentational approaches to the environment and the milieu of the individuation of agents. In the earlier chapter on ethology, I argued that Uexküll's theories of the *Umwelt* functioned through a more pragmatic coupling with the environment; the aforementioned Herbert Simon's approach similarly takes into account an interactional becoming with the environment much more than a mentalist conception of perception and action; Humberto Maturana and Francisco Varela's work from the 1960s has indicated that they took a similar direction. As part of the second wave of cybernetics, Maturana and Varela point toward an ethological realization of how crucial the work of construction is in the act of perception. Instead of there being a direct correlation between the world and perception, all environmental relations are constructed in a comovement of the milieu and the sense system of an animal. Perceptions are specified according to capacities of species. This is evident, for example, in the case of the cybernetically wired frog that Maturana and Varela used to analyze its specific capacities for perception of fast movements, like that of the fly.[60] This assemblage approach suggests why Deleuze and Guattari were also fond of Maturana and Varela, because this viewpoint seemed to be in line with Bergson and Uexküll: perception is not only a registering of reality but a much more complex and embodied relation in which the eye is coordinated with the rest of the body and these coordinations also extend outside the body to the world. In fact, some of Von Frisch's critics, such as Wenner, suggested that we need a hypothesis that takes into account the dynamics of population as part of an animal's environment. Instead of symbolic language, argued Wenner, bee orientation is a population-level process that suggests that the hive, its surroundings, and their history are "part of a dynamic system."[61] Instead of individual behavior producing intelligent-seeming results, the workings of the bee system stemmed from probabilistic patterns, argued Wenner in his attempt to dodge the dangers in detaching the individual from the environment.

However, writers such as Simon had already suggested a midway solution to the problem of the individual versus the population when he argued that the individual is already in any case structured and afforded by its environment (without suggesting complete adaptation). In a similar vein, we can appreciate the possibility of approaching Von Frisch's ideas relating to complex processes of environmental individuation. This way we can perhaps move from a disembodied view concerning communication, as promoted by Wenner and the wider cybernetic-influenced research fields, toward a materially grounded but dynamic understanding of communication as inherently part of perception and individuation as part of the milieu.

INDIVIDUATION, INFORMATION, MILIEU

In addition to the thinkers mentioned earlier, Gilbert Simondon approached similar conclusions in his distinctive take on information, milieus, and perception. Through Simondon's work from the 1950s and 1960s, which remains to a large extent not translated into English,[62] we can gain a better understanding of the intensive environmental relations of agencies from bees to speculating machines. Simondon was aware of Von Frisch's bee research and contributed some words on bees, perception, and communication in his course on perception, taught between 1964 and 1965 at the Sorbonne in Paris.

Simondon is interested in how bees are able to transform the measurement of distance into body movements that Von Frisch referred to as the communicating language. Simondon refers here not only to Von Frisch but also to Viaud's *Cours de Psychologie Animale* to explain the diminishing logarithmic relation between the amount and the nature of dancing and the number of possible voyages in a determined time frame. In other words, he explains that the "semantics" of this language are about correspondences between the distance, or the milieu, and the bee's body movements, which stand in a certain more or less fixed proportion to that milieu (although different dialects exist among bee species). Perception turns into body movements, which then turn into a collective perception that informs space and changes its dynamics because of its effects on the relations of bodies and milieu. Space turns into an active milieu of relations instead of only a backdrop for events and communication. Furthermore, the relation is not only that of spatiality, continues Simondon, but that of temporality and duration.[63] Another name for the process of unfolding through metastability is individuation.

With Simondon we are able to understand the intensive individuation that always takes place in the shifting boundaries of an entity and its milieu. Milieu is far from a stable background of individuation and is "characterized by a tension in force between two extreme orders of magnitude that mediatize the individual when it comes into being."[64] Thus we receive an account of the dynamic relationship between an individual embedded in a milieu of potential in which information becomes less a stable object to be transmitted than an indicator of change. Hence the notions of abstract information and language that characterized the understanding of communication in the cybernetic context can be reevaluated in the light of a more embodied notion.[65] Yet this embodiment is one that works through dynamics and the primacy of movement.

In his critique of hylomorphic notions of form and content, Simondon challenges the formalist ideas in information theories. Information is too often seen through conceptual dualisms of form and content, which brands communication as a stable process of transmitting content already in place. For example, the idea of bee communication is too easily formalized as a functionalist account of transmitting abstract symbols about the world rather than as an active becoming of animals within a milieu that is itself also an active part of the individuation. What Simondon proposes is to start with the individuation instead of the individuated entities and look at information as the intensive process of change at the border of different magnitudes. Information is not quantifiable in the way Shannon and Weaver and cybernetics proposed it to be but should be seen as an effectuating operation. In other words, information effects changes.[66] In another passage of his book *L'individuation psychique et collective,* Simondon argues that information is a dynamic notion that functions to "situate the subject in the world."[67] Information informs and guides as an intensive ongoing process, not as a stable form. It assembles agencies into positions in a parallel move as language shifts from a representational signification to a gathering in terms of relations, collectives, and transindividuals—a project of connection.[68] Instead of stable positions communicating—subjects talking (or dancing) about objects that are quantified as information—a focus on information and communication as individuation proposes a transductive notion of communication. The perceptions and orientations in the world of entities are about individuations, but similarly the second-order communications of those perceptions are individuations that gather up collectivities.

In this context, a key notion is that of "metastability," as Adrian Mackenzie explains. Ontogenetical metastability is the essence of transduction as a process of intensive encounters. The transductive nature of life owes to its temporal and topological characteristics, Mackenzie continues, pointing out that the transductive encountering of information is about responsiveness to problems. Living beings respond to problems of their milieu "through constant temporal and spatial restructuring."[69] Mackenzie uses the concept throughout his book-length analysis of technical culture, and we can similarly use it to understand the event of bee communication. Mackenzie argues that Simondon believes that the living beings' transduction also happens through interior milieus in which the body of the living can provide itself information and hence be characterized as metastable. This highlights the way the body of the living is a milieu, a medium in its own way, and also a collectivity instead of an individual. The processes of perception, movement, nutrition, excretion, communication, and dying are intensive processes of transductive nature that Mackenzie articulates as pertaining to the complex fields of biology and technicity. In other words, the body of a living being, or the life of a body, is defined by the metastability that signals a collectivity in place and manifests itself through individuation, change, and continuous foldings of various natures (perceptual, alimentary, semiotic, energetic, symbiotic).[70] As Matthew Fuller underlines, Simondon's way to bypass form–matter hylomorphism affords a way to understand the material process of individuation and "allows accounts of technicity and media to escape from a merely semiological reading of the world into an expanded involvement with and of it."[71]

Again we encounter the theme of the insect as a medium in itself. According to Simondon, "The living being can be considered to be a node of information that is being transmitted inside itself—it is a system within a system, containing *within* itself a mediation between two different orders of magnitude."[72] The body of the living being is thus an intensive carrier of change, which resonates with its environment. The transductive body of the living being works, then, not according to a predefined principle (whether termed instinct, intelligence, or whatever) but through drawing the solutions to problems from the process itself. In this sense, it is opposed to deduction, which operates with ready-made positions.[73] In the section on bees, Simondon notes that we should understand the bees' behavior through the register of perception. However, this perception works through a perception of distance that posits the perceiver as well.[74] The distances fix and inform positions for the perceiver in temporal terms of duration and bodies in duration so that Simondon seems to be also drawing from the bee lessons ideas regarding the temporal forces of situating the milieu; when the bees waggle and dance, so does the milieu through the medium of the bee in a double movement. The milieu is also a rhythmic refrain of a kind.

What Simondon and related perspectives provide, then, are ways to understand the fundamental and constitutive work of perception and individuation. Perception and communication seen as individuation are not separate modes of being in the world but processes constituting living beings as afforded by their milieus.[75]

But why this focus on bees and all the trouble finding an alternative explanatory context for those 1950s research objects, often framed in contexts of cybernetics and information theory? In order to provide an insight into nonrepresentational and intensive environmental relations that connect bees framed in scientific contexts, artificial animals like the environment-sensitive turtles of Walter and the potentials for using the bee bodies as philosophical tools to develop ways of understanding language less as information transmission and more, in a way loyal to Von Frisch's initial metaphors, as an embodied dancing that takes the world as its stage.

So far, the way Simondon paves an alternative way to understand the events of the living, information, and the intensive exchanges in fields of milieus (external and internal) has received little attention from scholars of media. Mackenzie's *Transductions* remains a pioneer work in this regard and offers an insight into the relevance of Simondon for media studies of technical culture embedded in discourses of biology. Contra mathematical theories à la Shannon and Weaver and cybernetics, Simondon focuses on the "genesis of the systems of relations,"[76] as Toscano writes. Individuation does not measure information, but information points to an orientation with it. All of this happens in the intensive environmental relation in which any "senders" and "receivers" are enveloped in the individuation taking place. To specify this point in terms of communication research, we are dealing with information as an arrangement and a creative relation between different states of reality. The pre-individual intensity affords a creation of dimensions "wherein the individual can come to exist and function, a dimension taking over from the scalar heterogeneity or energetic tension that precedes it."[77]

My intention has been to highlight, through this specific example of the communicative bees from the 1950s, the question of how to tap into a similar context of individuation and the milieu. Once again, tiny animals offer insight relevant not only to entomology and biology in general but also to the cultural theory of the cybernetic era as well as contexts of communication and media. Similarly, the new sciences of artificial life arising since the 1980s were much keener on emphasizing the connections with the embodied and less intelligence-oriented constructions of cybernetics than was the post-1956 AI research. For scientists such as Christopher Langton, the new machines of distributed nature paradoxically afforded much more than models of intelligence; they were closer to the simple but more effective processes of living organisms.[78] Indeed, next we will reconvene around the theme of nonrepresentational approaches to perception and work through the digital insects that infiltrated 1980s visual culture. We focus less on the representations of insects in the cinema of the 1980s (where, for example, David Cronenberg's films or Dario Argento's *Phenomena* would be obvious choices) than on the ways that neo-Darwinism and the emerging field of artificial life transposed insect life as an optimization of movements and perception and how this was framed through a reconsideration of the visual and perception in the algorithmic sphere.

BIOMORPHS AND BOIDS
Swarming Algorithms

I would like to thank flocks, herds, and schools for existing: nature is the ultimate source of inspiration for computer graphics and animation.

—Craig Reynolds, "Flocks, Herds, and Schools:
A Distributed Behavioral Model"

The previous chapter continued the ethological emphasis of this book. According to my argument, the "insect question" is one of relations of exteriority, temporal unfolding, and affects instead of just an expression of preformulated instinct-response patterns that denote a mechanical vision of the animal. Paradoxically, this is where the stance also digresses from some of the established notions of ethology. Figures such as Konrad Lorenz and Niko Tingbergen helped to establish the constancy of the instincts (or "movement forms," for Lorenz) that are structures of impulse-reaction. Such a position assumes that there is an already existing structural archive of possible responses that is called upon in specific environmental encounters. However, Uexküll's ideas, especially a Deleuze-Guattarian reading of Uexküll, as well as recent developments in ethology have underlined different perspectives. Instead of a spatialized archive of possible unfoldings, the reactions to the environment are seen as more varying and plastic. Ethology is reworked as a melodic conception of nature in contrast to a teleological and predetermined focus.[1]

Increasingly such a framework can be seen as applying to the nature of technics as well. The most obvious indication is the reformed AI and cognitive science discourse since the 1980s. Scientists such as Andy Clark can be seen as promoting an ethological understanding of the cognitive sphere in which the brain and cognition do not stop at the skin. In a similar vein as that suggested by Herbert Simon in the 1960s, the ethological understanding of the brain and the organism looks at the defining relations and temporal unfoldings of the agent. Like insect life, reason is distributed and always fundamentally intertwined, or afforded by, its collaborations with the world.[2] In fact, nature did not only provide good models for technological creation; for example, Rodney Brooks realized in the 1980s that the best robots might just be insectoidlike and also that nature in itself is creative. Clark used as one of his examples the tuna fish, which certainly was not ranked as one of the intelligent creatures of the world, but despite this prejudice he saw it as "paradoxically talented" as a swimming machine. Physically it should not be able to swim very efficiently, but its "parasiting" of the "fluid dynamics" of its environment produces the tuna as an intelligent creature of the watery milieu: "The tuna use naturally occurring eddies and vortices to gain speed, and they flap their tails so as to actively create additional vortices and pressure gradients, which they then exploit for quick take-offs, etc."[3]

W. Grey Walter's robotic creations addressed in the previous chapter already represented some pre-versions of the new robotics and technologies of milieu sensitivity. Brooks's design realization that "the world is its own best model"[4] implied that systems do not have to be built intelligent but that they can use their environment as a continuous backup and a catalyst. The previous chapter illustrated as well that informational environments do not have to be understood primarily through a representational vision. Embodied interactions, relationality, and motile activity responsible for a constant intensive creation of space as milieu are good modes by which to approach environments as information: informed by bodily intensities.[5]

A renewed interest in "low-level systems" in which insects and tuna could act as models, together with an appreciation of the continuity between bodies, actions, and milieus, as well as "special attention to issues concerning emergence and collective effects"[6] represented the direction in which research inspired by the New AI robotics and artificial life was going. Hence, in this context this chapter turns toward the coupling of nature and computing, as well as ethologies of code, but argues for the curious place of visuality in this assemblage of the 1980s digital culture.

The chapter shows that the media archaeological context of the budding digital culture of the 1980s is not only in mathematical gridding à la Cartesian knowledge but, just as much, an inheritor of the nineteenth-century discourse of evolution and the embodied faculties expressed through animal worlds. The entomological concepts of swarming and the like show an alternative way to understand the life of algorithms as objects in interaction—as evinced in object-oriented programming, for example.

Technology has increasingly shifted from an issue of matter (as stability) to one of variation and metamorphosis. In this sense, the insect potential of transformation, variation, relation, and intensive environmental relations has also characterized technology since recent decades. Bruce Sterling famously announced in the 1980s that technology is no longer celebrated through the grand designs of the Hoover Dam or any other modernist technological achievements but is intimately tied to the body much as the contact lens or the Sony Walkman. However, an updated description would see technology as perpetual variation evinced in the important figure of the computer virus, for example, which has been a key symbol of network culture since the 1980s.[7] In this context, the ethological perspective of temporal unfolding and primacy of variation infects not only biology, as it did already in the early part of the twentieth century, but also cognitive science and the design of technological culture.[8]

This chapter works through three perspectives and three different examples of visual culture and nature becoming an algorithm: biomorphs, SimAnt, and boids. From a mapping of the biological turn in software around the 1980s, we will move on to conclude with object-oriented programming (swarms) as one form of insect bottom-up technics.

THE POWER OF NATURE: BIOMORPHS AND NEO-DARWINIST VISUAL CULTURE

Revisiting Richard Dawkins's 1986 bestseller *The Blind Watchmaker* brings to mind an issue we addressed in chapters 1 and 2 already. The appreciation of nature as a perfection machine was a very strong part of the 1980s discourse surrounding neo-Darwinism. Admiration for the powers of nature was made evident most often in a neo-Darwinian framework such as that of Dawkins, who aimed his book against creationist explanations of the world. More closely, Dawkins argued against "arguments for design" inspired by William Paley, who was awed by the perfectness of nature and could not imagine that such a complex machine could have been created without conscious planning. Paley's *Natural Theology* from 1802 had explained that such complex technological objects as watches have always had to be designed by some intelligent creator. Paley believed that there is no artifice without an artificer and no artwork of nature without a designer. Nature easily parallels the complexity of watches for Paley, who also compared the eye with vision machines such as telescopes. He wrote that "there is precisely the same proof that the eye was made for vision, as there is that the telescope was made for assisting it."[9]

As noted in the chapter 1, much of the nineteenth-century discourse insisted on a theological interpretation of the powers of nature. However, Darwin introduced a very different mode of understanding nature, and similarly Dawkins, with the aim of revitalizing Darwin in the context of the 1980s, tried to argue that the living watches of the world are indeed a reason for wonderment but can be explained by the example of a blind watchmaker. This figure of thought is explained as having no "mind or mind's eye. It does not plan for the future. It has no vision, no foresight, no sight at all."[10] Dawkins thinks that living beings can be seen as perfectly designed machines (without implying that he sees them as mechanic machines). They seem to exhibit purposeful design as swimming, seeing, eating, reproducing, and replicating (gene) machines. Living beings can be seen as a response to a problem posed by their environment and through natural selection are the solution of that problem.

Bats are the ideal example for Dawkins. Comparing the bat machines to the engineers that developed the radar location systems during the twentieth century, Dawkins explains that natural selection has provided an immanent engineering of the bat as a location machine that uses sonar instead of radio waves but is still very effective in its echolocation. Emitting high-pitched sounds, bats are able to locate and maneuver at terrific speeds. This means that their brains are using echoes to "see" the world, to paraphrase Dawkins, which indicates that despite their seemingly simple lifeworlds, they are actually capable of performing highly complex calculations with their "computers," as Dawkins calls their brain-body systems. Indeed, the movement of the bat has to be synchronized with the world in which the rapid movements and locations require a huge number of calculations (a problem that the early robotic engineers of the 1950s and 1960s encountered):

> If the object reflecting the echoes were not a static tree but a moving insect, the Doppler consequences would be more complicated, but the bat could still calculate the velocity of the relative motion between itself and its target, obviously just the kind of information a sophisticated guided missile like a hunting bat needs.[11]

Contra Kittler (even though not explicitly), animals are akin to the environment-sensitive high-tech missiles of the 1980s, suggests Dawkins. In any case, all this distances them phenomenologically from us humans.[12]

One of Dawkins's key examples, or tools, in his *Blind Watchmaker* was the Biomorph software. With the program, Dawkins claimed to be able to demonstrate evolutionary processes and recursive branching that is an essential part of embryonic development. Desmond Morris's term "biomorph" referred to complex branching structures that evolve out of quite simple algorithmic rules. Dawkins describes the "genes" of the Biomorph program as a recipe that governs the emergence of the visual shapes. The genes produce segmented structures for which branching is the basic driving force, with genes controlling, for example, "Number of Segments" and "Distances between Segments."[13] In other words, the computer program is a digital coding of natural selection understood and coded as a probability function. Evolution unfolds in time because successive reproduction of forms is a key method that evolution is suggested to use in this model. Selection accumulates through reproduction and the various cycles in which survival or weeding out takes place. In this sense the program resembles similar computational ecologies that had been introduced since the 1960s: Ingo Rechenberg and Hans-Paul Schwefel's "evolution strategies" programming, Lawrence Fogel's "evolutionary programming," and the much more familiar examples since the 1970s, including John Conway's Game of Life and in general the genetic algorithm solutions that suggested design through breeding. John Holland had already come to the conclusion that a turn toward nature was needed and translated the "chromosomes" of nature

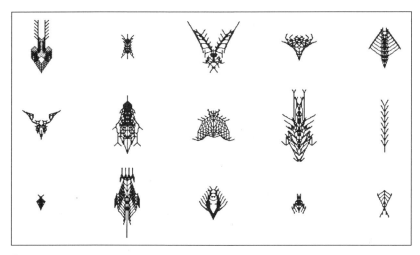

Segmented biomorphs created by Dawkins's software. The visual insectoidlike figures are an effect of the algorithms that take their cue from Darwinian principles. Reprinted from Christopher G. Langton, ed., *Artificial Life: Proceedings of an Interdisciplinary Workshop on the Synthesis and Simulation of Living Systems*, by permission of Westview Press, a member of Perseus Books Group.

into bits. A population of chromosomes or bits could then be let loose in ecologies governed by biooperators such as "crossover," "mutation," and "inversion."[14]

But biomorphs work as visual translations of genetic evolutionary processes, Dawkins claimed in the 1980s in the midst of the emerging network society that was soon to hail the power of neo-Darwinist processes. In other words, Dawkins translates processes of material nature into code instructions, which then translate into visual images that Dawkins claims are characteristic of the nature of the process itself. They are not just representations but simulations that, with the right environmental conditions, can be used to understand the powers of nonpersonal nature. This is where "insects," "spiders," "bats" and the like populate Dawkins's screen, which is much more than a screen of representation for the human eye. The screen becomes a *screening*, an interfacing of the enthusiasm for natural processes and the forces of nature, computer algorithms that were becoming an integral part of the artificial life discourses by Dawkins's time, and the human eye that is able to appreciate the complex patterns of things emerging on the screen.

I am paying attention to Dawkins and neo-Darwinism here because of their central status in the emerging digital culture of the 1980s and 1990s. What is curious is the assemblage of natural selection or the forces of nature expressed through the computer program that produces biomorphs. Here the program is a code filter that seems to fit a bit too perfectly with the power of the code of nature. Furthermore, in order to make this understandable for the phenomenology of the human being, the code must be translated into visual imagery as well. The blind watchmaker needs visual help. The sameness of nature and the computational environment is the assumption that glues these theories of biology and computation together, but at the same time the sameness needs continuous discursive framing in order to remain credible in the eyes of the public.

In other words, the material complexity of nature that for Darwin incorporated not only natural selection but also sexual selection of sights, sounds, and odors now became algorithmic.[15] For Dawkins, the computer code as a recipe became the pathway to the "evolution of evolvability" in his explanation of the Biomorph program from 1987.[16] The program became a model for population thinking that emphasizes that instead of the individual (the phenotypes) it is populations that are the object of selection, and hence genotypes are engines of evolution. Dawkins actually extended the notion of the phenotype to highlight that "individual" bodies reach far outside their bodies as well and that they are always composed of populations, or assemblages.[17] Bodies are drawn according to the genes, which act as creative limitations on the powers of the computer program (aka the forces of nature). The procedures "Reproduce" and "Develop" became the simple guidelines for the achievement of complex visual forms that transported Weissman's ideas about the continuity of the germplasm into a digital sphere codable in the Pascal programming language.

According to Luciana Parisi, this form of serial genetic algorithm imposed an image of evolution without change. The genetic lineage of accumulation weeds out change and anomalies in its emphasis on the binary settings of evolution that is not random, Dawkins insists, but is based on principles of mathematical probabilities. Hence, suggests Parisi, the

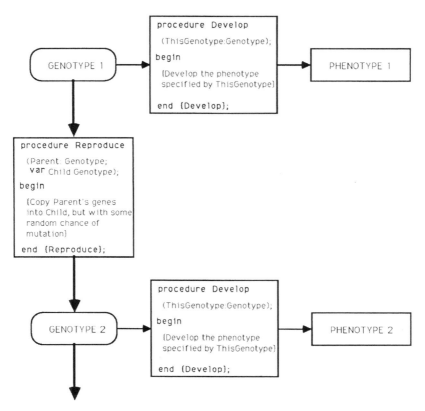

The principles of the Biomorph software are based on Weissmann's principle of the continuity of germplasm. Here this genotype–phenotype duality is expressed in Pascal programming language. Reprinted from Langton, ed., *Artificial Life*, by permission of Westview Press, a member of Perseus Books Group.

shapes, designs, and forms of Biomorph Land are combinatorics of 0s and 1s, and "what such digital binary logic assumes is that nature, like culture and the natural environments constructed artificially with CAD, operate through a genetic-digital programming that contains in itself all possible solutions for . . . design."[18] Whereas this kind of a view quickly became a channel for the emerging discourse of "breeding" and natural selection in digital culture, it still reflected a rigid image of digital spaces and design. It is perhaps more akin to the Cartesian space of coordinate systems as a reservoir of possibilities that was introduced in William Gibson's idea of cyberspace than it is an understanding of the relations of extensions and mutuality that other discourses have been trying to promote.[19] In other words, the intensity of animal relations that was part of the ethological paradigm is reduced in this kind of a biopolitical translation only to a gridlike framework of possibilities. Despite its reliance on population thinking, such "domesticated Darwinism"[20] is much too interested in the selection and fitness part of the creative process instead of the probing, erring, and aberrations having to do with the relational life of embodied entities. All seems to be predetermined and approachable in terms of spatialized relations of code/nature and where nature is the great database and calculator—or the blind watchmaker. In addition, what the hype around the powers of nature suggested was that natural selection does not work alone; it needs "populations and swarms of things"[21] that are able to perceive and exist through relationality.

SOFTWARE ANT FARMS

In the 1980s, the impact of Dawkins's neo-Darwinist views started to gain ground outside biology as well. Among computer scientists and in the emerging artificial life field, he represented a reinvigoration of the nineteenth-century optimism about harnessing nature.[22] Entomologists such as E. O. Wilson had made references to termites as examples of "dynamic programming,"[23] but Dawkins's ideas provided a way to frame the missing link between the genetic algorithms and the belief in the supremacy of nature as an *evolution* machine: both were about calculating populations. Of all the animals and insects, ants become the "unofficial mascots of the ALife field,"[24] with programs, search spaces, and various models for efficiency grounded in the industrious life of colonies.

In this context it is interesting to take SimAnt (1991) as our second example, or node, of this chapter. The game, designed by Maxis and Will Wright, was part of a successful simulation series with other titles such as SimCity and SimEarth. What all of these games entail is the need for the player to try to impose control on the unfolding events of the game, whether it is taking care of the various functions affecting the fate of a city, the conditions of life on a planet, or the niche ecology of an ant's life.

SimAnt's game play is about controlling one ant (at a time) and help-ing to build up a successful ant colony. What the player and her colony face are rival ants and other forms of insect life in the backyard of a nor-mal suburban home. The player has quite a limited range of "tools" to use in the game, including marking with a pheromone trail the pathways to food sources, picking up and leaving food, and attacking the other ant colony members. However, from such simple elements the complexity of the whole computational ecology is expected to emerge. Underlying SimCity, SimAnt, and other examples of the series is a sort of a cellular automata structure in which every action is surrounded by a set of simple predetermined functions, but this is still expected to result in emergent behavior on a larger level.[25]

In a way, besides making reference to 1960s and 1970s cellular autom-ata, SimAnt could be seen as a popularized version of the scientific simu-lation AntFarm, which had been designed and introduced some years earlier. Robert Collins and David Jefferson showcased their evolution-ary platform at the second artificial life conference in 1990 in Santa Fe. The "game" simulates artificial organisms that to some extent resemble ants. The environment is equipped with a nest, food, pheromones, and ants. The simulation consists of 16,384 colonies each of which includes 128 ants living in a 16 x 16 grid environment. The simulation functions as a costs-and-gains game in which food represents a gain of 1,000 points and, for example, dropping pheromone to mark a food source costs 0.1 points. The ants are not just random probe machines for food but are equipped with sensory arrays (3 x 3) that are able to sense food, the nest, and pheromone.[26] Whereas the basic settings for sensation and goals are set, the "ants still must evolve behavior to interpret and use"[27] their navigational systems, a compass of a kind. The behavior is encoded in "the genotype" of a kind so as to make the distinction between char-acteristics that are passed from one generation to another and the "liv-ing" phenotype bodies—a distinction that recalls the common ground of neo-Darwinism and genetic algorithms: genetics and embryology are to remain separated (even though mediated through genes/genotypic algorithm units). Indeed, the AntFarm is also a probing of optimal be-havior and what scientists have referred to as "evolution of cooperative"[28] behavior. The "space" of ants is of course not a space in the three- or four-dimensional phenomenological sense but a search space for algorithms.

Nonetheless, the authors insist on the importance of the insect aspect and references to pheromones and other traits of chemical characteristics that became a crucial part of the understanding of ant communication with Edward O. Wilson's work in the early 1960s. Pheromones appeared as the chemical substances of animal communication that signaled a whole alien world of communication—very much reminiscent of the aspirations of the earlier entomologists and writers. In this context, Wilson also engaged in a discourse close to science fiction, or at least speculative media theory:

> It is conceivable that somewhere on other worlds civilizations exist that communicate entirely by the exchange of chemical substances that are smelled or tasted. Unlikely as this may seem, the theoretical possibility cannot be ruled out. It is not difficult to design, on paper at least, a chemical communication system that can transmit a large amount of information with a rather good efficiency. The notion of such a communication system is of course strange because our outlook is shaped so strongly by our own peculiar auditory and visual conventions.[29]

Wilson calls for an interest in forms of communication that might seem unintuitive for the human phenomenological body and subsequently turns to insects. The external secretion of pheromones (in contrast to hormonal secretion internally) is a tool for regulation of the environment and relations to other animals, suggests Wilson. In various cases, the communication tool affects sexual behavior. Pheromones can cause physiological changes, writes Wilson, such as pseudo-pregnancies in female mice placed together with male mice.[30] But what is characterized as the best-developed form of pheromone communication is found in social insects such as ants, termites, wasps, and bees. Naturally Wilson's findings relate closely to the topic of our previous chapter on Von Frisch's bees, but I will ignore the internal lineage and the academic debates concerning insect communication.[31] Instead, what is worth noting here is that Wilson frames the ant chemicals as trailings and guidings for the colony. Pheromones lead other ants (in this case, fire ants, *Solenopsis saevissima*) toward "the source of emission"[32]—a new nest site or a food source. The pheromone trail is also a case of intensive and temporal environmental individuation. It diffuses very quickly, in a way described by Wilson as "volatile," and the threshold for following a trail is around two minutes. Hence, the guideline that unifies individual ants into a collective and emerging colony is a processual one, continuously renewed in fluctuating environmental relations and conditions. Here the communication is celebrated not only for its efficiency and goal-directed clarity (which would mark its resemblance to classical theories of communication) but because of its organizing role as well. Pheromones (read: communication) organize colonies. Communication is a medium in the sense of folding environments and relations between agencies, and the emergence of the superorganism is due to the communicative relations involved.

Already with Wilson the work of environmental relations is seen in terms of effects and efficacy. With the later informationalized understanding, the terrain of the colony becomes a grid of mathematical possibilities. The local relations between grids and agents produce global effects without a bird's-eye view (except for a game player of SimAnt or SimCity), which closely resembles the similar work done in genetic algorithms.[33] Simple rules that govern interactions between game grids produce patterns that are not only computational events but complex figurations on the screen. The grids "perceive" the other grids next to them and then react based on the simple rules already defined. The system turns into a self-reproductive ecology of a kind. AntFarm and other similar examples, such as the even earlier Tracker software (by Jefferson and Chuck Taylor from UCLA)[34] framed reproduction as a key trait that enables the subsequent evolution of actions. With AntFarm, which updated the focus on individual ants of Tracker to the colony-based models and parallel computing made possible by Danny Hillis's connection machines, the mode of digital behavior was changed. No more "rule-based lookup tables that accompanied finite state machines";[35] now the artificial ants were functioning as neural networks. Brains and ants found a common tune in the modeling of networks that are always, by definition, brainlike and reliant on the force of connections instead of on prefigured instruction lists. However, the simulation of pheromone trails in a mathematical search space is only a way to understand how to optimize search string patterns in a given environment. Here "perception" of an environment is transposed from an animal characteristic to an information relation with the aid of a visual interface to make it understandable to the human operator, so to speak.

It is curious, then, that increasingly since the 1990s popular culture has been filled with examples of swarming, cooperating entities and, for example, games that work through simulations of complex systems. Since then the enthusiasm for "smart mobs"[36] and collective intelligence in media design and network environments has found a seemingly apt example with Web 2.0 applications and hype. In the context of software, SimAnt is only one example, and perhaps not even the best one. In the game there is a persisting emphasis on the intelligent leader of the ant colony—the player in charge. Various other algorithmic objects such as other ants, trails, and insects continuously affect the overall flow of the game, but the player inhabits a singular place in the game environment. This is the "grammatical" illusion, à la Nietzsche, necessary to a translation of impersonal forces of social insects and algorithmic processes to a human popular culture. Nietzsche thought grammar and the structure of language produce the illusion of stable subjectivity; in digital culture, software and interfaces act at times to produce a similar illusion of control. The mode of subjectification inherent in the media culture of Hollywood productions and subsequent interpellations of game culture require this constant focus on the game play of the personalized user/viewer. Even if, as Alex Galloway has argued, the world of games is completely reliant on a plethora of other elements as well (e.g., nondiegetic machine acts), these are quite often subordinated to a representational logic of the personal pronoun. Swarm effects in games are still articulated as nondiegetic elements and remind us of the "current logic of informatics (emergence, social networks, artificial life, and so on)"[37] rather than being necessary for the narratives, explains Galloway.

Indeed SimCity (1989), for example, in which the simulation is about the complex interrelated processes involved in running a city, is much closer to swarms and emergent processes. Such claims are made in various journalistic popular science books such as Steven Johnson's *Emergence,* in which even the subtitle *(The Connected Lives of Ants, Brains, Cities and Software)* suggests the translatability of ant colonies to brains, cities, or software. Software acts as ants, and ants seem to suggest optimal and rational behavior that is algorithmic, or easily translated to such.

One way to understand the high visibility of such software objects since the 1980s and especially the 1990s is to see them as "objects to think with." This is how, for example, Mitchel Resnick's explorations into "massively parallel microworlds"[38] have been framed and how we might want to think the use of visuality in those software objects. Resnick taps into the same cultural niche as SimAnt and other similar software objects with his emphasis on the contemporary digital culture as an era of decentralization. From ethology and ecology to cybernetics and complex systems, Resnick's emphasis on creating software systems that feed us the new modes of thought of network society was in itself a transversal connecting of various discourses. Artificial life research, which in 1987 Chris Langton had emphasized as primarily focused on distributed systems,[39] was only one part of it, with buds spreading to and from economics to art. Langton had paved the way for a wider paradigm shift toward ALife models consisting of populations and emergence, and had even created the Swarm software platform that simulated such behavior.[40] In this context, various concrete projects with programming languages acted as vehicles that made such state-of-the-art scientific ideas part of the emerging software culture.

Resnick's use of object-oriented programming with the Logo language was meant as a tool for a hands-on understanding that emergent distributed systems were all around us—from the animal worlds of ants to traffic jams and of course software. Software acted as a vector to larger cultural trends that promoted the 1990s hyped idea of control without a controller. The environment was the active participant, local rules showed global patterns, and parallel processes from ant colonies to Resnick's software language gradually became intuitive to children as well. Resnick noted that SimCity and SimAnt were at the forefront of commercial software that aimed to teach decentralized behavior, but he was quick to add that they had a restricted take on the issue. Indeed, such programs were pretty much closed ecologies in terms of their functions. Resnick wrote:

> You can't change the underlying models that control the simulations, nor can you change the underlying context. What if you are interested in neither urban development nor ant behavior, but in cars and traffic? Today you are out of luck. What's needed are microworld construction kits, so that you can create your own microworlds, focusing on the domains you find most interesting. StarLogo is a step in that direction; more sophisticated *microworld construction kits* are sure to follow.[41]

Resnick tapped into a key issue of digital culture that was emerging as quickly as the boom around insects. Insects and distributed behavior might be easily represented on screens, but representations act only as framings and freezings of potentiality. A meta-level constructionism would be needed that would tap into the ontology of software creation— practically, for example, software kits that would be open social tools.[42]

What SimCity and SimAnt represented, after all, was the incorporation of insect themes into closed ecologies of software production in which tinkering with the code was prohibited and the more insectlike way of probing was to be found somewhere else. Many of the radical nonhuman procedures and processes were in a way "compromised" when turned into commercial software products. However, to continue to elaborate the transpositions of insects, software, and visual culture around the 1980s and 1990s, we will next turn to our third example, Craig Reynold's boids and swarm behavior.

BOIDS: SOFTWARE ECOLOGIES

What was continuously proposed since the 1980s was not only "software-to-think-with" but also "insects-to-think-with." Nature was framed as the ultimate external milieu for ethologies of software. From neo-Darwinism to software projects in the emerging digital culture, natural processes were the perfect dynamic models to track. People tinkering with computers were increasingly looking for entomology books in libraries and gradually realizing how to frame insects and the like as information machines. More concretely, we can observe how the computer stood as a key interface between various disciplines in the life sciences and sciences of control and informatics and worked not only as a tool but as a catalyst for a new way of thinking about nature and its phenomena. Perhaps it offered even a new ontology of nature.[43] The characteristics of artificial life based on population thinking, distributed nature, the primacy of local relations, and emergence led Langton to think of ant colonies as the perfect example for his proposal and vice versa: the ant society and the myrmecological research provided much of the background he needed to make the realizations that the second-order simulation of the swarms might actually function as a high-capacity computer of a sort.

The "antomata" was an exemplary low-level machine that showed that global-level behavior is a follow-up from both local units and "natural living systems."[44] After years of research into "intelligence," it was actually the nearly brainless insects that seemed to solve the puzzle for complex design and emergence.

Despite the seemingly deceitful naturality of the whole discourse, which is still all over the Internet and digital culture, we should think of this framing of nature as a specific kind of assemblage of technology + biology + nature + politics + economics + *n*. Indeed, to follow Andrew Goffey's line of thought, which borrows from Bruno Latour and Isabelle Stengers, this "intelligence" of nature is one in which nature does not just speak for itself (through software such as Biomorph and the like); the autonomous nature of the "insect-factor" in digital culture is fabricated through meticulous discourses and tactics.[45] In this case, Biomorph and other software programs are constellations that give nature a voice, enable its existence. However, it is important to note that software is itself continuously enabled by milieus external to it. In the context of this chapter, themes such as software and visuality are underlined, but they do not provide the exclusive truth about this framing. The characteristics of swarming, such as robustness, adaptability, and self-organization were suddenly the exact requirements of software-based systems that offered, I argue, the grounding for the representational theme of animal swarms in popular culture.

The popular cultural boom was spurred by scientific research into swarms and "the social insect metaphor"[46] from the early 1990s. Ant colony optimization research with scholars such as Marco Dorigo became a large field of interfacing ants with new technologies—for example, when routing British Telecom calls.[47] The field was based on the realization that there are various levels of complexity to simple things, such as ants, and their sensorimotor complexity is doubled by collective interaction. Swarm intelligence started to refer to "any attempt to design algorithms or distributed problem-solving devices inspired by the collective behavior of social insect colonies and other animal societies."[48] As Bonabeau, Dorigo, and Theraulaz explain in their book on the topic, the designs were about operationalizing insect capacities for optimizing certain search spaces. The fluctuations in their aberrant walks, errors, and so on were to be made use of as rational probeheading that enabled the discovery of solutions for complex mathematical tasks, such as the traveling salesman graph problem or vehicle-routing and graph-coloring problems.[49]

Ant-based algorithms promised efficient solutions for the emerging network society, which, for all its intelligence, needed a bit of insect instinct. For example, the pheromone trails ants used between nest and food were modeled into a virtual pheromone network in which the most efficient paths could be explored through antlike trackings. The ant colonies can be seen as continuously mapping the available food sources near the nest and marking the environments with pheromone trails—a certain kind of gridding of the environment. The environment was turned into a hierarchical space based on its potential usefulness for the ants. The intensity of the milieu became a marked space, a space for orientation and guidance.

However, despite the gridding, what is underlined is the temporal nature of the technical network, just as in the case of "real" ants. The network analyzers followed realizations from researchers such as E. O. Wilson. Even though pheromone trails persist as strong elements of the ant colonies, the virtual pheromones are made to evaporate more quickly for efficiency's sake—in order to take into account the continuous dynamics of technical networks.

> In several species of ants, cooperative foraging through trail laying–trail following allows decentralized selection of the food source that is closest to the nest. Despite its ability to select the closest food source, a colony may not be able to track a changing environment because trail reinforcement is too strong. Pheromone evaporation could, in principle, solve this problem, but real trail pheromones seem to be long-lived. Virtual trail pheromones in simulations of collective foraging can be made as volatile as necessary if biological plausibility is not an issue.[50]

Traffic flow and problems of routing were treated as distributed systems akin to insect colonies even through researchers were reluctant to be too hasty in making assumptions about parallels between ants and "real communication networks."[51] It was a question of finding the crucial patterns that were needed for optimizing behaviors. Also acknowledged was that of course insects were not the only animals that could be learned from, but that swarming was a form of collective behavior that could be learned from fish and birds as well. Interestingly, the basic characteristics of the object-oriented programming that emerged around the 1980s were based on the bottom-up emergence of individual interactions: swarming of a kind.

Birds are the animals that Craig Reynolds turned to. During the mid-1980s, Reynolds used the Symbolic Common Lisp programming language to create his by now famous "boid" figures, which simulated flocking behavior. With a background in computer graphics and animation, Reynolds represented another kind of initial context for the interest in animal worlds embedded in digital design. Animation experiments with flocks and groups had been around earlier as well, but Reynolds made important adjustments to the earlier ideas. What is curious is that later the boid animations were used in Hollywood productions such as *Batman Returns* (1992) and a number of other mainstream films including *Starship Troopers* (1997), *A Bug's Life* (1998), *Antz* (1998), and *The Lord of the Rings Trilogy* (2001–2003).[52] A parallel example would be the swarming mobs in the politically loaded video game *State of Emergency* (2002).[53]

The insects, bats, and other entities are afforded an autonomous life with the software forms, which take their algorithmic cue from insects, birds, and other forms of real life. The digital image is double in the sense of the processuality of the (animal) bodies providing the thematic cues for thinking about the digital image as processual as well. Lev Manovich's claim that the digital image provides an active interface to information is not enough, but we have to realize, in Mark B. N. Hansen's footsteps, that the bodily nature of interactions helps us to understand the ontology of processuality in images.[54] The swarming is a reminder not only of the animal "origins" of the ideas incorporated into digital languages but of the fact that the digital image is not itself a static representation but an algorithmic process, made of pixels that are refreshed on a constant basis. In addition, as Hansen argues, the embodied digital ontology of network culture has been grounded in a paradigm of motor activity instead of the virtual reality discourse focusing on representational contents and environments. Bodies in movement (or "bodies in code," to use Hansen's phrase) represent a "functional crossing between virtual and physical realms"[55] and the necessary interfacing of (human) embodiment and digital code. Whereas Hansen focuses on the inexhaustible virtuality of the human body as providing new individuations for digital images and space, I want to extend this focus on "motor activity" as providing intensity for digital creations from animal bodies. Indeed, it is the specificity of the intensive bodies as animal that needs attention here, and the realization of the extent to which the imagining of digital objects has been relayed through *nonhuman* bodies. It is not only the new modes of individuation that the human body finds with such code environments but also the modes of individuation of the digital code environments, ethologies of code, that rely on and are relayed through animal bodies.

In Reynolds's take on object-oriented programming, the flocking behavior that was to be transported from birds onto the computer screen was achieved by rules imposed on the bird-objects and their internal state. Without explicating the details of the animation too specifically here, I can briefly say that Reynolds programmed the birds to react to their local environment, which then fed into a coherent global flock behavior. In a way, the boids were equipped with "artificial vision," which referred to their ability to perceive their nearby flockmates. The neighborhood of every boid was designed as "a spherical zone of sensitivity centered at the boid's local origin" and "defined by two parameters: a radius and an exponent."[56] Hence the boid was governed by a zone of sensitivity, which was of course not a simulation of vision but still an arrangement of relations; such relations are experienced and hence affective.[57] It is curious, then, that even if the swarm enthusiasts of the 1980s and 1990s often underline the computational power of collectives and harnessing nature (as with neo-Darwinism), much of the power of the flock in Reynolds's model is based on perception and relationality. Chris Langton emphasized this as a new ontological realization: what connects the boids to real birds, or to other animals swarming, was the behavior of flocking. Both in nature and in computing systems, flocking is an emergent aftereffect instead of being modeled through a preset intelligent model. According to the argument, the artificial creations are real on the level of their lived relations, or behavior.[58] The ontology of such emergences stems from their relations, and the vision of nature becomes a bit different, changing from that of the database-calculating *blind* watchmaker to include perception and relations.

Indeed, in order to avoid the pitfalls of intelligence, Reynolds had to step out of the database way of providing the boids with perfect information about their position. Simulating real animals also meant imposing

A flock of boids avoiding cylindrical obstacles: a screenshot of a boids simulation running on a Symbolics Lisp Machine. Image by Craig Reynolds, 1986; printed with permission.

the same restrictions experienced by the real flesh-and-feathers birds. In other words, information had to be localized and the perception of positions had to be relativized in order to avoid problems having to do with concerted actions. To quote Reynolds, who explains why it was relevant to filter out the unnecessary "surplus information" and to "dumb down" the artificial birds:

> Simulated boids have direct access to the geometric database that describes the exact position, orientation, and velocity of all objects in the environment. The real bird's information about the world is severely limited because it perceives through imperfect senses and because its nearby flockmates hide those farther away. This is even more pronounced in herding animals because they are all constrained to be in the same plane. In fish schools, visual perception of neighboring fish is further limited by scattering and absorption of light by the sometimes murky water between them. These factors combine to strongly localize the information available to each animal.[59]

The flock object collectivities that are able to steer around obstacles and still keep formation are, then, *sensing algorithms* of a kind. As underlined by Reynolds himself, the visual perception of the boid is closer to a metaphor. There is no optics of software. Nonetheless, this fact does not deny that "sensitivity" in terms of location plays a key role in the algorithmic world of swarms. Indeed, this realization at the core of the swarm patterns signals the importance of relationality in an ethological manner. As a temporal unraveling and an ontology of relationality, ethological understanding of matter can help us to understand why it makes sense to talk about "affects" of algorithms.

Certainly when talking about perception in algorithms, we are talking of noncognitive and nonspatial perceptions. However, this leads us to consider a different take on algorithms, ethology, and nature than a neo-Darwinist version in which the visual is the end result of the calculation process and forces of selection. Instead, in ontology closer to Whitehead and, for example, Deleuze's Spinoza we can understand that matter is always about perception and relations and how this feeds into an ethology of matter that can be extended to software as well. What defines software but its capacities, its affects, its relationality? Software is not immaterial but a body of code being executed, existing through that temporal unfolding in technological and other milieus that support (or afford) its existence.[60] How different would software appear if we approached it as an ecological object that is capable of entering into specific relations (that are not only technical) and whose capacities for affect are due to certain internal and external milieus?[61]

What Reynolds's often-mentioned boids patterns suggest, then, is the importance of perceiving matter as an implication of the relationality of software objects (e.g., object-oriented programming objects) and the extensive relationality of software to issues relating to politics, economics, and aesthetics, for example. The swarming flocks of Reynolds and later ideas in "design by growing"[62] are embedded in histories and discourses of nature, computation, and digital culture, but at the same time they can be taken as "insect-models-to-think-with," with the ethological realizations of Deleuze–Uexküll–Spinoza taken into the sphere of software as well. Furthermore, these ideas are connected to a realization of the novel ontology of technological objects in network society. A jump into pre-Kantian ontologies in the manner of Bernard Cache has been taken to signal a need to reevaluate the status of the technological object not as one of molds and spatialized stability but as one of temporal unfolding.[63] This is evident in the ontology of object-oriented programming that is characterized less by a linear set of instructions governed by the programmer than by a multiplicity of objects (as if) in space that are semiautonomous.[64] As Casey Alt argues, this manner of programming presents an affectivity inherent in software objects whose functionality is defined by their correlations. They "occupy space," as Alt writes, in a curious mode of radical empiricism of software, where "spatialized" and embodied software objects are the ontological precondition to the era of object orientation. Alt explains how the "meaning" of such objects, defined by affects and, for example, "polymorphism," stems from this semiautonomous position but just as much from "each object's individual context"[65] and hence the topological arrangements between the objects.

Here swarms provide a very nice image of the technological object in the age of dynamic networks, but we have to understand the relational status of swarms. Such figures of collective decision-making and optimizing behavior—whether more physical swarm robots or software entities—have traveled a long way from insect worlds to digital culture as concepts and figures of scientific and philosophical thought, and we should be aware of the continuous translations and territorializations they are going through. Indeed, as Goffey points out, despite the supposedly revolutionary powers of emergence and ethological interest, the projects where such processes are made use of "remain absolutely territorial," ranging from retina scanning to such bounded processes as predator–prey relationships.[66] Indeed, swarms and interacting particle systems modeled on similar principles as boids have since become an important part of the governing of populations in network society. Movements of crowds are used in simulating evacuation scenarios for large populations, as well as in entertainment, for instance, in the movements of agent-based crowd simulations that demand very powerful processing capacities but also efficient and "instinctual" software.[67] Such software is seen as a perfect isomorphic tool for understanding and controlling processes involving large populations, such as the "old-fashioned fleshy populations" of humans, but also large and increasingly significant software populations that are no less important for the biopolitics of digital culture. With the centrality of population thinking, the emphasis shifted from both individuals and generalized types to the primacy of variation and deviation.[68] Hence it is crucial to understand that this corresponded to variation's becoming the primary focus for capture as well, providing mathematical and digital tools with which to understand and control such processes, which did not fit directly into categories of either "the individual" as something detached from collectivities or "the general" as an idealized type. Instead, difference and process become comprehensible and hence controllable.

What we should realize are the framings and historical positions through which the discourses of nature, collectivities, and ethological relations emerge. This methodological demand relates to some already existing approaches from which it draws inspiration. For example, the media ecology approach of Fuller but also John Protevi's "political physiology" as a take on the transversal assemblages across biology, technology, and the social are relevant here.[69] On the other hand, scholars such as Isabelle Stengers have pointed out the need for an ecoethological consideration of biology and, for example, Darwinism; such a call can easily be extended to the social framing of digital culture as well. Stengers's insistence on the radical dependency of entities on their affording milieus and vice versa becomes a way to understand the intensive life of software as well.[70]

In this vein, tracking the intensity of software as a multilayered network in itself, the next chapter continues the theme already begun here and elaborates the notions of affect, ethology, and visual figurations of insectlike forms of artificial life through the feminist media artist Lynn Hersman Leeson's film *Teknolust* from the end of the 1990s. *Teknolust* provides a continuation of the ethological mapping of relations of digital culture that in that chapter expand from biodigital creatures to feminist philosophy in network society and the new configurations of sexuality. The film also offers tools with which to understand the nonhuman individuation of network agencies by providing an account of embodiment that is not reducible to the human figurations that are at its surface. Instead it shows how individuation works through a conglomeration of bodies from animals to software, from biotech to human(ized) emotions.

SEXUAL SELECTION IN THE BIODIGITAL
Teknolust and the Weird Life of SRAs

The previous chapter concluded with the ethological question of relationality and sustainability. In what kind of relations and conditions can software persist? We pointed toward the affect relations between software objects and suggested that we think of software in itself not only as extensive spatialization of the intensive lifeworlds but as intensive individuation in which the lived perception of relations is a crucial feature. Such characteristics are not only part of the metaphorics of insect media but are quite materially incorporated in the logic of object-oriented programming.

In addition, the sustainability of software as a cultural form comes from nontechnical characteristics and points toward the ecoethological stance, where milieus afford animals/entities. As J. J. Gibson outlined in his nonrepresentational ecological theory, the world is not a physical gridding or a container of bodies in space but is better understood through intensive environmental relations and the notion of the medium. To be fair, Gibson is really talking about natural media, but this is quite relevant to our topic as well. For him, the environmental interfaces such as earth–water and water–air act as groundings for animal life. He continues to show that the notion of medium provides a way to understand how the surfaces and groundings afford different kinds of potentials for bodies. The air "affords locomotion to an animate body,"[1] imposing different kinds of active conditions for bodies than, for example, water, which forces the fish toward "streamlined anatomy." In addition to locomotion, air affords sights and sounds, permitting, for example, the "vibratory event."[2]

Indeed, we could add that for Gibson this amounts to almost a whole "milieu-medium theory" of a kind that culminated in these defining words in his 1986 book on the ecology of visual perception:

> If we understand the notion of medium, I suggest, we come to an entirely new way of thinking about perception and behaviour. The medium in which animals can move about (and in which objects can *be* moved about) is at the same time the medium for light, sound, and odor coming from sources in the environment. An enclosed medium can be "filled" with light, with sound, and even with odor. Any point in the medium is a possible point of observation for any observer who can look, listen, or sniff. And these points of observation are continuously connected to one another by paths of possible locomotion. Instead of geometrical points and lines, then, we have points of observation and lines of locomotion. As the observer moves from point to point, the optical information, the acoustic information, and the chemical information change accordingly. Each potential point of observation in the medium is unique in this respect. The notion of medium, therefore, is not the same as the concept of space as the points in space are not unique but equivalent to each other.[3]

This double notion of milieu-media reflects an intensive understanding of relationality that is familiar from the philosophy and cultural theory used throughout this book. It shares common traits with the ideas of Uexküll and Deleuze, Simondon's notions of individuation, and furthermore, for example, the Caillois-inspired ideas about space as not only a container for bodies but an active modulator, a medium, where bodies are folded and contracted, interacting and sensing. Gibson's ecological notion of the medium wants to underline the specificity and positionality of any act of perception, and hence the intensity at which perception is intimately connected to motility. Both the perceiving subject and the medium of perception are in constant double articulation, both taking part in the commonality of their event, shaping each other, and changing with each other.

Gibson has of course already been incorporated into some of the discussions in cultural theory, namely Manuel DeLanda's on science and philosophy,[4] but the ideas briefly outlined earlier characterize the way I see ethological relations of digital culture and software. Beyond being a "space" in the old container sense, the "cyberspace" of digital culture is one of intensive modulations and foldings of relations. Naturally sounds and smells might be nonexistent for software, but still relations can be seen outside the geometrical gridding as informed by their perceptions of other software objects and elements. Space becomes affective and affording: it allows potentialities to emerge, as well as specific compositions of objects that are "potential or activated relations."[5] Interactions are afforded as media, and here media can be seen working across the scales transversally. Here Félix Guattari's ecological ideas are relevant, as are Matthew Fuller's points about media ecology: media can be approached as a field of affordances that are not only standardized (as is, for example, standard industry software) but open to experimentation.[6] Similar is the point Ned Rossiter makes about processual media theory. Media processes might be increasingly rendered invisible (as is, for example, software), but therefore all the more needed is the process of translation and understanding the complex networked affordances across scales: "seemingly invisible forces, institutional desires and regimes of practice"[7] that always condition media processes.

After this short prologue or continuation of the previous chapter, we will turn to look at these ethological relations through an example taken from recent years of feminist media art. If the previous chapter started with a neo-Darwinist focus on digital culture as governed by the algorithms of natural selections, this chapter is much more tuned to sexual selection. Lynn Hershman-Leeson's film *Teknolust* (2002) is what I would call a peculiar intervention into the practices and representations of biodigitality as it has been discussed since the 1990s. In *Teknolust*, depicting a more than cliché image of a female scientist, the nerdy Rosetta Stone (Tilda Swinton) has succeeded in creating three SRAs, self-replicating automatons, Ruby, Marine, and Olive (also Tilda Swinton), which are, in biblical fashion, literally modeled on her image (and DNA). The broad theme of biodigitality is folded into a very micro-level analysis of relations, affects, and "cuddling," which is a repeated feature of the film. "Technology needs love" might be the Latourian slogan of the film, where the SRAs are trying to adjust to their liminal status between the organic and the digital. They have what

The three color-coded self-replicating automatons Ruby, Marine, and Olive. From *Teknolust* (2002), written and directed by Lynn Hershman-Leeson. Feature-length film, high-definition video, 85 minutes. Courtesy of Lynn Hershman-Leeson and Bitforms Gallery NYC.

could be called a continuous identity crisis of not fitting the technological categories as viruses, as financially profitable, or even as humans (considering themselves "such an improvement"). They are more akin to exploration machines, but what they explore are the gaps and undefined spaces between humans, machines, and biological life in general. Certainly the SRAs are not insects, but the theme is continuously present through the character of Ruby as a praying mantis–like femme fatale, as well as the framing of the intensive, explorative life of creatures biodigital.

Hence the film can be seen working through a certain dispositif or a discourse network of sexuality and reproduction where the move is from human-centric reproduction to "bacterial sex"[8] and other forms of abstract sex. In this emphasis on sexuality, it is also an exercise in becoming-insect, becoming-machinic in a Deleuzian-feminist sense,[9] as we will see. Another way to approach the film would be to think it as a probing into the affective, nonhuman, and subrepresentational subjectivities at work in network culture.

AFFECT

Teknolust is a curious assemblage of art, science, and technology that addresses the creation of digital culture as a visual (but not optical) process. Despite being framed in the subvisual techniques of manipulation of genetics and biodigitality, the film is a visual product that is very much characterized by its almost naïve iconographics. High-tech settings and equipment such as laboratories, test tubes, and efficient computers and networks are scaled down to the domestic spheres of biotechnology in the kitchen and the living worlds of the SRAs in a microwave oven–like habitat (not unlike the observation nests used in entomology for ages).

In *Teknolust,* the high-tech and high-profile science of biodigitality is rescaled because of concern for human–machine interactions and because the human stance toward technology seems to rely on fear, suspicion, or the capitalist need for profit. Instead of (re)producing sublimated images of genetic technology, *Teknolust* translates technology into intimacy, desire, and sexuality. Indeed, what is interesting is not only that the facialized processes of biodigitality are reterritorializing nonhuman desires into human emotions but that the theme of the face can at the same time transport us to rubrics concerning affect, software, and genetics as the field of affordance of nonhuman sexuality. The amusingly quirky face of Tilda Swinton does effectively humanize the explicitly subperceptual engineering of sexuality and reproduction (genetics) and network processes (software), but at the same time this face stands at a crossroads that allows us to think these figures as probeheads as well.[10] Despite the Deleuze-Guattarian stance that facialization works to attract the nonhuman forces of the cosmos into an investment in the human organization, the faces of the triplet SRAs are at the same time an interface where issues of human organization meet up with the nonhuman processes of genetics and software. Indeed, this is what sustains the film as a material instantiation of digital techniques (the use of specific software such as Maya) and as touching the new formations of what Parisi calls "abstract sex": sex beyond the human form of heterosexual coupling, continuously layered in the formations of "bacterial sex" and techniques of cloning.[11]

In the light of the narrative, this might sound paradoxical. After all, the film turns into a classical boy-meets-girl love story even if the "girl" is here a cloned piece of Rosetta Stone, half-software. Sex is seemingly reduced to the physiological need of the SRAs to acquire the male Y chromosome (from fresh male spermatozoa) to sustain themselves. However, this turns into something like existential questioning: Why are we supposed to live in this restricted ecology of a digital habitat? Why can't we interact with humans? Why are we seen as a threat to human life? What is the qualitative difference between biodigital life and human life? The vampish Ruby, who is responsible for acquiring the sperm samples, is especially interested in life beyond the sisters' restricted computer world. Although her sample-collecting copulations infect her male partners with a strange viruslike disease (at the same time infecting their computers), Ruby finds love with Sandy (Jeremy Davies), a shy copy clerk who lives with his mother.

The SRAs are out of bounds, perhaps even defiant in a juvenile manner, expressing a personified mode of technological agency very different from forms of AI found in earlier cinema. Their autonomy does not lead to sublime imaginings of machines' taking control, as, for example, in Kubrick's *Space Odyssey* (1968) or the Matrix series (1999–2003), but instead involves a curious probing of how technologies and organic forms might interact and cohabit in social reality. For Hershman-Leeson, writing at the *Teknolust* Web site:

> TEKNOLUST is a coming of age story, not only for the characters but also of our society's relationship to technology. The 21st centuries [sic] technologies—genetics, nanotechnology, and robotics have opened a Pandora's box that will affect the destiny of the entire human race. Our relationship to computer based virtual life forms that are autonomous and self replicating will shape the fate of our species.[12]

But when talking about "species," the film does it in a gender-specific way. For Ruby, Marine, and Olive, it seems to be hard to live in a man's world where technology and women are inert, functional, and compliant. Again quoting Hershman-Leeson from the movie's Web site: "Unlike Mary Shelley's monstrous creature in FRANKENSTEIN, or Fritz Lang's conflicted evil robot in METROPOLIS, all the characters in TEKNOLUST thrive on affection, and ultimately, reproduction."

Yet "affection" is a much more complex term in this context than that of everyday human emotion. It suggests, in fact, a much broader understanding of interaction, reproduction, and sexuality in which human affections are merely second-order expressions of more fundamental ontogenetic ties. In a take parallel to mine, Jackie Stacey approaches *Teknolust* as a movie of affects, but one that extends toward the "biomolecular affect," a term coined by Eugene Thacker.[13] Beyond the familiar organization of anthropomorphism on which our understanding of media has so strongly been based in theory and in practice, the molecular domain (and the domain of software, I would add) suggests that we need to reorient our analytical vectors to grasp the subrepresentational. In fact, this task of steering clear of the anthromorphic ontology of Western metaphysics is what a critical and innovative analysis of both animals and technical media share.[14] More concretely, the ideas surrounding object-orientated programming discussed in the previous chapter with Casey Alt's help are relevant here as well: object-oriented programming ecologies can be characterized through their relational unfolding and the intensive topological spaces where programs are, to quote Alt, more like "embodied communities"[15] than like linear scripts. Affect is the art of the interval where the semiautonomous software objects exhibit, at the same time, an internal subjectivity (encapsulation in software jargon) while unfolding only in situated, concerted contexts and time-spaces. The part-objects of programs, then, are more like potentialities through this defining affect-quality.

In the naïvistic visual style of the film, the names Ruby, Marine, and Olive alongside their costumes designate colors through which we can perceive the three protagonists of the film as intensities: force fields of potentiality. These are not proper names of individual persons but modes of biodigital agency. The cloned bodies of Rosetta are differentiated by the seemingly superficial theme of kimonos of different colors. The bodies of the SRAs might be anthropomorphic, and are emphatically feminine, but still their modes of operation are not constrained by the phenomenological world of humans. Indeed, as Stacey explains, the colors red, green, and blue denote not the individual bodies of the three SRAs but similarly the color coding of RGB as used in technical media contexts from video to computers.[16] Stacey notes that the theme of the movie is a reference to the modes of construction of the film nondistinguishable from its narrative: shot with a high-definition digital camera, the "comic sensibility" (Stacey's term) is a function of the coding mechanism brought to the fore as a visual theme as well. However, what I want to underline is the probeheading into subrepresentational themes that need to be articulated more closely. In this case it is the digital. The intensity of the information works through the components of any digital color image and the construction of a pixel from the primary elements of red, green, and blue. Through different *intensities* of each component, the visibility of the digital emerges.[17] Naturally anyone who has even tinkered around with Photoshop knows this: the image is "a three-layer combination of primary-colored channels."[18] Indeed, from the simple mode of digital images to the wider media ecological questions of affordance, layering and combinatorics are key processes of which *Teknolust* is an emblematic example.

Thus, *Teknolust* is certainly not to be read in terms of merely human emotions but as expressing a weird affectivity, something perhaps akin to animal or insect affects in their metamorphic ability to move from mathematical platforms to human worlds. This metamorphic status marks a liminal space separate from but approaching the human world. The digital organisms are agents of a particular combinatorial logic or, more accurately, a potential of affects: a potentiality to be related to various kinds of organic and inorganic bodies, corporeal and noncorporeal. They are "alien species" in the same manner as some media art installations and robots of recent years, such as Ken Rinaldo's *Autotelematic Spider Bots* (2006), which probe in real time the relations between the technological and the organic (the viewers) on emotional and affective levels.[19]

In addition, it is easy to see *Teknolust* as a probe for future sexualities given the narrative of the film. However, my focus is not merely on the question of (human) gender but on how *Teknolust* complexifies the scientific questions of biodigital creation in the context of sexuality while working through themes of software and genetics. My main concern is the way calculational, scientific processes translate into a wider cultural field on which biodigitality acts. Here, continuing the themes of the previous chapter, the "coding" of life in informatic units results not in a geometrical data structure, as in William Gibson's *Neuromancer,* but in an imaginative view of biodigital creatures as affective, interacting, folding in with various cultural forces.

REMEDIATING SEX; OR, COPY MACHINES

Copying is a constant theme in *Teknolust*. The film not only reproduces Tilda Swinton in quadruple form (as Rosetta Stone and three SRA copies of her) but takes the very process of reproduction, virality, and sexuality across various media as its main rubrics. Through the ironic take that is familiar from so much of the 1990s feminist media art on reproduction, virality, and sexuality, *Teknolust* could be seen as an imaginative take on artificial life as an ethology of social relations and as engaging with something that could be called a multiplication of forms of as-if life.[20] Released in 2002, *Teknolust* fits well the context of public discussions relating to genetics, bioengineering, and biocomputing, and it can be read as part of the genealogies of artificial agents, semiautonomous responsive computer systems, and modulations of desire that suggest agencies beyond the human form. Indeed, already the fact that we are dealing with molecular modes of reproduction is a vector that transports the narrative of the film to a much more encompassing framing of the piece as an event of digital technologies itself. The complex and subrepresentational processes from molecular biology to network software are ontologically "without a face" but are still insisted, throughout popular culture and undeniably in *Teknolust,* to engage with the facial world of human beings as well. In a way *Teknolust* is a facialization of what object-oriented programming is as a logic of software, but it also touches on the wider implications of such programming techniques and computational milieus to other areas of culture and embodiment.[21]

Hershman's works have consistently addressed the changes that new technologies of archiving, processing, and communication of information have effected on modes of individuation and hence subjectivity. Discussing the coupling of software and genetic modulation, *Teknolust* is very much anchored to the agenda of the last turn of the millennium. In this it can be seen as an example of the new modes of production inherent in copying or, more accurately, in cloning. This is evident in the film's narrative—the cloned SRAs are nearly exact replicas of Rosetta Stone, alluding to the cipher discovered in 1799 that helped unravel key traits of Egyptian hieroglyphs—and in its production mechanisms, where digital filming and editing techniques are used to create Tilda Swinton in quadruple form in one screen milieu. Yet *Teknolust* continuously refuses a grand narrative of "copying" and insists on the various inflections and levels of copying: the male protagonist Sandy is a copy clerk, burdened by repetitive copy work with Xerox machines but still developing a nearly erotic relationship with the rhythm of the copy machines.[22] In contrast, Rosetta makes high-tech machines for which copying is not mere repetition in carbon-copy fashion but a modulation of wetware with software.

To emphasize the theme, *Teknolust* is filled with duplicates but in a more humorous manner than in the earlier doppelgänger genres. Now the double is associated with twin helical strands of DNA, a recurring visual motive of *Teknolust*. In addition, copying is just as much a technique of sexuality and reproduction that the SRAs (especially Ruby) use in their adaptation to the human world. The film reads as an ironic version of classical Hollywood love stories (and, incidentally, the SRAs are addicted to such television narratives) in which artificial life automata gain subjectivity through their ability to perform female mannerisms. The film's computer-generated subjectivities remediate[23] older media forms such as television in their performative becoming. Dialogue from television ("motivational tapes," as they are called) become pickup lines and are part and parcel of the routines by which the SRAs try to adjust to the contours of modern human life in their quest to obtain spermatozoa. The phrase "You're looking good, Frankie, you've got a natural rhythm," borrowed from a 1950s movie (*The Man with the Golden Arm*, 1955), turns into a protocol that helps transport Ruby into the human world of copulation (picking up men in bars). In themselves such phrases reveal the media technological absurdity of heterosexual rites of romance and the machinelike copy character of Ruby the SRA. The mannerisms function through databases that, according to writers such as Lev Manovich, started to characterize the emerging digital culture.[24] Instead of narratives, new digital media are coordinated along database structures, which is illustrated from games to a wider culture of sampling and tinkering with already existing media pieces. Instead of possessing any ingrown psychology, SRAs pick their repertoire of emotions, affects, and actions from databases of human (media) history. Furthermore, such copying of human behavior recalls the Turing test or ELIZA the computer-program psychologist from the 1960s or, for that matter, Ruby's own Internet portal.[25] These all demonstrate the rise of intelligent agents as key figures of network culture inhabited not only by humans but by software bots of various kinds. Like insect colonies, software functions as a distributed force, an emergent layering. Both notions (insects and software) recall the nonhuman forces at play in the technical media culture of the Internet age, something governed by high-technological layerings of various kinds (from hardware to protocols and on to application software) and of conceptual figures that are created to tap into the complex ecological relationality of such layers. Hence the importance of insects for the era of technical media.

Like Hershman's 1970s performance project Roberta Breitmore,[26] Ruby is much more. She moves between medial scales and remediates her imitational behavior in a Web portal in the film and also on the Internet. Agent Ruby's E-dream Portal imitates the movie and the genealogy of calculational conversation. "Hello there User, type to me. Let's connect," invites the screen. However, as one usually expects of these "intelligent" agent encounters, Ruby's responses are very mechanical. What is interesting about this program is not how convincing it and similar programs are (Ruby's portal does not function very smoothly in terms of human communication) but what kind of powers and affects this mode of mediality and technological agenthood expresses and from what kinds of elements they are made. This "medial will to power,"[27] to use an expression of Matthew Fuller, is not a derivative of the human body in the manner of most cyborg media theories (e.g., that of McLuhan) but a body formed from a different organization, a material instantiation of forces positioned historically but not reducible to their place of origin. Nietzsche's call for a philosophy of perspectivism can be transposed into a media technological context and an understanding of the multiplicities of bodies of varying kinds, as well as the forces constructing, sustaining, and distributing the bodies. In order to further emphasize the nonhuman nature of such assemblages at cross-sections of biology, technology, and nonhuman bodies, the agents or bodies need not be thought in human terms but as a form of individuation that also applies to micro-relations between agents such as bacteria or certain software formations.

The three sisters of software and genes exist at a cross-section of digital databases (where the examples mimed are from Hollywood movies) and databases of biological material. To illustrate this double bind through a sort of mapping of the ethological ties of databases, we can look at how the already mentioned Turing and Weizenbaum examples relate to *Teknolust* and help us to understand the ethological relations in question.

In his 1950 paper "Computing Machinery and Intelligence," Alan Turing formulated the famous imitation test, whose original goal was to decipher whether an anonymous person responding to questions was a man or a woman. The goal of the digital version was to determine whether the responses were given by a machine or a human being. This mind game was designed to lead players to question the ability of computers to replace human functions: "The idea behind digital computers may be explained by saying that these machines are intended to carry out any operations which could be done by a human computer."[28] This is done by transforming (or coding) human-performed operations into instruction tables. In other words, the functions are programmed into algorithmic form: "To 'programme a machine to carry out the operation A' means to put the appropriate instruction table into the machine so that it will do A," as Turing expresses it.[29]

Somewhere between practical use and parody, Joseph Weizenbaum programmed his ELIZA program in the mid-1960s to simulate a psychoanalyst. ELIZA was an early experiment in responsive computing (in the MAC time-sharing system at MIT) and interactive database structures, showing how machines could respond to human input and how to produce responses that would seem human (or at least as convincing as possible). For Weizenbaum, a typical conversation proceeded as follows:

Men are all alike.
IN WHAT WAY
They're always bugging us about something or other.
CAN YOU THINK OF A SPECIFIC EXAMPLE
Well, my boyfriend made me come here.
YOUR BOYFRIEND MADE YOU COME HERE
He says I'm depressed much of the time.
I AM SORRY TO HEAR YOU ARE DEPRESSED.[30]

ELIZA was built as a software program that consisted of a database of keywords and transformative rules governing their use depending on input. Fundamental questions included how to identify the most important keywords expected to occur in a conversation, how to place such keywords depending on context, and how to choose the right rules and responses in case no keyword was given. The program was restricted by the size of its database and by the vastness of the archive of potential keywords and responses it could handle. Technically Weizenbaum identified the functioning of the ELIZA program as formed around two elements: decomposition of data strings it received and reassembly into an output. So when in *Teknolust* Ruby uses keywords (or passwords) to activate social situations, she is part of a certain genealogy of imitation based on database structures. The question for Ruby, as it was for Turing, is how such programs or artificial entities entwine into a complex web of interaction or an ecology of networks that does not consist merely of technological or biological parts. Indeed, even some of the classical approaches in AI rely not on a purely disembodied notion of calculational intelligence but on a much more noncognitive sphere of intelligence of bodies related. Furthermore, in such ecologies of heterogeneous bodies we are dealing not so much with thinking or intelligence in the human sense but with how to cope sensitively and responsively as part of an information environment. For an increasing number of media theorists, such as Mark B. N. Hansen, this liminal sphere of translations between information and body phasing with the digital technologies (images are a key concern for Hansen) is the primary field in which embodiment is being reconfigured.[31] Ruby is a liminal body par excellence, phasing between her human genealogy and the informational spheres represented both through the software and database logic of DNA and through the screen technologies remediating old media. In fact, this is how the Ruby Web site functions as well: as a remediation of ELIZA and other earlier examples but now in an online form embedded in Flash animations.

What *Teknolust* tries to underline is that the software protagonists are not predetermined pieces of code either, but they exemplify code as "affect," a mode of contact with an outside that is determined only by the SRAs' encounters with other pieces of code and other milieus of interaction. Echoing the shift of emphasis in digital culture around the 1980s and especially the 1990s, this anticipates the turn from intelligence-centered AI to artificial life and to New AI, in which dumb interacting agents take advantage of their surroundings to complete tasks. In other words, we are back to the ants again. On one level, the challenge to produce intelligence is an interface problem solved by programming: how to develop sufficiently responsive and sensitive feedback routines that can "react" to the user's input in a fashion that gives the impression of interface-level intelligence. Reactions signal information processing: identifying input, classifying it, and fetching a proper response from a database (despite the objection in the film by the SRAs that "we do not do menial labor"). On another level, the challenge of programming intelligence is to couple the algorithmic procedures, the code level, with an environment.[32] The software program, although composed of algorithmic code strings, must constantly stretch beyond its computer habitat. In fact, code exists only through its execution, and the focus moves toward executability and processuality, which already conceptually flags the need to take into account the milieus and environments of interaction in which code is embedded.

For the SRAs, language is not only the representational, signifying regime but a code that can be executed in order to achieve desired results. Code is an order-word,[33] language that has the remarkable ability to actually, by definition, do things. This is what takes the SRAs far beyond the hermeneutic understandability of "normal languages" and where the imitational nature of the SRAs turns into much more than pure imitation. In the early scenes of the film, when Ruby is fed "motivational tapes," the projected film surfaces not merely on the wall but also on Ruby's face. The two faces, of the woman on the film and Ruby asleep, form a common surface: the images and speech fold into Ruby's dream. This is not, however, "a meaningful implementation" in a hermeneutical sense but an affective folding at the limits of language.[34] As with ELIZA, the question is how to fold alternative modes of rationality. The becoming-calculational of language and speech in the mid-twentieth century related both to the assemblages of desire around AI projects and, more contextually, to the ways such programs function in environments and handle tasks.[35] In this the SRAs and ELIZA recall the original Eliza Doolittle in George Bernard Shaw's *Pygmalion* (1916), in whose case the powers of psychophysiology and the modeling of cultural techniques such as speech can be reduced to technological modulation.[36] In the age of technical media, language is a matter of technological modulation, and in the age of digital modulation, there is no need for the organic mouth in the speech act. Bodies and brains exist beyond the human organization: "They are everywhere you look, bodiless brains breathing down your neck

Ruby's sleep folds with the remediations of old film media, an archive of human emotions, and modes of social behavior. From *Teknolust.* Courtesy of Lynn Hershman-Leeson and Bitforms Gallery NYC.

and controlling your desires. Where do they come from, how do they replicate, how can I get one, why do they look human?"[37]

INSECT WORLDS

There is a long history of feminist theory engaging with animals and insects, more recently embraced by writers such as Sadie Plant, Rosi Braidotti, Luciana Parisi, and Elizabeth Grosz. Sadie Plant raised the connection between weaving as a characteristic activity from spiders to women and on to digital culture. Plant saw weaving as a synthetizing concept, in the manner of Deleuze and Guattari's "machinic phylum," by which to approach the techniques of digital culture as trackings of matter-flows. Hence, concepts such as "folding, plying, multiplying threads"[38] became key feminist notions for an ontology of processes and antidualism. Joanna Zylinska has picked up on the Derridean threads of the notion of weaving and argued that the notion of the spider's web is suitable for a complex understanding of the epistemologies of in-betweenness and mimicry. As Zylinska points out, mimicry, citation, and repetition are part and parcel of the poststructuralist feminist toolbox although in different ways from Butler to Irigaray. As a focus on constructiveness and construction, those tactics are, for example, for Irigaray ways of converting "subordination into an affirmation"[39] and looking for the ontogenetic moment in a specifically feminine mode of production. Zylinska then tracks the cyberpolitics of representation, as she calls it, where "women challenge the teleological rational of the IT discourse with a circular logic of the repetitive spin."[40]

For yet another example of the link between animals and feminist critique, Braidotti's notion of "becoming-insect" draws from Deleuze's notion of becoming, which Braidotti takes as an ethiconeomaterialist vector for subjectivities outside that of the human. Becomings activate agencies that are nonunitary, multilayered, and dynamic.[41] Braidotti takes the notion of the feminine and the animal in a bit different direction that is less occupied with representations and more with materialist becomings and interactions of bodies. For Braidotti, the insect or the animal is not a figure of representation that is important for the feminist theories of corporeality but a marker of intensities and a reminder of the layered ethological and environmental subjectivities that are defined by their intensities. Animal bodies are interesting for any theory of becoming due to the fact that they do things differently. Braidotti speaks of insects' "technological performativity" to refer to the fact that these animals offer alternative ways to understand communication, visuality, acoustics, and, for example, temporality.[42] To quote Braidotti's *Metamorphoses* and her take on insects:

> They pose the question of radical otherness not in metaphorical but in biomorphic terms, that is to say as a metamorphosis of the sensory and cognitive apparatus. In this regard, the insect provides a new paradigm for discontinuous transmutations without major disruptions. The key elements of this are: larval metamorphoses; the speed of their reproductive system; the propensity to generate mutations; the faster rate of genetic recombination. Moreover, not having any major neuronal reservoir, insects are free from the hold of memory and of the socially enforced forms of sedimented memory, known as institutions. In Deleuze's terminology, they are multiple singularities without fixed identities. All of these have been amply explored and documented in literature, cinema and culture.[43]

Teknolust is one of those films that could be said to be an exploration, or a probing, into alternative singularities and agencies that are emerging in contexts of new technologies of reproduction, memory, and networks. The question of the insect is then not merely a figurative or a representational necessity but can be seen as a vector to a wider, multilayered understanding of the ethological relations of agencies.

This is where we return to affect and a technoaffective interpretation of the multilayered notion of agency that *Teknolust* suggests in a Braidottian vein. Love, cuddling, and other themes of affectionate relations are ever present in *Teknolust,* which uses these "feminine" (to play with the cliché) characteristics to scale down high technology and science. But beyond the narrative themes, these notions can be read as pointing toward affect as a more general notion of relationality. This is where the Deleuze-Spinozan understanding of affects and affective relations can help us to turn away from the solely human understanding of the term and use it to encompass a multiplicity of heterogeneous relations, which I see as crucial for a full-fledged understanding of digital network culture. From insects and animals to technology and social relations, affect can point toward the needed complexity of relationality, the primacy of relations.[44]

In their defining relationality, the SRAs recall swarms, insect robots, and other "dumb AI" creatures that we addressed in the previous chapters and that already acted as interfaces between animals and technologies of emergence. Relationality was the factor that Morgan emphasized as the key to understanding emergence, and since the 1980s the old AI has been set apart from the way of connections, multiagent interaction, and types of behavioral systems that resemble hydrodynamics[45] and insect societies. In other words, the goal in such responsive and dynamic systems, as was already discussed in chapter 5, is to build not an intelligent unit of action that has a representation of the external world in which it should act but a distributed system of "dumb agents" that resemble, for example, insects (ants, bees, cockroaches) and their social interactions.[46] Local insect interactions have large-scale repercussions that are often approached in terms of emergent intelligence. This discourse of emergence had already commenced in the early twentieth century but persisted and was adopted as part of high-tech media design as well. From robot design by Rodney Brooks[47] to biology interested in self-organization and structural coupling (Varela) and on to more recent examples in responsive swarm art installations[48] and military creations, insects indeed provide an alternative model for design.

We have already discussed the notion of perception in this context of software and dynamic media entities. Also, Brooks uses the term "perceptual world" to characterize the interactive relationship that AI programs can have with their environment, adapting the concept from ethology. As John Johnston notes, the term stems from Jakob von Uexküll's *Merkwelt* term, which designates the way perceptual worlds define the affective relationships in which animals are embedded. These perceptional worlds are "constrained by each animal's unique sensory apparatus, morphology, and capacity to move."[49] In the familiar example used by Delezue and Guattari, the tick as analyzed by Uexküll becomes a way to understand the power of ethological analysis as an analysis of affects. The tick is characterized not by its genus or species but by its orientation toward light, its smell of mammals, and its perception of skin topology. For Deleuze and Guattari, ethology provides the perfect example of the Spinozan quest to map potentials of bodies in interaction and defined by the relations into which they enter.[50] This ethological perspective focuses on tendencies to act and to receive action, that is, on the interactions of bodies with other bodies (the milieu). In short, bodies are defined by the connections they make or tend to make. Instead of starting the ethological mapping of affects from individuals or any other transcendent forms of organization, one starts on a plane of immanence that does not recognize a fundamental difference between nature and artifice, subject and object. In fact, this was the challenge that Gilbert Simondon (as discussed in chapter 5) tackled as well: the need to start to analyze individuation not from the prefabricated individuals but from the process of individuation that is always folded into a wider pre-individual milieu that the individual "carries" with it. For Deleuze and Guattari, insects have in this sense acted as good concepts with which to approach the molecular variations present in different constellations, even though their prime example in the insect context is the medium of sonic phenomena, as Patricia Pisters explains. Indeed, insect music and swarms are embedded in "vibrations, chirring, rustling, buzzing, clicking, scratching and scraping"[51] that are reminders of the elements that make up the more stable forms. They are what Deleuze and Guattari call dissolutions of forms and expressions of the fact that all production works through forces and their combinations in speed and slowness.[52] What I argue is that the insect analysis gearing toward molecular becomings and mappings of ethological relations is a good way to approach not only music and sonic media but a variety of media from visuality to software and networks.

When the feminist figurations of software of *Teknolust,* the SRAs, individuate, their milieus consist not only of human social relations.[53] This event of the SRAs involves various scales and overlapping milieus from overdetermined social relations to the intensive fields of software and digital techniques, not forgetting the media technologies of visuality such as cinema. As noted in chapter 4 and by other scholars,[54] the insect was in close relation with the emergence of a whole media technological discourse at the time when cinema was still fresh. Then the focus of the biopower mechanisms of cinema was the *physiological real*[55] (also analyzed in the earlier chapters of this book), but now the object of biopower is the *informatic real* as well.

The cinematic apparatus also cuts into biodigitality (with the tools of software design part and parcel of cinema production, as well as digital video shooting and nonlinear editing). Hershman-Leeson as a cinematic cartographer? Perhaps, but cinema as a folding point of various regimes, just as it has been since its inception at the crossroads of intensities of animal life, science, and experimentality. Now another level of digital processing is added to the multilayered agencies that seem to run loose from the habitat of the screen, whether of the cinema or a computer. Some call these runaway entities viruses, some biogender warfare, and that is the topic of the last section of this chapter.

MULTIPLICATION: A THOUSAND SEXES

What the SRAs exhibit are nonhuman affects. Very explicitly, in the SRAs' take on the "identity politics" of difference, humans have a different horizon or mode of orientation with the world:

> MARINE: Humans are so different from us. They can't repair themselves, they age, they die, they live . . . they hurt each other, they even kill each other. I don't understand their engines, we are such an improvement: why aren't there more of us? We are supposed to be self-replicating, she has erased our code for that. I want to hear the ticking of my biological clock!

RUBY: Stop it. When you sound defensive and aggressive, you sound completely human. That is a recessive trait, you remember?

However, despite the recessive nature of Marine's longing for biological clocks and the overdetermined discourses and practices of heterosexual coupling, the SRAs' milieus are also multilayered in this field. On one obvious level, some of the visual and narrative themes pinpoint the SRAs to the already mentioned Hollywood films and performative discourses of gender. This is the Butlerian moment of the SRAs, evincing the power of the performative as argued by Judith Butler in her influential writings since the 1990s. As Stacey argues, Ruby in particular is an exaggerated figure of the femme fatale and "female desirability," with long hair and red nails and lipstick.[56]

Furthermore, Elizabeth Grosz has grounded her material feminist take in a productive processuality and sees the politics of sexual difference in terms of the multiplication of practices, discourses, and concepts folding around the term sex. For Grosz, beyond heteronormative reproduction, sex is a more open and more fundamental mode of becoming. To desire is to open oneself to a movement of co-animation that engenders new encounters, new bodily zones, new affects.[57]

Here Grosz's ideas are related to her reading of Caillois's theories of insects. In chapter 4 we discussed the mimicry of insects as a particular tactic of space and disorientation, but another key theme with which Caillois and the surrealists were infatuated was that of the femme fatale and the praying mantis. Grosz sees Caillois as promoting notions of the feminine and of insects as vampiric and parasitic entities of the femme fatale genre. As said, this theme is used in *Teknolust*'s figuration of Ruby as vamp(iric) but also as a mantislike femme fatale who almost kills her mating partners. Ruby's deadly feminine being actually resonates quite well with Caillois's mix of feminity, sexuality, animality, and technology; for Caillois the praying mantis uncannily figured feminine sexuality as devouring (decapitating) the male and as a machinelike automaton, "a fucking machine."[58] Such an emphasis is found directly in Caillois's article "The Praying Mantis" (1937). First referring to the early twentieth-century French physiologist Léon Binet's idea about the insect as a machine, he wrote:

> Indeed, it strikes me that likening the mantis to an automaton (to a female android, given the latter's anthropomorphism) reflects the same

emotional theme, if (as I have every reason to believe) the notion of an artificial, mechanical, inanimate, and unconscious machine-woman—incommensurate with man and all other living creatures—does stem in some way from a specific view of the relations between love and death and, in particular, from an ambivalent premonition of encountering one with the other.[59]

Through the insect as an intensive figure of overflowing sexuality and death, Caillois already affirmed an articulation of sexuality, machines, and insects. *Teknolust*'s SRAs, with their ethological modes of affectivity, embody different scales and modes of reproduction and act throughout the film in complex layerings of sexuality, agency, and gender. Recent feminist theory, primarily that of Braidotti,[60] has insisted on the need to inclusively think not only the cultural figurations of life through sociability known to us humans *(bios)* but also the intensive layerings of animal life *(zoe)* that have been addressed in this book through insect life. To complement this, I want to suggest that another level of life, that of technology, should be added in order to make up a triangle of forces of life *(bios–zoe–techne)* of which the SRAs are a good example. To be accurate, such ideas have already been suggested, explicitly through the notion of sex. Here I am referring to Luciana Parisi and her highly original cyberfeminist take on how sex has been layered and is appropriated in the biodigital practices of contemporary network society.

Parisi has called the transformation of sexuality in biodigital culture "abstract sex," that is, decoupled from reproduction. Instead of taking sides in the long ongoing debate between advocates of "fleshy bodies" and those of "disembodied information," her "cybersex" points toward a new formation of biodigital sexuality that captures the flows of bacterial sex (surpassing human desires) and constitutes something that can be called "symbiotic sex." This emphasis on symbiosis as an ontogenetic force stems from Lynn Margulis's work on endosymbiosis, which in Parisi's take is extended in order to grasp in novel terms not merely sexuality or reproduction but also information, understood as an affective event that takes place between bodies.[61] Parisi also draws heavily on Simondon's notions of individuation, which is placed in the context of feminist theory in the age of biodigitality and cloning. I would like to think that in a way Parisi is talking about such creatures in a liminal zone of life as Ruby, Marine, and Olive. The SRAs are to my thinking exactly mutations of the way sexuality works and is remediated in the age of new technologies. In other words, beyond a linear fantasy of a transhumanist future, there is the element of bacterial, insect, and in general non-anthropomorphic life that plays an active part in the individuation of creatures of network society.

Indeed, Parisi's position on the "mutations of desire" in the age of bio-technology approaches sex and sexuality as a kind of a layering. In her tripartite conception, sex has gone through three levels of stratification: the biophysical stratification of bacterial and meiotic sex (3.9 million years ago), the biocultural stratification that focused on heterosexual reproduc-tion and so-called human sex (in the nineteenth century), and finally clon-ing and recombinant desire, which is not simply a new level but a capturing of the earlier tendencies and their folding with contemporary biodigitality. According to Parisi, if disciplinary societies were keen on controlling sexuality and reproduction and channeling sexual flow via strict proce-dures of power (e.g., spatially), control societies or the informatic modula-tion of desire are more akin to the turbulent space modeled by complexity theorists. What I would like to accentuate is that if the mode of discipline familiar from the earlier modern technologies of spatialization and enclo-sure were specifically targeting the human body (both as an individual and as a population, as Foucault explained), the modes of control of network society are increasingly focusing on bodies that are not so clearly visible in terms of phenomenology: we are talking about subrepresentational bodies of codes, genes, and other animal and technological processes.

Parisi sees in her Deleuzian vocabulary bioinformatics as a mode of multiplication that accelerates turbulences and deterritorialization. It "feeds on the proliferation of turbulent recombinations by modulating (i.e., capturing, producing, and multiplying) rather than repressing (i.e., excluding) the emergent variations. It marks the real subsumption of the body-sex unfolding the autonomy of the variables of recombination from organic sex and entropic pleasure."[62] In short, turbulence and metastabil-ity become engines of creativity and variation. Bioinformatics taps into the intensive qualities of matter and turns them into a process of production.

Following Parisi's stratifications of sex, in *Teknolust* the SRAs can be seen to express a layering of (at least) three modes of sexuality: they (1) imitate human forms of coupling (human sex) but (2) function as high-tech machines built from software and DNA (molecular sex) and then (3) act as bioinformatic creations that tap into biophysical modes of cellular trading (called meiotic sex). Biodigital creatures like the SRAs are not without histories but are part of an archaeological stratification whose biodigital modulations capture earlier flows. As noted earlier, biogenetic modulation relies on a 3.9-million-year-old mode of bacterial sex that was an early way of transmitting and reproducing information.[63] This was, according to the work of Parisi, Lynn Margulis, and Dorion Sagan, a form of genetic engineering. Such a stance comes from seeing evolution as a symbiotic event: reproduction happens as a network of interactions and involves the coevolution of microbial actors. The SRAs' mode of becoming, then, is also a network, or an assemblage, that draws its being from phylogenetic remediations and ontogenetic connections (with their biodigital environment). The SRAs' human form is not solely a comic element but expresses the nineteenth-century stratification of sexuality as heterosexual reproduction that is usually taken to be norma-tive sexuality, part and parcel measures of governing the population. As the film explains, software also needs a bit of intimacy and cuddling.

In *Teknolust*, however, heterosexual coupling remains a phylogenetic memory of an earlier stratification (but something not left behind). The need for spermatozoa cannot, then, be reduced to a mode of sexuality in which boy meets girl but is perhaps a channel for biodigital sex or for an insect sexuality of crossing borders (mixing actual and virtual, digital spaces, and various phenomenological levels from human to insect af-fects). Like viruses, which have been used as biotechnological vehicles for transmitting DNA between cells since the 1970s, figures such as the SRAs can be used to question the very basics of what sexuality is and to which scales it pertains.[64]

Teknolust does not fail to address the social political contexts of these modulations of desire, either. The mutations are part of the medial drive of biogenetic creatures and are also conditioned on the networks in which they are formed. These networks include material infrastructures and other networks of various scales, as noted in a conversation between Rosetta and a male laboratory scientist:

ROSETTA: It takes only one cell to make a living thing human.
SCIENTIST: Well, what about a synthetic human cell? Then you would have to patent it.

ROSETTA: Why?
SCIENTIST: Because it makes it legal, financially viable, proprietorial.
ROSETTA: How do you patent life?
SCIENTIST: Well that, my dear, is a very profound question.

In such scenes *Teknolust* emphasizes that networks of reproduction and multiplication are not merely about physical or local material connections but depend just as much on incorporeal actions. Patenting, financial backup, and consumerization are incorporeal acts that "breathe life" into material beings (in a contemporary capitalist version of the hylomorphic schema). As the scientist of the film explains to the puzzled Rosetta, Iceland is patenting its citizens' genetic codes, and multinational corporations are pirating and collecting trees in the Amazon and poisonous spiders in China for medicines. These are examples of how geographically and conceptually stretched the biodigital networks that tap into nature's material flows can become. Such networks present curious kinds of corporeal flows (flows of matter-energy) that are intensified by incorporeal events: the potential of biogenetic modulation is not an artificial invention of high technology but is already part of the virtual sphere of nature. Yet it is tapped by the deterritorializing machinations of capitalism and by biodigital techniques of power that move and reterritorialize this potential to new contexts, including the surveillance of citizens and productions of new medications. This kind of "nurturing nature" takes advantage of the abstract processes of cellular sex and underlines the continuity from nature to culture and also between creation and capture.

The context of capitalist appropriation is not left unnoticed in terms of resistance, either. According to Parisi, this multiplication of sex is also at the heart of microfeminist warfare. Abstract sex, sex as a mode of endosymbiosis operating on various scales, from bacterial to biodigital, is also about multiplying the possibilities to think feminine desire. Resisting identity politics as molar, already defined formations, feminine micropolitics attaches itself to the molecular compositions that form the molar (as the secondary capture of creative potential). Similar to the ways that various other feminists have appropriated the notion of becoming as part of their politics and ethics, Deleuze and Guattari's concept of becoming-woman is important in Parisi's take on biodigitality, which affirms the powers of mutating bodies beyond pleasure (as a stabilization of affects into emotions and feelings) and beyond the man-woman binarism. In a parallel move, Parisi's philosophy is doubled in *Teknolust,* where the viral behavior of the SRAs is dubbed "biogender warfare"—a bioterrorism that attacks only males and their machines, infecting them with a bar code. In medical examinations, the bodies of men show signs that they are prone to reject new forms of sexuality that turn into biological threats. The disease of the body is at the same time a disease of the machine; the computers of the infected men succumb to viruses as well. This feminist intervention echoes the 1990s VNS Matrix poetics on viruses as tactics of disorder. However, instead of disorder, what *Teknolust* proposes are slight reorderings and subtle differences. This is part of its weird atmosphere of contrasts, and one could hardly describe the film as a threatening call to arms. The mode of warfare here could be understood as a micropolitics that moves at the level of molecular flows, not the molar forms of organization (male, female); it is a molecular movement that follows the "tendencies of mutation of a body rather than focusing on stable levels of difference."[65] This means that modes of sexuality multiply beyond the one difference-model: sexuality spreads across scales.

These constructions of sex, multiplication, and sexual difference are powerful metaphors used as philosophical concepts, which can also be taken as concrete modes of creation. For instance, *Teknolust* as a cinematic product can be seen as a multiplication machine of "a thousand tiny sexes" that promotes new perspectives of humans, machines, love, sexuality, and biogenetics. In my view, it is related to such recent projects as Isabella Rossellini's at least as quirky Green Porno online/mobile short film series (2008), which introduces in a naïvistic animation style the sex lives of insects.[66] Green Porno feels like an intuitively natural realization of the thousands of tiny sexes of the insect world, where penises, anuses, and erogenous zones in general are wandering from the territories familiar to us humans to new, unimaginable combinations. Even less threatening, Green Porno is hilarious in this modulation of desire, which takes elements from nature films but also contributes to a wider discourse on sexuality.

To conclude, in addition to biogender warfare or the micropolitics of desire, I want to emphasize in the context of this chapter the issue of becoming-animal. As argued earlier, the modes of affectivity in *Teknolust* feed on the "conceptual figures" of the animal and the insect. In *Teknolust* they act as force fields of weird affectivities reminiscent of the alternative modes of sex and superfolds that pierce the human form. They function as vectors (like viruses transmitting DNA) that interface with affective worlds in the context of digital technology and software.[67] Object-oriented programming is one evident concrete media technological context for this new class of social computational objects, but *Teknolust* wants to expand this diagram of ecologies of code outside the computer and networks as well. In other words, the networks expand far outside the material technics toward technics of incorporeality.

The micropolitics of mutating desire meets the worlds of bacteria, insects, and animals in a circuitous relation of force fields to create new becomings. These relations are always composite, not merely imitating some animal or becoming *an* insect or *a* technological organism but individuating assemblages of insects, animals, technologies, sexuality.[68] Here the force of becoming-woman is composite and appears in relation to other forces, those technological and bestial, for example. Feminist theory has already grabbed hold of these intensive forces of materiality and animality, and we can further emphasize the forces of media technologies as well—including software and network technologies. I see these forces as interconnected assemblages of heterogeneous nature: insectoid–woman–technology. As part of a media ecological twist, the forces of animality are continuously layered and cut through other sets of forces without neglecting the forces of imaginary creations. I want to see this as an exercise in ecosophy of a kind that draws from the incorporeal species of music, the arts, and cinema, as Guattari puts it.[69] Such ecological objects are conceptual tools that "open and close fields of the possible, they catalyse Universes of virtuality."[70] Indeed, through a production of novel singularities in different ecological assemblages, we are able to summon a different kind of politics—a politics aiming for the not yet existing in the sphere of bodies, sensations, and ethological relationality. What follows is an epilogue that not only summarizes and draws together the argument of this book but points toward some of the recent practices in media arts in which an ecosophy of technology and animality can be seen working.

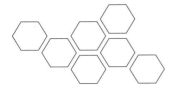

EPILOGUE
Insect Media as an Art of Transmutation

The insect does not belong to our world. The other animals, even the plants, do not seem total strangers to us, despite their silent lives and the profound secrets they cherish. We feel in them somehow a certain terrestrial fraternity. They surprise us, they fill us with wonder often, but they do not amaze or overwhelm our very mode of thought. But the insect seems far removed not merely from our own habit of life, but even outside the morale and psychology of our globe. One would say it had come from another planet, more energetic, more monstrous, more unfeeling, more atrocious, more infernal than ours.

—Maurice Maeterlinck, *New York Times*

Sarah Peebles's electroacoustic recording *Insect Grooves* (2002) is an exemplary mix of imaginary media and high technology. Indeed the humming, ticking, scratching, vibrating, chirping, and flapping sounds make up a groove reminiscent of something that we might believe an insect orchestra could fabricate. For example, crickets make their noise through a vibratory rubbing of their wings, a sound that can be described as a combination of "a stringed and a percussion instrument." However, they can also tune their chirping with other crickets, which produces a pulsating synchrony.[1] The pulse is an index of granules finding common relations that turn into a rhythm, a sound; it raises the question, What kind of body is this teeming multiplicity that is not easily localizable? In Peebles's work, the sounds, which were partly improvised, partly semi-composed, present a sonic take on grooves imperceptible before. A *New York Times* story from 1880 of a woman with a cricket orchestra[2] seems here to have found a body of resonance with techniques of sampling and electronic sounds that in themselves seem to heavily draw on "insect worlds." Of course sonic insect bodies are only an imaginary medium in the sense that the notion of the insect presents a motif whereby the creation of sounds is territorialized, made intelligible. The sound of a body almost too tiny to see, or to hear, is here brought into worlds of perception of technical media. But what is important is that the swarm is not represented or even visualized but rather emerges as the body of the sound. It is not a theme in media, but the medium itself, teeming with a multitude of lines and pulsations that draw it in so many directions.[3]

Mira Calix's sound piece "Nunu" (2003) also features insects. Performing with live insects, Calix produced soundscapes that bear a screeching resemblance to the aesthetics of modernism in the wake of György Ligeti as much as to the ticking, tapping, mysterious worlds of the microsounds of animals. Calix's music is an amplifier of a kind that taps into the too-silent-to-hear worlds of animals vibrating in their environments. It is also, along with Peebles's work, a venture into what is too small to be heard, imperceptible, beyond the human phenomenology. In addition, it is the result of an archival experiment in which the Museum d'Histoire Naturelle in Geneva commissioned Calix to use their archives of insect noises (from those of wasps and flies to those of hatching larvae).[4] It is important to note that the collection of insect sounds already represented an excavation into what the ear does not normally hear; the rapid pulses and specific frequencies, patterns, and intensities of sounds produced by insects are picked up only with special recorders and technical modes of analysis (originally oscilloscopes and audiospectrometers).[5]

As a further layer of technical media, Calix's collaboration with the collections represents a wonderful point about transposition in the fuzzy interzone between sciences, entomology, and the technical arts of digital media culture. Its way of using "found objects of nature" resembles, to some extent, a project of the artist trio Graham Harwood, Richard Wright, and Matsuko Yokokoji that looks at "free media" of nature. For the artists, in a manner that is reminiscent of the discourses of "insect technics," the ecosystem is a communication network of atmospheric flows, tides, reproductive hormones, scent markers, migrations, or geological distributions.[6] Their project(s) does not focus solely on the ecological crisis that has been a topic of media representations for years, but they seem to engage with a more immanent level of media ecology in a manner that resembles Matthew Fuller's call for "Art for Animals."[7] They approach media from the viewpoint of the animal and such perceptions, motilities, and energies (they mention, for example, wind) as escape from the frameworks of "human media." In this context I find their rhetorical question concerning nonhuman media intriguing: "Can 'natural media' with its different agencies and sensorium help to rethink human media, revealing opportunities for action or areas of mutual interest?"[8] This question, in a way, indicates the problem that I have tried to map throughout this book. And, in a way, this question, which I have approached historically, can be seen reworked through various contemporary media art pieces as well. Even though my method has been media archaeological, it resonates strongly with the media ecological methods of current media art practices, which aim to displace and transpose

Garnet Hertz's Cockroach-Controlled Mobile Robot, version 1. Equipped with a special harness, the cockroach is able to control the robot vehicle. The robot art system investigates technological development through the living animal, integrating the evolutionary powers of insects with high-tech design. Courtesy of Garnet Hertz.

notions of nature and technology. It is not only dead media and the history of obsolescent technology but nature as well that has been framed as a "storehouse for invention" at least since the nineteenth century.[9]

As a rethinking of perception and sensation, music has been a key field in which the worlds of entomology have found resonance with creative practices and technical media. Most often, this is through meticulous algorithmic practices such as swarm granulation. As Tim Blackwell explains, in such practices granulation refers to

> the process of packing very short samples of sound into tiny grains, which are subsequently rendered into dense clouds. In this technique, the flow and dynamic patterning of a virtual swarm is matched to the sonic properties of the grain cloud by a relationship between particles and grains; the organization of the swarm in the space of grain parameterisations is manifest as a sonic organisation in a space of textural possibilities.[10]

Drawing from discoveries in visual algorithms such as Reynolds's boids, Blackwell outlines the key idea of granulation techniques as the ability to create new sound textures from existing "natural sounds." Such techniques are fascinating in underlining the rich material connections that enable phenomenological perception. Aptly, the idea draws from the insect world of swarms in its complexity-theory-oriented manner of looking at the patterns of sounds in terms of topologies of sound that revolve around attractors and flows. Just as visuality is detached from the realm of phenomenology, as noted in chapter 6, sound is revealed to consist of various weird nonhuman materialities in which animality and technical media meet. However, there remains the challenge of how not to treat the "swarm" only as an abstract and discrete pattern and hence a spatial algorithmic form but also as incorporeal materiality. This means thinking it as a folding between the topological multiplicity and as a phenomenal entity that unfolds in time, as Thacker writes, pointing to the necessity to rethink materiality: "What is interesting in the case of sonic swarms is the way in which the incorporeality of the swarm as a phenomenal entity in itself is tied to a materiality that is unseen, unbodied, and only reductively localizable."[11]

In addition to sound, recent years have seen various examples of "insect media art" that involve explorations into new forms of motility, sensory and communicatory practices in which the "insect" is a conceptual and embodied focal point. A perfect example is the Bug City exhibition in Winnipeg, curated by Gary Genosko, Doug Lewis, and Mary Reid in 2005–6. In a move parallel to my book, the exhibition pieces explored and experimented with themes from insect robotics and new sensory interfaces to the cultural imaginary around insects as an alien world beyond our two-legged, two-eyed existence. Maria Fernanda Cardodo's *Flea Circus* frames wonderfully and in a true media archaeological style the nineteenth-century enthusiasm for the microworlds of these alien media; Craig Walsh's *Contested Space* is a rethinking of the nature of space and "infests" it with the teeming bodies of cockroaches, underlining how all space is lived through relations of bodies; and, for example, Joelle Ciona's live art piece works through insect principles that are reminiscent of Bergson. Ciona frames her body installation *In Habitation* as an insectlike becoming-with space in which, through her repetitive actions and movements, she is continuously creating the space. The installation space, which she calls "a nest," consists of weblike structures of ropes with Ciona as the weaver of those spaces. The processuality of the becoming of space through her movement is a framing of the space and a focusing on the intensity of the relations that are mostly made visible with the structures. However, the tensions in the relations encompass the whole of the space in this insectlike exercise in the reality of relations (radical empiricism) as an individuation from topology to phenomenal agency.

Such projects, along with the genealogy I have been mapping in this book, challenge some of the claims made by Mark B. N. Hansen in his *New Philosophy for New Media*. Hansen argues that "the most significant aesthetic experimentations with new media carry on the legacy of Bergson's valorization of intelligence over instinct, and specifically, his understanding of technology as a means of expanding the body's margin of indetermination."[12] Hansen's take on mostly image-based new media projects aims to offer a phenomenology of the human body (as "viewer-participant") embedded in circuits of information that are produced in the works. Hansen remains critical of any disembodied notion of information and maps the bodily frames of any project of information that always has to provide such images—not only visual but auditory and tactile as well—which screen the information for the human body. In this context, apprehension through the body is a key notion for Hansen.

However, it would be justifiable to approach some of the media art of recent years, as well as other trends in media design and theory, through a quite opposite path. Following Bergson's notion of the instinct, as outlined in chapter 1, we can approach a different kind of an understanding of space as intensive, immanent to the lived body, and defined by the relationality of the process of living that space. Chapters 1 and 2 address this intensity of space, which works outside a human-centered understanding of media technology and toward an understanding of architectures defined by movement and variation. It was actually a very modern way to understand the beginnings of technology through consciousness and human imagination—as did such writers as Karl Marx, who acknowledged that bees and spiders are fine laborers but different from the human architect, who can erect structures in imagination as well.[13] This is also the context of ideas in which several theories of technology and media started to emerge. Yet there is another tradition that starts from a much more modest assumption about instinct. It is not only through detachment from lived bodies through abstraction that current media art works but through embodied technics in which the bodies involved become experiments and probings in nonhuman technics in themselves.

To be fair, Hansen's more recent book *Bodies in Code* fits quite nicely into this idea of pre-personal organism-environment coupling, being a key area of interest for contexts of digital creation.[14] Here Hansen's focus is on the noncognitive operations of embodied and pre-individual modes of tapping into the virtuality of bodies in becoming, interfacing with digital media. This is a stance toward a transmutational entanglement of bodies of various "substances" in a manner in which Bergson's notions on instincts and immanent technics become relevant. Hansen draws heavily on Simondon's notions of transindividuality, individuation, and the emphasis on pre-individual potentiality that every living individual carries with it. Individuals are in excess of themselves, and the notion of affectivity in this context helps Hansen to extend the human being as part of technics and the outside world. Yet what needs more emphasis is the primacy of animality as a regime of the pre-individual. Far from a mystical experience of the primordial animal within us, it refers to the various potentials of becoming outside our established bodily coordinates and the differing potentials of sensation of which animals have been good reminders. Simondon's points afford an even more radical nonhuman position in which individuation also happens in media culture outside the human center and through machines, images, and processes of various technological scales. Technology does not individuate only from or through the human being; rather, there are relatively autonomous engines of individuation, memory, and affects as well—organic and nonorganic. As Hansen himself acknowledges through a reading of Bernard Stiegler and Simondon, technics can be "understood as a quasi-autonomous domain of being" that resides "between the organic and the inorganic."[15]

In addition to understanding that Simondon's view lends itself to a posthuman media theory, we have to understand the Bergsonian vocation for instinct and immanence as technics of nature of a kind. Such technics resonates with much more recent notions surrounding animal models used in media design, from media art pieces as mentioned earlier to, for example, networks and distributed agencies. The Bergsonian position does not necessarily lead to thinking instinct as a dumb mechanism of repetition but rather to thinking it as an unfolding individuation that connects it to the themes in chapter 5 of bees as well as to the cultural theory of embodiment of recent years. Instinct becomes in this sense the marker of the pre-intelligent—perhaps in resonance with the recent brain sciences that emphasizing that tools actually afford intelligence, not the other way round—and hence an apt concept to take into account the pre- and nonhuman modulations of milieu. Such ideas were used in the fields of New AI as well, for example, in Rodney Brooks's adaptation of Francisco Varela's insistence on the embodied nature of cognition. The environment affords intelligence, and cognition and perception are results of the coupling of the embodied "system" with its milieu.[16] In such various contexts of practice and theory, instead of a predetermined image of a teleological goal as in intelligent design, the notion of instinctual becoming leads toward a nonrepresentational individuation that deals much more with affects and relations between vibrating bodies in milieus than with diagrammatic gridding and control.[17] It furthermore bypasses the potential dangers in spatializing the intensities of bodies of swarms and other multiplicities to an abstracted set.

However, as underlined throughout this book, I want to steer clear of any dualism between intensive animal bodies and diagrammatic control as a vampiric capture of those potentials. The overall picture is much more complex, involving a feedback loop into the research into animal bodies that is part of the biopolitics of technical modernity but that at the same time reveals the potentiality, the virtuality, in such animal bodies or, more widely, bodies defined by ethological relationality. It is through the diagrammatic framing of animals' bodies that an understanding of the intensities, an excess, of those bodies emerges. Theorists such as Jakob von Uexküll, addressed in chapter 3, have acted as a crucial beacon for later developments into radical empiricism, and Uexküll's research into animal perception is a key conduit in the exchanges between animals, nature, and media (theory). His systematic research into the perceptual worlds of animals in their milieus is an enterprise parallel to the later practical developments in, for example, artificial life robotics, in which perception and local information are set as primary to any intelligent global and representational understanding of the surroundings. Furthermore, as noted in chapter 6, the software culture emerging since the 1980s can be seen in terms of reliance on neo-Darwinism but, perhaps more interestingly, in terms of what I have called the "ethology of software": the notion that software can also be understood through perceptional (though of course not optical) relations and sensitivity to milieus.

Unfortunately, in my mapping of the coupling of animals and technology, I have to neglect various themes relevant to media studies that have been crucial in framing the milieu approach. Various key distinctions between embodied robotics (as practiced by Brooks and designers such as Luc Steels and Pattie Maes) and, for example, cognitive approaches (such as Douglas Hofstadter's use of an ant colony as a way to understand subcognition) are not thoroughly discussed. This is why books such as John Johnston's *The Allure of Machinic Life* are good mappings of those histories for anyone interested in a more detailed account of the New AI and robotics. Hence, the tracking of ethologies of artificial creations could have justifiably touched not only software but also physical-world robot design or "simulated physical environments."[18]

In a more direct connection to network culture studies, Alex Galloway and Eugene Thacker's *The Exploit* is one of the most recent enterprises into nonhuman media theory, drawing on ideas similar to those I have been mapping in this book. The authors approach the politics of network culture through Simondon and individuation as a creation of a multiplicity. Hives and swarms are individuated not according to old models of "subjects" but as nodes that furthermore connect them to other networks; subjectification is transformed into individuation, becoming subject into "networking."[19] Swarming is exemplary of the future forms of diagrammatic control in bioinformatic networks and represents for Galloway and Thacker a particular emerging form of diagrammatics of network biopolitics. Or, to be more exact, we could underline that swarming is not so much a form as a mode of individuation, and this mode of individuation toward hives, collectives, and, for example, social networks is pinpointed as the defining characteristic across scales and different phenomena of network society. This is the point at which animal studies meets up with media theory via the intermediation of posthuman discourse. Because animals have already served for a long time as key modes for thinking about the intensities and possibilities of bodies anyway, and hence fed into the discourse and practices of government and the biopolitics of modernity,[20] it is crucial to recognize their position in the history of media and their value for a media theory of individuation and nonhuman animal bodies. We have to be aware of the material specificity and framing of contemporary digital technologies, where the specificity stems both from an account of the singularities in current network protocols and software and from the "'animal' mode of digital culture."[21]

Posthuman media theory should in this sense not neglect the animal as a concept and vector of affectivity. As in the most interesting approaches to the discourse on posthumanism, for example, those of Serres, Braidotti, Haraway, and others,[22] posthumanist media theory is less about what comes after the human than what constitutes the nonhuman forces inside and beyond the form of the human. However, whereas such writers as Roberto Esposito pay special attention to, for example, Nazism in their accounts of biopolitics, I started from fields of knowledge and practice that are by definition nonhuman: the animal worlds, especially that of entomology, and media technologies of modernity that are defined by wavelengths, speeds, and slownesses that are beyond the world of the unwired human being. Despite the emphasis on Simondon, Hansen fails to articulate this link to the worlds of animals beyond the human being. Even if Hansen acknowledges the role of digital technologies in expanding, folding, and twisting bodily potentials and as a tapping into the pre-personal, he does not broaden his reach to discuss the specificity of the animality in contemporary discourses in media arts. And yet, from biomedia art to various insect art pieces that deal with the modulations of the sensorial, it is exactly through the animality of perception and "being-with" that the metamorphosis of the human being takes place. In short, digital technologies and art expose the animal in the human being. Bodies such as swarms are radically nonhuman.

This claim concerning the logic of swarms becomes clear through scanning some recent projects on swarms and evolutionary media design. It is exemplary of the way swarms and genetic algorithms have been adopted as optimization procedures. The radicality of a nonlinear evolution of form and structures is, on a more mundane level, often pinned down with a teleology of, for example, the increased efficiency of network traffic, as in the case of developing "discrete particle swarm optimization algorithms" to solve the traveling salesman problem.[23] Incidentally, the usual examples of collective behavior adopted from insect lives are seen in terms of business, as with organizing database information:

> An example of this is a bank trying to determine which people will receive approval for loans based on various application data. Other problems that might benefit from this approach include stock analysis, product line design, analysis of online auction purchase patterns, and the dynamic placement of Web advertisements based on user behavior within a particular site.[24]

This is not meant to downplay the complexity of the design software but to pinpoint how effectively the intensities, the topological forms and singularities, and the emergent behavior are framed through well-specified diagrammatics. Furthermore, what various contemporary philosophers argue is that biopower is able to tap into the processes of the virtual as well and modulate them not only on and through a capturing of actuality of bodies. Potentiality and creativity are also the targets of the subtle forms of control, an argument proposed by writers such as Paolo Virno and Maurizio Lazzarato, among others.[25] Control is just as interested in the machinics and assemblages of the intensive materialism of potentiality. Capitalism works by cultivating differences and creating potentialities. Actualities are surrounded by the clouds of potentialities that are future-oriented and exemplary of the logic of control and the new logic of technoculture as a perpetual variation. This keenness to track intensities is what forces any critical ethos of difference and ecosophy to keep a focused eye on the wider ecological and ethological connections of their discourses and practices as they move on the same ground as the capitalist wish to tap into reformulations of desires, bodies, and politics of relationality.

Certainly art is one form of tapping into the forces of metamorphosis and a creation of novelty through modulation. Grosz highlights this Deleuzian stance clearly when she writes:

> Each of the arts is concerned with a transmutation of bodily organs as much as it is with the creation of new objects, new forms; each art resonates through the whole of the sensing body, capturing elements in a co-composition that carries within the vibrations and resonances, the underlying rhythms, of the other arts and the residual effects of each of the senses.[26]

I want to acknowledge that such an understanding of the arts, and of course specifically contemporary media art pieces revolving around the question of the animal and the insect as specific modes of individuation and sensation, is parallel to my more historically tuned excavation. For example, the analysis in chapter 4 of some of the themes surrounding Roger Caillois's thought introduced ideas that resonate strongly with contemporary artistic discourses. Variation and modulation can be seen as the crucial tactics of creation, and such ideas can take their strength from an understanding of the processuality of metamorphosis as well. But, in the contemporary context, we cannot avoid the question about the political stakes of thinking in terms of metamorphoses, difference, and intensities; they are far from self-evident promises of resistance but need to be framed and understood in wider assemblages of enunciation. Here, for example, the contact with capitalism and the diagrammatics of biopower cannot be neglected. The modulation, variation, and intensification of certain processes of life within the human body and other animal bodies and also outside them becomes a crucial motor for various practices, from biotechnology to new media technologies.

"Insect media," then, is a transversal field that has moved from the historical examples from the nineteenth century discussed early in the book to the more recent discussions concerning swarms and network culture, and from the discourses surrounding art and the transmutation of bodies and their sensoriums to new diagrams of tapping into and capturing such bodies in technocapitalist projects. It is defined by this complexity, and by the media ecological relationality that demands an insectlike compound vision system and the alternative senses of the cultural analyst as well, to be able to take into account the various planes on which the notion of insect media is organized and distributed but also finds its lines of flight. As tracked throughout this book, insects are not only the theme of the book but also the subjects of a body of thought that emerges from various sources, some explicitly, some implicitly present here: Michel Serres's notions concerning parasites, animals, and theories of information; Deleuze and Guattari's biophilosophy; Foucault's analysis of the regimes of power and the body; Simondon's way of thinking the living as a process of individuation; and the ideas of various more recent theorists, from Rosi Braidotti to Eugene Thacker, who have helped to bridge gaps between "wetware" and "techware" approaches to posthumanism. The way some insects are defined by metamorphosis connects them to a conceptual agenda of cultural analysis and media archaeology keen on developing conceptual tools to open up "universes of virtuality"[27] and ecosophic cartographies that are less about interpretation than about creating potentials for "assemblages of enunciation capable of capturing the points of singularity of a situation."[28] In this case, the singularity resides in ethological relations, metamorphosis, and bodily intensities and potentials of communication that are not captured from an anthropomorphic perspective. Incidentally, these points are what connect contemporary network culture and the much older techniques of environing that we find in animals such as insects.

NOTES

INTRODUCTION

1. See the project homepage for DARPA: http://www.darpa.mil/ (accessed April 10, 2009). For another example of insect robotics, see "Robots Scale New Heights," *BBC Online,* July 8, 2008, http://news.bbc.co.uk/ (accessed April 10, 2009).

2. John Arquilla and David Ronfeldt, "Swarming and Future Conflict," *RAND National Defense Institute Document Briefings 311* (2000), http://www .rand.org/ (accessed April 10, 2009).

3. For a short summary of insect robotics, see, for instance, "The Buzz about Insect Robots," *Nova: Science in the News,* http://www.science.org.au/ nova/084/084key.htm (accessed April 10, 2009).

4. Ki-Hun Jeong, Jaeyoun Kim, and Luke P. Lee, "Biologically Inspired Artificial Compound Eyes," *Science* 312 (April 2006): 557–61. For example, compound eyes were already being discussed at the end of the nineteenth century. See, for example, R. T. Lewis et al., "On the Use of the Compound Eyes of Insects," *Science 20* (December 2, 1892): 314–15.

5. David Blair, *Waxweb,* http://jefferson.village.virginia.edu/wax/ (accessed February 24, 2009).

6. Eric Bonabeau, Marco Dorigo, and Guy Theraulaz, *Swarm Intelligence: From Natural to Artificial Systems* (New York: Oxford University Press, 1999), xi. See James Gleick, "Why Can't a Robot Be More Like a Man?" *New York Times,* December 11, 1988.

7. "Sci/Tech Cockroaches: World Champion Side-Steppers," *BBC News,* February 17, 1999, http://news.bbc.co.uk/ (accessed April 10, 2009).

8. Rodney A. Brooks and Anita M. Flynn, "Fast, Cheap and Out of Control: A Robot Invasion of the Solar System," *Journal of the British Interplanetary Society* 42 (1989): 479.

9. Ibid., 478–85.

10. John Johnston, *The Allure of Machinic Life: Cybernetics, Artificial Life, and the New AI* (Cambridge, Mass.: MIT Press, 2008), 340.

11. John Johnston, "A Future for Autonomous Agents: Machinic Merkwelten and Artificial Evolution," *Configurations* 10 (2002): 490–92. A short note on sensation and perception: perception can be understood as the mapped and coordinated regime of the body "being in the world," whereas sensation is the element that exceeds that. Sensation is the element of becoming that cannot be pinpointed to one register or organ. See Elizabeth Grosz, *Chaos, Territory, Art: Deleuze and the Framing of the Earth* (New York: Columbia University Press, 2008), 72. Sensation is the element of virtuality and creativity that feeds perception, which underlines that the two are continuously tied together, informing each other.

12. Eugene Thacker, "Biophilosophy for the Twenty-first Century," in *Critical Digital Studies: A Reader,* ed. Arthur Kroker and Marilouise Kroker (Toronto: University of Toronto Press, 2008), 132–42; Michael Hardt and Antonio Negri, *Multitude: War and Democracy in the Age of Empire* (New York: Penguin Press, 2004), 91–93; Rosi Braidotti, *Metamorphoses: Towards a Materialist Theory of Becoming* (Cambridge, England: Polity, 2002). On early social theory and insects, see Diane M. Rodgers, *Debugging the Link between Social Theory and Social Insects* (Baton Rouge: Louisiana State University Press, 2008).

13. See Pasi Väliaho, "Bodies Outside In: On Cinematic Organ Projection," *Parallax* 14, no. 2 (2008): 8–9.

14. See Gilles Deleuze and Félix Guattari, *What Is Philosophy?* trans. Graham Burchell and Hugh Tomlinson (London: Verso, 1994), 212–13.

15. Media archaeology as a term and as a method has more or less been attached to research by Erkki Huhtamo and Siegfried Zielinski, as well as several approaches trying to open up cinema history into a more multimedial understanding, like that of Thomas Elsaesser, but also in recent years the materialist media archaeology of Wolfgang Ernst. Ernst continues Friedrich Kittler's agenda to approach technical media in terms of their technological capacities to record and transmit beyond the human senses. On media archaeology, see Erkki Huhtamo and Jussi Parikka, eds., *Media Archaeologies* (Berkeley: University of California Press, 2011). See the introduction for an archaeology of media archaeology.

16. "Studies of the Spider," *New York Times,* May 9, 1897. See also, for ex-

ample, this book from the nineteenth century: Eliçagaray, *Beautés et merveilles de la nature et des arts,* 3rd ed. (Paris : Philippart, n.d.), which lists among the marvels of artifice and nature both technological and animal wonders, for example, bees and other insects. We should note, however, that according to present understanding spiders are not insects but part of a different subclass of arthropods, namely arachnids.

17. "Two Hundred Crickets," *New York Times,* May 29, 1880.

18. Michelle Tolini, "'Beetle Abominations' and Birds on Bonnets: Zoological Fantasy in Late-Nineteenth-Century Dress," *Nineteenth-Century Art Worldwide: A Journal of Nineteenth-Century Visual Culture* 1, no. 1 (2002), http://www.19thc-artworldwide.org (accessed February 11, 2009).

19. William Kirby and William Spence, *An Introduction to Entomology,* vol. 2 (London: Elibron Classics, 2005), 270, facsimile of the 1843 edition; orig. 1815–1826.

20. Ibid., 272.

21. See Laura Otis, *Networking: Communicating with Bodies and Machines in the Nineteenth Century* (Ann Arbor: University of Michigan Press, 2001).

22. J. H. Fabre, *Social Life in the Insect World,* trans. Bernard Miall (Harmondsworth, England: Penguin Books, 1937), 151.

23. Steven Shaviro, *Doom Patrols: A Theoretical Fiction about Postmodernism* (New York: Serpent's Tail, 1996), http://www.dhalgren.com/Doom/ch11.html (accessed January 22, 2009).

24. Akira Mizuta Lippit, *Electric Animal: Toward a Rhetoric of Wildlife* (Minneapolis: University of Minnesota Press, 2000), 187.

25. See Jeffrey Sconce, *Haunted Media: Electronic Presence from Telegraphy to Television* (Durham, N.C.: Duke University Press, 2000).

26. Eric Kluitenberg, ed., *Book of Imaginary Media: Excavating the Dream of the Ultimate Communication Medium* (Rotterdam: NAi Publishers, 2006).

27. See, for example, Christian Jacob and Gerald Hushlak, "Evolutionary and Swarm Design in Science, Art, and Music," in *The Art of Artificial Evolution,* ed. Juan Romero and Penousal Machado (Berlin: Springer, 2008), 145–66.

28. See Monika Bakke, "Zoe-philic Desires: Wet Media Art and Beyond," *Parallax* 14, no. 48, July–September 2008, 21–34.

29. Matthew Fuller, "Art for Animals," in *Deleuze/Guattari and Ecology,* ed. Bernd Herzogenrath (Basingstoke, England: Palgrave, 2008), 267.

30. Zielinski, *Deep Time of the Media: Toward an Archaeology of Hearing and Seeing by Technical Means,* trans. Gloria Custance (Cambridge, Mass.: MIT Press, 2006), 6.

31. Keith Ansell-Pearson, *Viroid Life: Perspectives on Nietzsche and the Transhuman Condition* (London: Routledge, 1997), 162. Ansell-Pearson writes that

consciousness is merely "one means by which the powers of life unfold and extend." Beyond such human, oh so human enterprises, for example, Bergson posited his idea that life comes up with various solutions to problems it encounters. These are analyzed in chapters 1 and 2, among others.

32. This can also be related to Michel Serres's approach to the posthuman. It is less about a figure that comes after the human than about a mode of rethinking key notions at the core of agencies such as unity and rationality. See Michel Serres, *The Parasite*, trans. Lawrence R. Schehr, with a new introduction by Cary Wolfe (Minneapolis: University of Minnesota Press, 2007). See also Wolfe's introduction, in which this idea is elaborated. In addition, see Robert Esposito's point about Nietzsche, which underlines a similar approach, in *Bios: Biopolitics and Philosophy*, trans. Timothy Campbell (Minneapolis: University of Minnesota Press, 2008), 101–9.

33. Lippit, *Electric Animal*, 2.

34. Anna Munster and Geert Lovink, "Theses on Distributed Aesthetics, or What a Network Is Not," *Fibreculture*, no. 7, http://journal.fibreculture.org (accessed February 11, 2009).

35. See J. Macgregor Wise, "Assemblage," in *Gilles Deleuze: Key Concepts,* ed. Charles J. Stivale (Chesham, England: Acumen, 2005), 77–87.

36. Cf. Gilles Deleuze and Félix Guattari, *A Thousand Plateaus*, trans. Brian Massumi (Minneapolis: University of Minnesota Press, 1987), 309.

37. See, for instance, Patricia Ticineto Clough with Jean Halley, eds., *The Affective Turn: Theorizing the Social* (Durham, N.C.: Duke University Press, 2007).

38. Stacy Alaimo and Susan Hekman, eds., *Material Feminisms* (Bloomington: Indiana University Press, 2008).

39. See, for instance, Manuel DeLanda, "Deleuze, Diagrams and the Open-Ended Becoming of the World," in *Becomings: Explorations in Time, Memory and Futures,* ed. Elizabeth Grosz (Ithaca, N.Y.: Cornell University Press, 1999). In general, see also Cary Wolfe, *Critical Environments: Postmodern Theory and the Pragmatics of the "Outside"* (Minneapolis: University of Minnesota Press, 1998).

40. Karen Barad refers to *"things"-in-phenomena* to bypass the things/phenomena dualism. The world is for Barad a process of dynamic flows and mattering from which "differential agential" positions emerge and suggest posthumanist notions of matter in a state of "congealing an agency." Barad, "Posthumanist Performativity: Toward an Understanding of How Matter Comes to Matter," in *Material Feminisms,* ed. Stacy Alaimo and Susan Hekman (Bloomington: Indiana University Press, 2008), 139.

41. As Constantin Boundas explains, we need not fear that Deleuze's ontology is dualist: "virtual intensity exists nowhere else but in the extended that it constitutes." Intensity is not identical to the extended terms, nor does it re-

semble them, but is rather the creative difference, force as a creative relation. Boundas, "Intensity," in *The Deleuze Dictionary,* ed. Adrian Parr (Edinburgh: Edinburgh University Press, 2005), 131.

42. Peter Hallward, *Deleuze and the Philosophy of Creation* (London: Verso, 2006), 11–18.

43. For some, such as Elizabeth Grosz, a rethinking of the connections of modern biology (such as Darwinism) and cultural theory is a crucial requisite for new concepts and practices of the body as an open-ended system that functions "with other huge systems it cannot control, through which it can access and acquire its abilities and capacities." Elizabeth Grosz, *The Nick of Time: Politics, Evolution, and the Untimely* (Durham, N.C.: Duke University Press, 2004), 3. Others, such as DeLanda, frame their "new materialism" more closely through a physics of self-organization.

44. Braidotti, *Metamorphoses,* 126.

45. Rosi Braidotti, *Transpositions: On Nomadic Ethics* (Cambridge, England: Polity, 2006), 38–40. However, passages from Foucault's later lectures suggest a way to incorporate this openness to the "natural running of things" as part of his theories of biopower. As he outlines, already early on a certain breach in the disciplinary apparatus of the police provided the need not only to impose objective regulations on the socially crucial issues from grain to safety but to find a way of flexible regulation: "So a regulation based upon and in accordance with the course of things themselves must replace a regulation by police authority." Michel Foucault, *Security, Territory, Population: Lectures at the Collège de France 1977–1978,* trans. Graham Burchell (Basingstoke, England: Palgrave Macmillan, 2007), 344. This relates in general to the sketching of the logic of security as one of intervening in the natural course of things—an alternative logic to that of discipline.

46. Also, nonorganic life "evolves," differentiates, and resonates with its adjoining milieus in order to further develop new assemblages and territories. Assemblages work through cutting flows and selecting from milieus (which can be external or internal). As J. Macgregor Wise notes, the elements of an assemblage are not just things but processes: qualities, speeds, and lines—and hence temporal becomings and milieus resonate as rhythms ("Assemblage," 78).

47. For sure, their biophilosophy has encountered severe criticism from writers such as Mark B. N. Hansen, who has pointed how their approach fetishizes the molecular becoming at the expense of organization. Mark B. N. Hansen, "Becoming as Creative Involution? Contextualizing Deleuze and Guattari's Biophilosophy," *Postmodern Culture* 11, no. 1 (September 2000): 22–23. Hansen hopes to flag the different modes of engaging with the body to which contemporary biology and complexity thinking adhere as well as the different

modes of thinking the body in some cognitive theories. Instead, writes Hansen, Deleuze and Guattari address a philosophical mode of conceptualizing bodies as ethological systems of relationality.

48. Mark B. N. Hansen, *Bodies in Code: Interfaces with Digital Media* (New York: Routledge, 2006), 13.

49. I am indebted throughout the book to Bergson, whose thinking is well summed by John Mullarkey, who writes that "organisms should not be regarded as natural kinds but as collections or nexuses of different tendencies, for no species, genus or kingdom uniquely possesses any one characteristic." Mullarkey, *Bergson and Philosophy* (Edinburgh: Edinburgh University Press, 1999), 65.

50. In Deleuze and Guattari's words: "We know nothing about a body until we know what it can do, in other words, what its affects are, how they can or cannot enter into composition with other affects, with the affects of another body, either to destroy that body or to be destroyed by it, either to exchange actions and passions with it or to join with it in composing a more powerful body." Deleuze and Guattari, *A Thousand Plateaus*, 257. Hallward, *Deleuze and the Philosophy of Creation*, 19.

51. Hansen, *Bodies in Code*, 86–87. On the computational assemblage, see Johnston, *The Allure of Machinic Life*.

52. Lippit, *Electric Animal*, 49.

53. See Luciana Parisi, "For a Schizogenesis of Sexual Difference," *Identities: Journal for Politics, Gender and Culture* 3, no. 1 (Summer 2004): 67–93.

54. Deleuze and Guattari, *What Is Philosophy?* 164.

55. Here, as Matthew Calarco explains, Deleuze and Haraway have much to offer with their ontological stances. Matthew Calarco, *Zoographies: The Question of the Animal from Heidegger to Derrida* (New York: Columbia University Press), 141. See also Cary Wolfe, ed., *Zoontologies: The Question of the Animal* (Minneapolis: University of Minnesota Press, 2003). More specifically, Haraway distances herself from both Derrida and Deleuze-Guattari in her recent *When Species Meet* (Minneapolis: University of Minnesota Press, 2008), 31. Her focus on the multiplicity inherent in "companion species" eventually extends into a Whiteheadian ontology of events and, more specifically, draws from Lynn Margulis's idea that every solid organism is always an ecosystem in its own right. Without going into a discussion of her disagreement with the aforementioned thinkers, I find this ecological realization resonating with the affect-relationality, a politics of ecology, that I am trying to express through the following chapters.

56. Cf. Wise, "Assemblage," 84.

57. Ansell-Pearson, *Viroid Life*, 180–81.

58. Keith Ansell Pearson notes a resonating theme in his reading of Deleuze

and Guattari and von Uexküll. Prior to having functionally determined that organisms are closed units, we have the intensive molecular level of nonorganic life in which the "form" of matter is immanent to it. This immanent view of reality (of humans, animals, technologies, etc.) bypasses the dichotomies of form and matter, subject and objects, and taps into flows constituting stable entities. Beyond subjects and objects, or form and matter, there are "forces, densities, and intensities. . . . In short, this is to arrive at 'the immense mechanosphere' beyond the opposition of nature and artifice (technics, assemblages) in which the 'cosmicization of forces' is harnessed." Ansell-Pearson, *Viroid Life,* 120. This is a mode of intensive abstract or spiritual materialism in which everything remains immanent to material instances yet irreducible to any actualized entity. Every actuality, or graspable "thing," is surrounded by its potential for change, movement, sensation, and becoming. Here Ansell-Pearson is contrasting a machinic view of reality with Heidegger's notion of how "the animal is poor in the world." For Heidegger, echoing Hegel, the animal in its lack of recognition of itself is doomed to a life of mere repetition short of potentiality. Only self-recognizing beings can have a history, and hence a potentially nondetermined future. As Ansell-Pearson notes, Heidegger's reading, marked by "bad biology," fails to take into account the "affective relationships between heterogeneous bodies" and is in danger of operating on mere molar concepts and at the level of predefined organisms (Man, Technology, Nature). Instead, with von Uexküll we have the possibility to bypass such rigid terms.

59. See Manuel Delanda, "Deleuze and the Use of the Genetic Algorithm in Architecture," online essay, n.d., http://www.cddc.vt.edu/host/delanda/ (accessed April 10, 2009).

60. See, for example, Jonathan Crary, *Suspensions of Perception: Attention, Spectacle, and Modern Culture* (Cambridge, Mass.: MIT Press, 2001). See also Otis, *Networking.* For a brilliant analysis of the aparallel evolution of the biological sciences and informatics, see Johnston's *The Allure of Machinic Life.*

61. Adrian Mackenzie, *Transductions: Bodies and Machines at Speed* (London: Continuum, 2002), 25 n. 2.

62. Donna J. Haraway, *Simians, Cyborgs, and Women: The Reinvention of Nature* (New York: Routledge, 1991), 11.

63. See Rosi Braidotti, *Metamorphoses,* 117–53. See also Braidotti, "Of Bugs and Women: Irigaray and Deleuze on the Becoming-Woman," in *Engaging with Irigaray,* ed. Carolyn Burke, Naomi Schor, and Margaret Whitford (New York: Columbia University Press, 1994), 111–37.

64. Thacker, "Biophilosophy for the Twenty-first Century."

65. Cf. Donna J. Haraway's defense of the culture of canines in her *When Species Meet.*

66. Steven Connor, *Fly* (London: Reaktion Books, 2006), 163.

67. On ecosophy, see Félix Guattari, *Chaosmosis: An Ethico-Aesthetic Paradigm,* trans. Paul Bains and Julian Pefanis (Bloomington: Indiana University Press, 1995).

68. I use the idea of autonomous affect to refer to the facts that (a) affects are not inclusively of the human and (b) they are pre-individual events. See Paul Bains, "Subjectless Subjectivities," in *A Shock to Thought: Expression after Deleuze and Guattari,* ed. Brian Massumi (London: Routledge, 2002), 101–16. Brian Massumi, *Parables for the Virtual: Movement, Affect, Sensation* (Durham, N.C.: Duke University Press, 2002).

1. NINETEENTH-CENTURY INSECT TECHNICS

1. Cf. Mieke Bal, *Travelling Concepts in the Humanities: A Rough Guide* (Toronto: University of Toronto Press, 2002).

2. William Kirby and William Spence, *An Introduction to Entomology; or, Elements of the Natural History of Insects,* 4 vols., unabridged facsimile of the 1843 edition (London: Elibron, 2005), 1:7.

3. Ibid., 9.

4. Kirby and Spence, *Entomology,* 1:14.

5. An early example was Reverend William Gould's 1747 *An Account of English Ants,* in which ants were raised up as idols of modern pious society. The order of nature paralleled that of divine creation and remained influential long after the presumed Darwianian secular turn. Charlotte Sleigh, *Ant* (London: Reaktion Books, 2003), 64–68.

6. Étienne-Louis Geoffroy, *Histoire abrégée des insectes, dans laquelle ces animaux sont rangés suivant un ordre méthodique,* tome 1 (Paris : C. Volland, 1799), iii.

7. Quoted in "Say's American Entomology," *North American Review* 21, no. 48 (July 1825).

8. J. J. Bourassé, *Esquisses entomologiques; ou, histoire naturelle des insectes plus remarquables* (Tours: A. Mame, 1842), 1–2. Also, William Paley's early nineteenth-century text *Natural Theology—or Evidences of the Existence and Attributes of the Deity Collected from the Appearances of Nature* (1802) argued a similar point, that intelligent design was to be thanked for the complex technics of nature. See chapter 6 for a continuation of this discussion.

9. Kevin Murray, "Glass Angels and Data Insects," in *International Symposium on Electronic Art,* Chicago, October 22–27, 1997, http://kitezh.com/texts/isea.html (accessed January 10, 2009).

10. Charles Darwin, *Origin of Species,* ed. with an introduction and notes by

Gillian Beer (Oxford: Oxford University Press, 1996), 395. Some commentators have argued, however, that Darwin gives natural selection an anthropomorphic face, a theme that stems from Darwin's keen interest in artificial breeding. Here Darwin's rhetoric is seen to be translating the power of the breeder into natural selection. Instead of a theological view of a divine breeder, Darwin introduces the technological idea of a machinery of evolution, a version that suited his social context of thriving industrialization. See John F. Cornell, "Analogy and Technology in Darwin's Vision of Nature," *Journal of the History of Biology* 17, no. 3 (Fall 1984): 303–44. For an alternative view, which I find more interesting for its emphasis on experimentality, see Hans-Jörg Rheinberger and Peter McLaughlin, "Darwin's Experimental Natural History," *Journal of the History of Biology* 17, no. 3 (Fall 1984): 345–68. These authors criticize the view that Darwin saw natural selection merely as analogous to artificial breeding and try to find a richer view in which the human being is not detached from nature but also subject to its forces. Here artificial breeding is perhaps more accurately seen as a tracking of the tendencies inherent in nature. It was actually Arthur Russel Wallace, in his ideas of variations in nature, who proposed a view of humans as conscious actors who could turn nature to their ends, emphasizing the supremacy man enjoys over matter. See Rheinberg and McLaughlin, "Darwin's Experimental Natural History," 355 n. 23.

11. Kirby and Spence, *Entomology*, 1:85–86. Of course, anthropomorphizing insect and animal behavior was a continuous theme throughout the nineteenth century (as it is now). Often it was connected to a desire to somehow make sense of otherwise meaningless-appearing devastation by insects. Locusts and the like were a continuous threat, especially in the Unite States. Consider, for example, this depiction of crop-destroying army worms from 1880: "Encouraged by this official recognition [by the Agricultural Bureau], the army-worm has begun a most energetic campaign, and is displaying a degree of enterprise and a knowledge of strategy and tactics that are extremely creditable." "The Army-Worm," *New York Times,* June 14, 1880.

12. Kirby and Spence, *Entomology,* 1:120.

13. Ibid., 2:330.

14. Michelle Tolini, "Beetle Abominations" and "Birds on Bonnets: Zoological Fantasy in Late-Nineteenth-Century Dress," *Nineteenth-Century Art Worldwide—A Journal of Nineteenth-Century Visual Culture* 1, no. 1 (Spring 2002), http://19thc-artworldwide.org/ (accessed April 24, 2009). In addition, Richard Marsh's novel *The Beetle* from 1897 introduced a horrifying insect figure that connected archaic mythic creatures and rites to contemporary London mysteries.

15. Steven Connor, *Fly* (London: Reaktion Books, 2006), 82–83.

16. Fred W. Saxby, "How to Photograph through a Fly's Eye," *Knowledge: An Illustrated Magazine of Science*, n.s. 13 (1898), 189. Quoted in Connor, *Fly*, 89.

17. Jean-Jacques Lecercle, *Philosophy of Nonsense: The Intuitions of Victorian Nonsense Literature* (London: Routledge, 1994), 204. For a stimulating idea of the double logic and co-presentness of sense and nonsense, see Gilles Deleuze, *Logic of Sense,* trans. Mark Lester with Charles Stivale, ed. Constantin Boundas (London: Continuum, 2004). Moving from Lewis Carroll to Friedrich Nietzsche, Deleuze analyzes the intertwining of incorporeal events and corporeal bodies, a process in which the sense subsisting in language becomes continuously expressed through bodies. Here bodies or subjects also became released from their usual positions and move as nomadic singularities beyond fixed individuals. With Nietzsche, Deleuze writes: "The subject is this free, anonymous, and nomadic singularity which traverses men as well as plants and animals independently of the matter of their individuation and the forms of their personality" (123). This Deleuze identifies as the discourse of the Overman, a movement of forces across established subjectivities: a movement of bodies and events at their surfaces and encounters.

18. Lewis Carroll, *Alice's Adventures in Wonderland and Through the Looking Glass,* ed. with an introduction and notes by Roger Lancelyn Green (Oxford: Oxford University Press, 1998), 42. Lippit notes Carroll's interesting relation to themes of Darwinian evolution. One could speculate to what extent Carroll's morphings of the human and animal worlds are a response to the Darwinian discussions of the era. Lippit, *Electric Animal*, 137.

19. Ernest van Bruyssel, *The Population of an Old Pear-Free; or, Stories of Insect Life* (New York: Macmillan, 1870), 2.

20. Ibid., 4.

21. "A Storehouse of Invention," *New York Times,* August 4, 1901. Later, in the 1920s, William Wheeler saw this even as a defining instinct of ants: the instinct of craftsmanship (and also the instinct of communication). William Wheeler, "Scientific Observations of Ants and Etymologists," *New York Times,* July 29, 1928.

22. Kant, quoted in Georges Canguilhem, "Machine and Organism," in *Incorporations,* ed. Jonathan Crary and Sanford Kwinter (New York: Zone Books, 1992), 60.

23. Ernst Kapp, *Grundlinien einer Philosophie der Technik: Zur Entstehungsgeschichte der Cultur aus neuen Gesichtspunkten* (Braunschweig: George Westermann, 1877), 21. In Kapp's anthropological philosophy of technology, the human being's key focus was to be on itself. "Der Gegenstand des Menschen nichts anders ist, als sein gegenständliches Wesen selbst" (138). Kapp's influence was later acknowledged by, for example, Alfred Espinas, who in 1897

adapted Kapp's ideas of organ projection as the key element of the philosophy of technology as action (what he called *praxeologie*). The worker remains unconscious of his intertwining with his tools, which seem to be natural extensions of his capabilities. The machinic ensemble is not merely an extension but an articulation. As Espinas notes, the machine is a coordinating system that has to remain unconscious in order for the worker to work. Alfred Espinas, *Les origines de la technologie* (Paris: Ancienne Librairie Germer Baillière, 1897), 45–46, 84–85.

24. Kapp, *Grundlinien,* 18–20. The ideas also amounted to a hierarchy of morphological elements, so to speak, and were cultivated later in France by Espinas. Lowest were the reflex-bound and instinctive forms of will, highest the voluntary and (self-)conscious appropriation of technology as a mastering of nature. Espinas, *Les origines,* 281–83.

25. Kapp, *Grundlinien,* 34.

26. Kapp, *Grundlinien.* Frank Hartmann, *Globale Medienkultur: Technik, Geschichte, Theorien* (Vienna: Webster University Vienna, 2006).

27. Canguilhem, "Machine and Organism," 61.

28. Jonathan Crary, *Techniques of the Observer: On Vision and Modernity in the Nineteenth Century* (Cambridge, Mass.: MIT Press, 1992).

29. Johannes Müller, *Handbuch der Physiologie des Menschen für Vorlesungen,* 2nd ed. (Coblenz: J. Hölscher, 1840), 255.

30. In developmental biology, resonating views of organs as tools and organisms as complexes of instruments were proposed by Wilhelm Roux at the turn of the twentieth century but later criticized by Martin Heidegger. Martin Heidegger, *The Fundamental Concepts of Metaphysics: World, Finitude, Solitude,* trans. William McNeill and Nicholas Walker (Bloomington: Indiana University Press, 1995), 213. Among Roux's works relevant in this context is *Der Kampf der Theile im Organismus: Ein Beitrag zur Verwollständigung der mechanischen Zweckmässigkeitslehre* (Leipzig, 1881). What Heidegger embraced to some extent, however, was Jakob von Uexküll's appreciation of Müller's ideas and his development of them into his own ethological approach to the world, analyzed in chapter 3.

31. Crary, *Techniques,* 88.

32. Ibid., 89.

33. See Müller, *Handbuch,* 305–12.

34. Crary, *Techniques,* 92. Italics in the original.

35. Etienne-Jules Marey, *La machine animale: Locomotion terrestre et aérienne* (Paris: G. Baillière, 1873), 6.

36. Marta Braun, *Picturing Time: The Work of Etienne-Jules Marey (1830–1904)* (Chicago: University of Chicago Press, 1992), 320–50.

37. Marey, *La machine animale*, 188. Etienne-Jules Marey, "Note sur le vol des insectes," *Comptes rendus des séances et mémoires de la Société de biologie*, 4th ser. 15 (1868): 136–39. Etienne-Jules Marey, "Lectures on the Phenomena of Flight in the Animal Kingdom," *Annual Report of the Board of Regents of the Smithsonian Institution* for the year 1869, Washington, D.C., 1871, 226–85. Even though Marey's studies on insects were done fairly early in his career, at the end of the 1860s, he also returned to the analysis of their movements in the 1890s, cutting into their movements at a camera speed of 1/25,000 of a second. Braun, *Picturing Time*, 166; Etienne-Jules Marey, "Le vol des insects étudié par la chronophotographie," *La Nature*, 20th year, 1st half (January 30, 1892): 135–38.

38. Marey, "Lectures on the Phenomena of Flight," 227.

39. Ibid., 235. For Marey, insect flight was not a phenomenon of the muscles and their organization but of their interaction with other elements, especially currents of air. Insect wings, for example, those of the dragonfly, were optimized to adjust to air currents: "Thus the reaction of the air, which combines its effect and acts perpendicularly upon the surface which it strikes, can be decomposed into two forces, a vertical and a horizontal force; one serving to elevate, and the second to propel the animal" (ibid., 244). The insect was then a folding of forces of physiological organization and the environment.

40. Marey, "Lectures on the Phenomena of Flight," 246.

41. "The Velocity of Insects' Wings during Flight," *Scientific American* 20, no. 16 (April 17, 1869): 241–56; "Velocity of Insects' Wings during Flight," *Manufacturer and Builder* 3, no. 1 (January 1871). Marey himself also engaged with plans for engine-powered aircraft. Around the end of the 1870s he collaborated on such plans with his assistant Victor Tatin. Braun, *Picturing Time*, 49–51. See also E. P. Felt, "Bugs and Antennae," *Science*, May 19, 1922.

42. War provides an exemplary context for the workings of biopower as a mobilization of population(s) but also of research into efficient solutions for organization and projectiles. If a crucial part of the analysis of moving bodies by Marey and others was to focus on the problem of perceiving bodies in motion, the solutions in the military context to propelling bodies into motion and subsequently catching them in their motion was of utmost importance. This is related to Paul Virilio's often articulated ideas on war and the logistics of perception. Paul Virilio, "The Aesthetics of Disappearance," in *The Paul Virilio Reader*, ed. Steve Redhead (New York: Columbia University Press, 2004), 63. For example, the French War Ministry was supporting research into flying apparatuses at the end of the nineteenth century. One of the examples that could be cited includes Clément Ader's 1890s design, which was modeled on biological movements (resembling those of a bat) and aimed to produce a new kind of a war machine: the Avion III. Jyrki Siukonen, *Uplifted Spirits, Earthbound*

Machines: Studies on Artists and the Dream of Flight, 1900–1935 (Helsinki: SKS, 2001), 53–56.

43. "Flight of Birds and Insects," *Harper's New Monthly Magazine* 41, no. 246 (November 1870).

44. Siukonen, *Uplifted Spirits,* 38–40.

45. J. Bell Pettigrew, *Animal Locomotion; or, Walking Swimming, Flying with a Dissertation in Aeronautics* (New York: D. Appleton, 1874), 170.

46. Pasi Väliaho, "Simulation, Automata, Cinema: A Critique of Gestures," *Theory and Event* 8, no. 2 (2005): 15.

47. Lippit, *Electric Animal.*

48. Marey, *La méthode graphique,* 108, quoted in Väliaho, "Simulation, Automata, Cinema," 19. On severing perception from the human body and the regime of vision, see also Crary, *Techniques.*

49. Giorgio Agamben, *The Open: Man and Animal,* trans. Kevin Attell (Stanford, Calif.: Stanford University Press, 2004), 14–15. With, for example, the early research into the principles of life by Xavier Bichat, the organism as a whole was divided into its constituent parts, making life a phenomenon of interrelated processes that resisted death. The life of an organism was viewed in Bichat's *Recherches physiologies sur la vie et la mort* (1800) as one of locomotion + respiration + sense perceptions + the brain. Life, in itself indefinable, was to be analyzed via its traces and the interactions of the internal with the external. Death functioned as the limit of an organism but also as the limit of biopolitics, not so keen on inflicting death as on cultivating life. Hence, both life and death as events of a biological organism (system) were distributed and divisioned on the levels of both individual bodies and the body politic, where the human species was integrated as part of the networks of knowledge and power. Crary, *Techniques,* 78–79; Xavier Bichat, *Recherches physiologiques sur la vie et la mort* (Paris: Bechet jeune, 1822), 2–3; Pasi Väliaho, *The Moving Image: Gesture and Logos circa 1900* (Turku, Finland: University of Turku, 2007), 60–64.

50. Braidotti, *Transpositions,* 55. Braidotti criticizes the negative "towards-death" ontology of Agamben and Heidegger for its overevaluation of death as the horizon of life, because this would allow us to forget the continuous innovation and creativity of life as a process of positive difference that succeeds individual life.

51. Darwin, *Origin of Species,* 149.

52. Elizabeth Grosz, *The Nick of Time: Politics, Evolution, and the Untimely* (Durham, N.C.: Duke University Press 2004), 215–16.

53. Ibid., 218. Bergson addresses this in terms of tendencies. Even though life is the differentiation and emergence of specialized tendencies, the traits of elementary directions are preserved. See Henri Bergson, *Creative Evolution,*

trans. Arthur Mitchell (Mineola, N.Y.: Dover, 1998), 112–19. Bergson writes: "There is no intelligence in which some traces of instinct are not to be discovered, more especially no instinct that is not surrounded with a fringe of intelligence. . . . All concrete instinct is mingled with intelligence, as all real intelligence is penetrated by instinct. Moreover, neither intelligence nor instinct lends itself to rigid definition: they are tendencies, and not things" (136).

54. Grosz, *The Nick of Time*, 224; Bergson, *Creative Evolution*, 142.

55. Bergson, *Creative Evolution*, 142.

56. Ibid., 140.

57. Grosz, *Nick of Time*, 13.

58. Grosz, *Time Travels*, 137.

59. Bergson was very familiar with Marey's work, and the two men were also personally acquainted when working on psychic phenomena in experiments organized by the Psychological Institute of Paris in the early years of the twentieth century. Braun, *Picturing Time*, 279–80. Yet Bergson's ideas produced an emphasis radically different from that of Marey, who believed in overcoming the human vision by dissecting movement into discrete observable images and graphs. For Bergson, surpassing the human senses was part of the ontology of duration and continuity that defines the way bodies fold and mutate with the world. Bergson, *Creative Evolution*, 28–31. In *An Introduction to Metaphysics* (1903), an essay he wrote before *Creative Evolution*, Bergson defines the difference between analysis and intuition as methods. Whereas analysis cuts duration into predefined categories for practical ends, intuition is a method for thinking through the object itself. It is hence a tracking of its extending and enduring becoming. Henri Bergson, *An Introduction to Metaphysics*, trans. T. E. Hulme (Basingstoke, England: Palgrave Macmillan, 2007).

60. Bergson, *Creative Evolution*, 140.

61. Ibid., 140–41. See Grosz, *Time Travels*, 137–38.

62. Bergson, *Creative Evolution*, 141.

63. Ibid., 151.

64. Grosz, *Time Travels*, 138.

65. John Mullarkey, *Bergson and Philosophy* (Edinburgh: Edinburgh University Press, 1999), 79.

66. Ibid.

67. Charlotte Sleigh, *Six Legs Better: A Cultural History of Myrmecology* (Baltimore, Md.: Johns Hopkins University Press, 2007), 52–53.

68. See Jessica Riskin, "The Defecating Duck; or, the Ambiguous Origins of Artificial Life," *Critical Inquiry* 29 (Summer 2003): 599–633. The question of instinct was already of interest to the the early natural philosophers such as Aristotle, who saw the life of social insects such as bees and ants as governed

by the instinct that he likened to the growth of a plant. In other words, the social insects work and build as a plant grows, according to a development plan. Bees and ants lack imagination and a future-orientated anticipation. Aristotle called this quality *phantasia aisthètikè,* and it is found only in the higher animals, explains Gilbert Simondon in his lectures from 1967. With the modern age and Descartes, spiders and other animals were stripped of their instinctual status and reduced to automata. Animals are fixed to their capacities, whereas the human being is an entity of plasticity and reflection. See Gilbert Simondon, *Deux leçons sur l'animal et l'homme* (Paris: Ellipses, 2004). In this context, we can understand how much of the later discourse on instinct adopted the language of the Cartesian spatiality and mechanistic worldview and approached instinctual life in terms of the machine analogy. In this book, in the way I approach technology and machinology I try to find an alternative to the overly straightforward mechanistic notions that were discarded during the twentieth century, replaced with notions such as emergence and swarming in discourses in biology and technology.

69. C. F. Amery, "Instinct," *Science,* November 25, 1892, 300–301.

70. Ibid., 302.

71. William James, "What Is an Instinct?" *Scribner's Magazine* 1, no. 3 (1887): 355.

72. Ibid., 359–61. Schneider's book, familiar to Nietzsche as well, classified animal actions and psychological principles. Schneider was arguing that instinct and will are not exclusive modes of animal orientation: instinctive actions can have a conscious side, and voluntary actions stem from instinctive impulses. Schneider's Darwinian analysis suggested approaching instincts as "sensori-motor arrangements fixed by natural selection together with association," which implies the historical nature of formation of instincts. See James Sully, "A Review of *Der Thierische Wille,*" *Mind* 5, no. 19 (July 1880): 424–28, quote on 428.

73. Cf. Massumi, *Parables for the Virtual,* 72–75. This line of thought could lead us to discuss the territorial tendencies of art, a theme on which Deleuze and Guattari contrast Konrad Lorenz's ethological ideas of "fixed action patterns" that determine behavior and environment with the idea of the priority of relations and territoriality. Specific functions/instincts, such as aggressivity, emerge only from the relations of temporality and spatiality, that is, rhythmicity and expressive marking. See Gary Genosko, "A Bestiary of Territoriality and Expression," in *A Shock to Thought,* ed. Brian Massumi (London: Routledge, 2002), 47–59. Elizabeth Grosz addresses the relations between nature and art. Grosz tracks the Deleuze-Guattarian idea of art as contracting the forces of the cosmos. Both nature and art are vibrations whose animality marks a forceful

creation, an open-ended becoming, from bird songs to colors of fish. According to Kontturi and Tiainen, "We as humans get the raw materials to produce art: sonorous cadences, intense colours, from birds, fish, and plants." Such ideas relate to the early entomological and popular discourse themes of insects and other animals as "storehouses of invention." Katve-Kaisa Kontturi and Milla Tiainen, "Feminism, Art, Deleuze and Darwin: An Interview with Elizabeth Grosz," *NORA—Nordic Journal of Women's Studies* 15, no. 4 (2007): 246–56, quotes on 254.

74. Diane M. Rodgers, *Debugging the Link between Social Theory and Social Insects* (Baton Rouge: Louisiana State University Press, 2008), 98–102.

75. Gilles Deleuze, *Bergsonism,* trans. Hugh Tomlinson and Barbara Habberjam (New York: Zone Books, 1991), 28.

76. "Concerning Spiders," *New York Times,* July 9, 1880.

77. My point is parallel to Grosz's argument that art does not begin with the "creativity of mankind but rather in a superfluousness of nature." Elizabeth Grosz, *Chaos, Territory, Art: Deleuze and the Framing of the Earth* (New York: Columbia University Press, 2008), 10.

2. GENESIS OF FORM

1. For example, George Romanes divided his interest in the "intelligence of insects" into sense of direction, memory, emotions, modes of communication, habits common to various species, habits of particular species, and intelligence in general among different species. See George John Romanes, *L'intelligence des animaux: Précédée d'une préface sur l'évolution mentale,* vol. 1 (Paris: F. Alcan, 1887), 29.

2. Charlotte Sleigh, *Ant* (London: Reaktion Books, 2003), 45.

3. Cf. Joost van Loon, "A Contagious Living Fluid: Objectification and Assemblage in the History of Virology," *Theory, Culture, and Society* 19, nos. 5–6 (2002): 107–24. Hannah Landecker, "Cellular Features: Microcinematography and Film Theory," *Critical Inquiry* 31, no. 4 (2005): 903–37.

4. Some films are available through the British Film Institute Web site, http://www.screenonline.org.uk/ (accessed January 20, 2009).

5. For a more detailed account, see John Johnston, *The Allure of Machinic Life: Cybernetics, Artificial Life, and the New AI* (Cambridge, Mass.: MIT Press, 2008), 375–84. Such contemporary artists as Ralf Schreiber (in the context of his "Living Particles, version 45") have referred to the differences of swarms created artificially and the added advantage of nature: "However, swarm sounds of living populations are usually much more intensive, since sound production and especially the development of maximum volume and maximum inten-

sity has been exposed to millions of years of evolution." "Interview with Ralf Screiber," *Neural IT* 32 (2009): 18.

6. Kevin Kelly, *Out of Control: The Rise of the Neo-Biological Civilization* (Reading, Mass.: Addison-Wesley, 1994), 340. Italics in original.

7. Richard Dawkins, *The Blind Watchmaker* (London: Penguin, 2006), 21.

8. Kelly, *Out of Control,* 342.

9. On accidents and "viral capitalism," see Jussi Parikka, *Digital Contagions: A Media Archaeology of Computer Viruses* (New York: Peter Lang, 2007), 96–100.

10. Christian Nottola, Frédéric Leroy, and Franck Davalo, "Dynamics of Artificial Markets: Speculative Markets and Emerging 'Common Sense' Knowledge," in *Toward a Practice of Autonomous Systems: Proceedings of the First European Conference on Artificial Life,* ed. Francisco J. Varela and Paul Bourgine (Cambridge, Mass.: MIT Press, 1992), 185–94.

11. Cf. Charles Darwin, *Origin of Species,* ed. with an introduction and notes by Gillian Beer (Oxford: Oxford University Press, 1996), 149.

12. Ibid., 69.

13. Ibid.

14. Bergson, *Creative Evolution,* trans. Arthur Mitchell (Mineola, N.Y.: Dover, 1998), 58.

15. Ibid., 51.

16. Kirby and Spence, *An Introduction to Entomology,* 2:379.

17. Ibid., 2:382.

18. Ibid.

19. Ibid., 2:388. One also has to note the difference of this view from that of Bergson, who underlined that nature approximates the precision of mathematics and geometrics but is not reducible to them. Instead, these are mere scientific trackings of the creative evolution inherent in nature, which is not restricted by any (human-) posited laws of physics, for example. This relates to the idea that creative evolution "transcends finality." This is the vitality inherent in the difference engine of nature, a pattern that seems to be as ingenious as one of mathematics but actually even exceeds it as a creative enterprise. Bergson, *Creative Evolution,* 218–24.

20. Jakob von Uexküll, "Bedeutungslehre," in *Streifzüge durch die Umweltern von Tieren und Menschen* (Hamburg: Rowohlt, 1956), 110–12. See also the example from *La nature* of a beetle who labors to form a leaf into a cigar-shaped housing with such precision that it is seen as a natural geometrician. "Un insecte géomètre," *La nature,* 30th year, second half, nos. 1515–40 (1902): 180–82. See also the short, anecdotal account of "an insect that counts," a story of an insect that moved with dancelike precision of movement. "Un insecte qui compte," *La nature,* 27th year, second half, nos. 1358–83 (1899): 90.

21. Lewis Mumford, *The Myth of the Machine: Technics and Human Development* (London: Secker and Warburg, 1967), 5.

22. Kirby and Spence, *An Introduction to Entomology,* 2:396. Italics in original. Also Louis Figuier, in *The Insect World* (1868), saw bees as incorporations of ideal harmony yet not mechanical (instinctlike) habits. Figuier thought they exhibit premeditation that signals intelligence. We can perhaps translate this premeditation as a sensitivity to environmental tendencies and the singularity of the organism of the hive, an emergent phenomenon. Louis Figuier, *The Insect World: Being a Popular Account of the Orders of Insects* (London: Cassell, Petter, Galpin, s.a.), 326. Figuier wrote: "The construction of their cells, always uniform, is, they say, the result of instinct. However, it happens that under particular circumstances, these little architects know how to abandon the beaten track of routine, reserving to themselves the power of returning, when it is useful to do so, to the traditional principles, which ensure the beauty and regularity of their constructions. Bees have been seen, indeed, to deviate from their ordinary habits in order to correct certain irregularities—the result of accident or produced by the intervention of man—which had deranged their work" (346).

23. Lorraine Daston, "Enlightenment Calculations," *Critical Inquiry* 21 (Autumn 1994): 182–202.

24. See Riskin, "The Defecating Duck,"628–30.

25. Darwin, *Origin of Species*, 183.

26. Ibid., 191.

27. The optimized use of wax, a spectacle of nature that was underlined, as part of their architecture was underlined in the early nineteenth century (1732) by the clergyman Noël-Antoine Pluche in his *Spectacle de la nature; ou, Entretiens sur les particularités de l'histoire naturelle qui ont paru les plus propres à rendre les jeunes gens curieux et à leur former l'esprit:* "They use this wax with a wonderful frugality; for it is easy to observe that the whole family is conducted by prudence, and all their actions regulated by good government. Everything is granted to necessity, but nothing to superfluity; not the least grain of wax is neglected, and if they waste it, they are frequently obliged to provide more; at those very times when they want to get their provision of honey, they take off the wax that closed the cells, and carry it to the magazine." Quoted in James Rennie, *Insect Architecture,* new enlarged edition (London: Bell and Daldy, 1869), 117. The innate mathematics and calculating capabilities of bees and wasps were noted by George Romanes in *L'intelligence des animaux*. Romanes placed an emphasis on the remarkable capacities of orientation of bees and wasps, noting how they are able to adjust to change in their environment (if, for example, the hive is shifted to another location). In addition, their innate navigation coordinates imply for Romanes, drawing on research by John Lubbock,

that bees and wasps are able to find the shortest routes for their movement from one place to another. This is explained by their instincts but also by their sense of direction (Romanes also admires the perceptual capabilities of bees). Hence, in tones reminiscent of mathematical modeling, for example, graph theory and the traveling salesman problem in which ants were used as calculational models, here bees and wasps are already implicitly imagined as such calculation machines, able to find the most rational singular vector and also to fold as part of their environment. See Romanes, *L'intelligence des animaux,* 133–40. Similarly, the industrious life of bees is shortly marveled in a curious old book about the beauty and ingeniousness in nature and artifice, underlining the common genealogy of creations in nature and artifice. Éliçagaray, *Beautés et merveilles de la nature et des arts* (Paris: Philippart, s.a.), 3–4. However, it is interesting to note that in addition to mathematical accuracy and patterns, Rennie paid attention to the way insects deal with materials. For example, wasps were subtle papermakers much before humans. Rennie, *Insect Architecture,* 100–102.

28. Rennie, *Insect Architecture,* 59.

29. Ibid., 113.

30. Maurice Maeterlinck, *The Life of the Bee,* trans. Alfred Sutro (New York: Mentor Book, 1954), 29.

31. Quoted in Juan Antonio Ramírez, *The Beehive Metaphor: From Gaudí to Le Corbusier,* trans. Alexander R. Tulloch (London: Reaktion Books, 2000), 67.

32. Ibid., 97.

33. Ibid., 93–98, 131–47. Le Corbusier believed that the machine aesthetics and functionalism of spatial creation is connected to the perfected order already found in nature. Artifice, then, does not differ from natural creation but tracks the optimal points already existing in material. "Here we have, in rational France, the call to nature; analysis. The entomologist Fabre shakes us up. He perceives that order is a natural phenomenon, our eyes open. The year is 1900. Effusion. Truly a beautiful moment!" Quoted in Ramírez, *The Beehive Metaphor,* 128.

34. A good example from Rennie is the building of the cells: "When bees begin to build the hive, they divide themselves into bands, one of which produces materials for the structure; another works upon these, and forms them into a rough sketch of the dimensions and partitions of the cell. All this is completed by the second band, who examine and adjust the angles, remove the superfluous wax, and give the work its necessary perfection; and a third band brings provisions to the labourers who cannot leave their work." Rennie, *Insect Architecture,* 131–32.

35. William Morton Wheeler, "A Neglected Factor in Evolution," *Science,* May 16, 1902, 770.

36. Quoted in Sleigh, *Ant*, 73.

37. Ibid., 66.

38. Ramírez, *The Beehive Metaphor*, 28. This represents the crucial realization of biopower and modulation of life: life becomes graspable only in its modulation, which in a way gives an expression of a fleeting life; in other words, whereas modern power functions via a cultivation of life, an organization, this also implies that there is no way of grasping and framing life beyond its organization. What would an organized space be without life inhabiting it, and what would life be if it were not organized in architectural spaces, temporalities, and other forms of modulation? Of course Giorgio Agamben, among others, has pointed toward these articulations of bare life and organized life.

39. Diane M. Rodgers, *Debugging the Link between Social Theory and Social Insects* (Baton Rouge: Louisiana State University Press, 2008), 80–90.

40. See also the story about the early filming of *The Adventures of Maya*, the story of an industrious bee. "The Screen: Bees, a Beetle, and a Spider," *New York Times*, April 23, 1929. The Belgian novelist Maurice Maeterlinck presented the life of the bee in his 1901 novel as one in which the community overruled the individual: "The bee is above all, and even to a greater extent than the ant, a creature of the crowd. She can live only in the midst of a multitude. . . . From the crowd, from the city, she derives an invisible aliment that is as necessary to her as honey. This craving will help to explain the spirit of the laws of the hive. For in them the individual is nothing, her existence conditional only, and herself, for one indifferent moment, a winged organ of the race. Her whole life is an entire sacrifice to the manifold, everlasting being whereof she forms part." Maeterlinck, *The Life of the Bee*, 23. Another early example of a model bee, from Victorian Britain, was presented in a 1884 children's reader, L. and M. Wintle's *Books for Young Readers* (London: George Bell and Sons, 1884), where "Mrs Bee" was an idealized worker without a will of her own. See J. F. M. Clark, " 'The Complete Biography of Every Animal': Ants, Bees, and Humanity in Nineteenth-Century England," *Studies in the History of Biology and Biomedical Sciences* 29, no. 2 (1998): 260.

41. Brian Massumi, *A User's Guide to Capitalism and Schizophrenia: Deviations from Deleuze and Guattari* (Cambridge, Mass.: Swerve/MIT Press, 1992), 31.

42. Sleigh, *Ant*, 148–52. The image of the beehive as the ideal political entity has long roots in various contexts. For example, the early proponents of liberal democracy and laissez-faire economics in the beginning of the eighteenth century already saw the beehive as a model for constitutional monarchy. Bernard Mandeville's 1705 *The Grumbling Hive; or, the Knaves Turn'd Honest* proposed such images of hives as ordered communities living in prosperity, ruled not by "wild Democracy" but by kings whose "power was circumscribed by Laws." In

addition, in another context, for the National Socialists of Second World War Germany the nation functioned as a superorganism where individuality was subordinated to the welfare of the people. Ramírez, *The Beehive Metaphor*, 19–24; quotes on 20.

43. Maeterlinck, *The Life of the Bee*, 24.

44. Eugene Thacker, "Networks, Swarms, Multitudes, Part Two," *CTheory*, May 18, 2004, http://www.ctheory.net/ (accessed April 10, 2009).

45. See Deleuze and Guattari, *A Thousand Plateaus*, 259. Also, Adorno and Horkheimer, although with differences, note the modern tendency to stabilize processes of nature in terms and concepts anthropomorphic. They see this as part of the Enlightenment's narcissistic tendency to make nature mirror humans. See Lippit, *Electric Animal*, 78–79.

46. Massumi writes on the relation of affects (as intensities) and singularities. Both are "critical points," or "turning point(s) at which a physical system paradoxically embodies multiple and normally mutually exclusive potentials, only one of which is 'selected.' 'Phase space' could be seen as a diagrammatic rendering of the dimension of the virtual. The organization of multiple levels that have different logics and temporal organizations, but are locked in resonance with each other and recapitulate the same event in divergent ways, recalls the fractal ontology and nonlinear causality underlying theories of complexity." Massumi, *Parables for the Virtual*, 32–33. This is also how Sanford Kwinter has approached the modern (futurist) architecture of (especially) Antonio Sant'Elia; in his designs, space turns from a hierarchical ordering of elements according to stable building blocks to a mosquito cloud–like centerless, groundless becoming in which space is more akin to that of an intensive field. As Kwinter notes, space is here closer to "hydrodynamics and laminar flows than . . . statics, metrics, or the physics of solids." Sanford Kwinter, *Architectures of Time: Toward a Theory of the Event in Modernist Culture* (Cambridge, Mass.: MIT Press, 2002), 92. The centers and flows of the architectures are shifting and distributed across the milieu, where the whole complex becomes a swarming assemblage instead of a solid building. Here architecture becomes a distributed organism of a sort, not a unity but a pulsating "cloud."

47. Deleuze and Guattari, *A Thousand Plateaus*, 367–74. Deleuze and Guattari also mark the importance of Bergson's separation between modes of intelligence and modes of intuition. Indeed, Bergson's ideas in *An Introduction to Metaphysics* do offer a similar way of distinguishing between the science of analysis (gridding, predefined concepts, and forms) and intuition (placing oneself inside the object in order to track its singularities).

48. Kwinter, *Architectures of Time*.

49. Manuel DeLanda, "Deleuze and the Genesis of Form," available online

at http://artnode.se/artorbit/issue1/f_deleuze/f_deleuze_delanda.html (accessed January 13, 2009).

50. Such discourses had specific appeal to engineers such as Charles Janet (1849–1932), who spent time observing wasp lives (*Observations sur les guêpes*, 1903). As Sleigh explains, for Janet, optimization was a process without one agency behind it—a certain force of the assemblage connecting on its own. Charlotte Sleigh, *Six Legs Better: A Cultural History of Myrmecology* (Baltimore, Md.: Johns Hopkins University Press, 2007), 57–58.

51. Maeterlinck, *The Life of the Bee*, 82. "'Again, it has been demonstrated that, by making the bottoms of the cells to consist of three planes meeting in a point, there is a saving of material and labor in no way inconsiderable. The bees, as if acquainted with these principles of solid geometry, follow them most accurately. It is a curious mathematical problem at what precise angle the three planes which compose the bottom of a cell ought to meet, in order to make the greatest possible saving, or the least expense of material and labor. This is one of the problems which belong to the higher parts of mathematicians.'"

52. Ibid., 84. Maeterlinck notes, however, that several entomologists have also disagreed, among them Kirby and Spence.

53. Thacker, "Biophilosophy for the Twenty-first Century," 132–42.

54. Thacker, "Networks, Swarms, Multitudes, Part Two."

55. "Insect Swarms," *Science*, September 15, 1893, 151.

56. Claire Preston, *Bee* (London: Reaktion, 2006), 139.

57. See Lippit, *Electric Animal*, 13.

58. Maeterlinck, *The Life of the Bee*, 27.

59. The bees' swarming becomes in Maeterlinck's prose an *event*, one related to clouds passing, a mystery that is pinpointed to a certain time and place but at the same time overflows the explanatory contexts. As Deleuze and Guattari write, "Climate, wind, season, hour are not of another nature than the things, animals, or people that populate them, follow them, sleep and awaken with them. This should be read without a pause: the animal-stalks-at-five-o'clock. The becoming-evening, becoming-night of an animal, blood nuptials. Five o'clock is this animal! This animal is this place!" Deleuze and Guattari, *A Thousand Plateaus*, 263. Bodies are considered in such an ethological perspective not as carriers of predefined capacities or characteristics but as potentials that actualize in interaction with other bodies. "At most, we may distinguish assemblage haecceities (a body considered only as longitude and latitude) and interassemblage haecceities, which also mark the potentialities of becoming within each assemblage (the milieu of intersection of the longitudes and latitudes). But the two are strictly inseparable" (263–64).

60. Maeterlinck, *The Life of the Bee*, 31.

61. "Vast Swarms of Locusts," *New York Times,* February 16, 1896. For another typical newspaper story, originally from the *London Times,* see "A Destructive Insect," *New York Times,* August 26, 1880. Also consider this short newspaper description from 1903, which could as easily be from a much later science-fiction film: "The northwest part of this city [New Bedford] is suffering from an invasion never known before. Myriads of insects have suddenly appeared, and houses, barns, fences, and sidewalks and streets are literally alive with them. In some cases the insects are so numerous that it is almost impossible to tell the color of the houses." "Flies Invade New Bedford," *New York Times,* June 9, 1903. Or this one: "They Come in Swarms," *New York Times,* October 19, 1894. The article focuses on germs but underlines their dangers with a reference to insects: "If you have ever seen a swarm of bees, you will realize how many insects it is possible to get within a small space. When you stop to think, though, that there are a million insects in an atom of air as large as the head of a pin, you will be able to understand what germs are."

62. Charlotte Sleigh, "Empire of the Ants: H. G. Wells and Tropical Entomology," *Science as Culture* 10, no. 1 (2001): 46.

63. Rodgers, *Debugging the Link,* 87.

64. Kelly, *Out of Control,* 11–12.

65. William Morton Wheeler, "The Ant Colony as an Organism," *Journal of Morphology* 22, no. 2 (2005): 307–25. For Wheeler, the ant colony was an individuated actant comparable to a cell or a person due to its ability to maintain "its identity in space, resisting dissolution and, as a general rule, any fusion with other colonies of the same or alien species" (310).

66. Sleigh, *Six Legs Better,* 70–71.

67. William Morton Wheeler, "Emergent Evolution and the Social," *Science,* November 5, 1926, 433. In a short text, "Contemporary Organicists," Wheeler also listed research that dealt with or commented on ideas of emergence. According to Wheeler, the idea that an organism as a whole is more than the sum of its parts could already be tracked in the early work of such writers as G. E. Stahl (1660–1734), J. C. Reil (1759–1813), and C. A. Rudolphi (1771–1832). Wheeler discussed more closely nineteenth-century physiologists du Bois-Reymond and Claude Bernard, both of whom marked the strange reality of the organism—constituted of material particles yet differing from the world outside this singular organism. For example, in *Introduction to the Study of Experimental Medicine* (1865) Bernard presented this assembling as a process of summoning virtual elements that otherwise would remain imperceptible: "In a word, when we unite physiological elements, properties appear which were imperceptible in the separate elements." Quoted in Wheeler, "Contemporary Organicists," in *Emergent Evolution and the Social* (London: Kegan Paul, Trench, Trubner, 1927), 44.

68. Kelly, *Out of Control*, 12.

69. C. Lloyd Morgan, *Emergent Evolution* (London: Williams and Norgate, 1927), 22. For a critical contemporary evaluation of Morgan's idea, see Flora I. MacKinnon, "The Meaning of 'Emergent' in Lloyd Morgan's 'Emergent Evolution,'" *Mind*, n.s. 33, no. 131 (July 1924): 311–15. MacKinnon noted that curiously Morgan problematically saw some forms of relatedness as noneffective, that is, as not changing the dynamics of a system they enter. MacKinnon wrote: "Space-time relatedness (24), quantitative relatedness as expressed in numbers (88), and relations of perceptual refexence in cognition (79), are noneffective, that is, 'they induce no change in the nature of the things which thus function as terms.' On the other hand physical, vital, and conscious relatedness are 'effective' in that they do induce changes which without them would not have occurred. Perception, for instance, is non-effective because although the perceived object is, as object, largely constituted by perception (41), the thing as it is in itself, a complex of matter and energy and their correlates, is not affected by that relation (77)" (314). But as Morgan notes (216), his interest was mainly in the reception of physical impressions of vision, the recipient organism, what he saw as corresponding to Whitehead's percipient event. Again, what is interesting is the autonomy of perception Morgan granted to nonhuman forms of "percipient events." He mentioned modern technical media of photographic perception, but thought it could perhaps be extended to other animal forms of life as well. See also Morgan's answer to Mackinnon: C. Lloyd Morgan, "Emergent Evolution," *Mind*, n.s. 34, no. 133 (January 1925): 70–74.

70. Morgan, *Emergent Evolution*, 64. With Morgan, however, there is a constant danger of succumbing to a quasi-mystical linearism in which the human being is the end of evolution. But Morgan did try, for example, to deny that there is any kind of end to this type of evolution and was reluctant to see God as a substancelike end point for emergent movements and differentiations.

71. Ibid., 69.

72. Wheeler, "Emergent Evolution and the Social," 434.

73. Ibid.

74. Ibid., 435.

75. See again Bergson's *An Introduction to Metaphysics.*

76. However, sociology beyond the human form was already practiced by Gabriel Tarde in his microsociology. Even though the lessons in zoology, Darwinism, and even the entomology of social insects were transported into sociological considerations—Herbert Spencer is naturally one of the key names associated with such ventures—more interesting are the parallels with the sociology of "primitive processes" of Tarde.

77. Sleigh, *Six Legs Better*, 72–73.

78. In 1902, Kropotkin wrote in *Mutual Aid*: "Sociability—that is, the need of the animal of associating with its like—the love of society for society's sake, combined with the 'joy of life,' only now begins to receive due attention from the zoologists. We know at the present time that all animals, beginning with ants, going on to the birds, and ending with the highest mammals, are fond of plays, wrestling, running after each other, trying to capture each other, teasing each other, and so on. And while many plays are, so to speak, a school for the proper behaviour of the young in mature life, there are others, which, apart from their utilitarian purposes, are, together with dancing and singing, mere manifestations of an excess of forces—'the joy of life,' and a desire to communicate in some way or another with other individuals of the same or of other species—in short, a manifestation of *sociability proper,* which is a distinctive feature of all the animal world." Peter Kropotkin, *Mutual Aid: A Factor of Evolution* (London: Freedom Press, 1987), 58–59.

79. Wheeler, "Emergent Evolution and the Social," 436.

80. Grosz, *Time Travels,* 140. As Grosz notes, drawing on Bergson, this phenomenal and primordial intensity is beyond the calculable: the Bergsonian duration, or virtual.

81. Thacker, "Biophilosophy for the Twenty-first Century," 135.

82. Eugene Thacker, "Networks, Swarms, Multitudes, Part One," *CTheory,* May 18, 2004, http://www.ctheory.net/ (accessed April 10, 2009).

3. TECHNICS OF NATURE AND TEMPORALITY

1. Thacker, "Networks, Swarms, Multitudes, Part One."

2. See Parikka, *Digital Contagions,* 285–95.

3. See Mullarkey, *Bergson and Philosophy,* 63–67.

4. Henri Bergson, *Matter and Memory,* trans. Nancy Margaret Paul and W. Scott Palmer (Mineola, N.Y.: Dover, 2004), 275. Also, for C. Lloyd Morgan the paradigm of emergence seems to have been inherently a temporal one—in contrast to the mechanistic-spatial ways of understanding interaction of entities where only mixtures result. Morgan, *Emergent Evolution,* 8.

5. Brian Massumi, *Parables for the Virtual,* 16, 258 n. 11.

6. Ibid., 276.

7. This resonates with Robert Hinde's notion of ethology and species diversity as means of solving problems. "A number of ethological concepts refer, like 'bridge', to the solution of a problem, but not to a particular means to an end. In this they resemble terms like 'leg' or 'eye': there is no suggestion that the legs of caterpillars or cows, or the eyes of ants and antelopes, involve similar structures." Robert A. Hinde, *Ethology: Its Nature and Relations with Other Sciences*

(New York: Oxford University Press, 1982), 20. Ethology presents itself here, then, as a science of variation of functions and solutions to problems posed by nature.

8. See Mullarkey's point concerning Bergson: "Organisms should not be regarded as natural kinds but as collections or nexuses of different tendencies, for no species, genus or kingdom uniquely possesses any one characteristic" (*Bergson and Philosophy,* 65). Elizabeth Grosz has also recently used Bergsonian ideas to come up with neomaterialist ways of understanding cultural reality. As Grosz noted in an interview: "Nature or materiality have no identity in the sense that they are continually changing, continually emerging as new. Once we have a dynamic notion of nature, then culture cannot be seen as that which animates nature. Nature is already animated, and culture borrows its energy from nature." Kontturi and Tiainen, "Feminism, Art, Deleuze, and Darwin," 248.

9. Thacker, "Networks, Swarms, Multitudes, Part Two."

10. See Michael Halewood, "A. N. Whitehead, Information and Social Theory," *Theory, Culture, and Society* 22, no. 6 (2005): 73–94; Michael Halewood, "On Whitehead and Deleuze: The Process of Materiality," *Configurations* 13, no. 1 (Winter 2005): 63–64.

11. Gilles Deleuze, *The Fold,* trans. Tom Conley (Minneapolis: University of Minnesota Press, 1993), 20.

12. A. N. Whitehead, *Process and Reality: Corrected Edition,* ed. David Ray Griffin and Donald W. Sherburne (New York: Free Press, 1978), 28, 88.

13. Ibid., 88.

14. Erin Manning elaborates Whitehead in the context of movement and dance in her *Relationscapes: Movement, Art, Philosophy* (Cambridge, Mass.: MIT Press, 2009), 66–68.

15. Claire Colebrook, "The Sense of Space: On the Specificity of Affect in Deleuze and Guattari," *Postmodern Culture* 15, no. 1 (September 2004), http://www3.iath.virginia.edu/pmc/ (accessed April 10, 2009). This resonates with the Bergsonian conviction that there is no life in general and that evolution is not a neat form of progress but a messy affair of disparities, failures, and deviations. In this sense, against Spencer, for example, we should note that biophilosophy should not gather the pieces from the already evolved and extrapolate based on that but should rather find the cuts and setbacks inherent in life. Mullarkey, *Bergson and Philosophy,* 65–67.

16. See Johnston, *The Allure of Machinic Life,* 337–84.

17. Steven Shaviro, *Without Criteria: Kant, Whitehead, Deleuze, and Aesthetics* (Cambridge, Mass.: MIT Press, 2009), 40–41.

18. William James, *Essays in Radical Empiricism* (Mineola, N.Y.: Dover, 2003), 37. James also shares the primacy of temporality as a defining ontologi-

cal feature, connected here to the reality of relations. James saw experience as a "process in time, whereby innumerable particular terms lapse and are super-seded by others that follow upon them by transitions which, whether disjunc-tive or conjunctive in content, are themselves experiences, and must in general be accounted as real as the terms which they relate" (33).

19. Edmund Husserl, *Cartesian Meditations: An Introduction to Phenome-nology,* trans. Dorion Cairns (The Hague: Martinus Nijhoff, 1982), 26. To be fair, here we do not have the possibility of engaging as thoroughly in phe-nomenology as we should. Instead of seeing Husserl as reducing the world to a determined apriority of the transcendantal ego, we see that he makes interest-ing references concerning the nature of the "infinity of apriori forms": "The universal Apriori pertaining to a transcendental ego as such is an eidetic form, which contains an infinity of forms, an infinity of apriori types of actualities and potentialities of life, along with the objects constitutable in a life as objects actually existing" (74).

20. Grosz, *Time Travels,* 133. Perhaps Charles Darwin could also be seen as a proponent of "ethological experimentation" in his focus on nature as an ex-perimenting force that is embedded in a complex web of interdependency. See Hans-Jörg Rheinberger and Peter McLaughlin, *Journal of the History of Biology* 17, no. 3 (Fall 1984): 345–68. Such an interpretation might allow us to think of nature as a probehead of a kind, as a *natura naturans* in Spinozian terminology—probing for "what works" instead of acting due to innate laws of transformation, something that Darwin himself argued in *The Variation of Animals and Plants under Domestication.* We can see nature as acting for Darwin as a patchwork mechanism, governed not by laws of physics or physiology but by specific eco-logical laws in which adaptation is always a relative enterprise with a remainder, a surplus, which leaves out the possibility of further change. See Rheinberger and McLaughlin, "Darwin's Experimental Natural History," 359, 366.

21. Whitehead acknowledges Lloyd Morgan's importance for his *Science and the Modern World* (New York: Mentor, 1925).

22. Related to this idea, see Stengers's explication of the notion of White-head's abstractions. Isabelle Stengers, "A Constructivist Reading of Process and Reality," *Theory, Culture, and Society* 25, no. 4 (2008): 91–110.

23. Jakob von Uexküll, "An Introduction to Umwelt," *Semiotica* 134, no. 1/4 (2001): 109. However, Steven Shaviro provides an important note regarding Kant and his Third Critique, whereby, according to Shaviro, radical ideas of affect and singularity are introduced. Hence, this Third Critique is of special importance when reading A. N. Whitehead and perhaps also Uexküll. Shaviro, "Without Criteria," in *Sensorium: Aesthetics, Art, Life,* ed. Barbara Bolt et al. (Newcastle, England: Cambridge Scholars Press, 2007), 2–14.

24. See Crary, *Techniques of the Observer*, 92. Cf. Jakob von Uexküll, *Theoretische Biologie*, 2nd ed. (Frankfurt: Suhrkamp, 1973), 7–11; 174–79. Uexküll appreciates Müller as proposing the animal not as a machine but as an autonomous entity, stretched between its specific energies and the perception of the environment.

25. Uexküll, *Theoretische Biologie*, 70.

26. See Shaviro, "Without Criteria," 10.

27. Colebrook, "The Sense of Space," 32.

28. Georges Canguilhem, "The Living and Its Milieu," trans. John Savage, *Grey Room*, no. 3 (2001): 16. In this presentation, originating in 1946–1947, Canguilhem wrote about the central place occupied by the concept of milieu in understanding living systems. However, he notes the strong roots the concept has in mechanistic theories, originating from Newton's physics, where milieu was the needed mediating fluid that explained the possibility of action from distance. Here we see the concept's interesting resonance with the idea of media. Also, Uexküll refers to Loeb. For Uexküll, there is no direct reflexive link between milieu and an animal; the animal has always to perceive the impulse from its environment. Uexküll, *Theoretische Biologie*, 327–29. On the history of ethology, with a special emphasis on the contested sites of observing behavior from Frédéric Cuvier at the end of the eighteenth century to Niko Tingbergen at the middle of the twentieth, when the field of ethology was more officially established, see Richard W. Burkhardt Jr., "Ethology, Natural History, the Life Sciences, and the Problem of Place," *Journal of the History of Biology* 32 (1999): 489–508.

29. William Morton Wheeler, "'Natural History,' 'Œcology' or 'Ethology'?" *Science*, June 1902, 971–76.

30. Adolf Portmann, "Vorwort: Ein Wegbereiter der neuen Biologie," in *Streifzüge durch die Umwelten von Tieren und Menschen*, by Jakob von Uexküll and Georg Kriszat (Hamburg: Rowohlt, 1956), 8–9. Konrad Lorenz and Niko Tingbergen, the key founders of ethology, have been described as key critics of reductive, structure-oriented models for the explanation of living entities. See Hinde, *Ethology*, 30.

31. Jakob von Uexküll and Georg Kriszat, *Streifzüge durch die Umwelten von Tieren und Menschen* (Hamburg: Rowohlt, 1956; trans. *A Foray into the Worlds of Animals and Humans* [Minneapolis: University of Minnesota Press, 2010]), 24. The functional cycle, or circle, functions as a double articulation, "the two arms of a forceps (receptor and effector)." Irenäus Eibl-Eibesfeldt, *Ethology: The Biology of Behavior*, trans. Erich Klinghammer (New York: Holt, Rinehart and Winston, 1970), 6. Meaning (in the sense of significance) is the product of this double articulation, a grasping of the world that can be understood not as a mental operation but as a very material event, of affects.

32. Uexküll, *Streifzüge*, 28–29. Giorgio Agamben, *The Open: Man and Animal*, trans. Kevin Attell (Stanford, Calif.: Stanford University Press, 2004), 47.

33. Uexküll, "An Introduction to Umwelt," 108. For Heidegger, even if the bee is able to coordinate itself with the help of the sun, it does not perceive the sun but is merely captivated by it, interlocked in a functional closed system, so to speak. Martin Heidegger, *The Fundamental Concepts of Metaphysics: World, Finitude, Solitude*, trans. William McNeill and Nicholas Walker (Bloomington: Indiana University Press, 1995), 241–47. Here Heidegger drew on E. Radl's 1905 study on "animal phototropism," *Untersuchungen über den Phototropismus der Tiere*.

34. Samuel Butler, "The Mechanical Creation," *Reasoner* (London), July 1, 1865. Quoted in George B. Dyson, *Darwin among the Machines* (Cambridge, Mass.: Helix, 1997), 25.

35. Richard le Gallienne, "The Homer of the Insects," *New York Times,* January 8, 1922. Good examples are the views of Professor Riley, presented in the *Washington Post* in 1894. According to Riley, insects possessed powers of sight, touch, taste and smell that "could not be compared with the like senses in man, for they undoubtedly possessed others which man does not have." For example, the ant was presented as having superior forms of communication, intuition, and orientation. Riley also hinted at a posthuman vision: "In closing Prof. Riley indulged a dream, which he said he is fond of, in speculating what other forms of animal could surpass man and drive him from the face of the earth if endowed with his intelligence. He thought it was not impossible that on some other sphere other organisms with a brain like that of man ruled supreme and were far more powerful than is man. He would have eyes of telescopic power, organs more specialized, wings for flight, power to suspend life and take it up again at will, and other limbs, which would fit him for more special acts. Such a creature could triumph over man and make the earth and the fullness his own." "Power of Insects," *Washington Post,* January 30, 1894. Such ideas were continued in twentieth-century science fiction, for example, in *Amazing Stories* and Frank R. Paul's cover art for the magazine. For a glimpse of his illustrations from the 1920s on, see the online archive at http://www.frankwu.com/paul1.html (accessed November 22, 2007).

36. See Väliaho, "Bodies Outside In," 7–19. It is as if the animal worlds have found their corresponding double in the awe the film camera inspired in certain avant-garde theorists and directors, such as Jean Epstein and Dziga Vertov. In addition to philosophy, both discourses, the biological and the cinematic, were keen on finding alternatives to the one-eyed Cartesian model. Such models of insects/technology proposed distributed subjectivities in which insects could function as new "eyes" to the world, and camera eyes (Vertov) produced similar

detachments from the phenomenological human being. For example, in 1926 Jean Epstein theorized this turn as one of becoming an "eye outside of the eye," the possibility that with new media technologies we could "escape the tyrannical egocentrism of our personal vision." Jean Epstein, "L'objectif lui-même," *Écrits sur le cinema 1* (1926), 128–29, quoted in Trond Lundemo, *The Intelligence of a Machine—Jean Epstein and a Philosophy of Cinema* (Stockholm: Svenska Filminstitutet, 2001), 18. New technologies discovered common ground with the developments in the arts (e.g., cubism) but also with animals as the equivalent of the breakout of single-eyed geometry. Gilles Deleuze, *Cinema 1: The Movement Image,* trans. Hugh Tomlinson and Barbara Habberjam (London: Continuum, 2005), 24–25. In Deleuze's reading of cinema and overturning of phenomenology, Bergsonian ideas of distributed, acentered perception are seen as fundamental to this media technology—and also a wider ontological stance of the universe as a metacinema. Deleuze turned Bergson's own reluctance to embrace cinema into an interest in the eye that is distributed from the I to things themselves. See Keith Ansell-Pearson, *Germinal Life: The Difference and Repetition of Deleuze and Guattari* (London: Routledge, 1999), 71.

37. For example, William Patten, a professor of zoology who in 1900 wrote "The Organs of Sense and Their Limitations," in a positivist manner believed in man's ability to come up with technological equivalents of sense perception. He wrote of the new ways of measuring the wave movements that form the basics of our perception and added: "It is well known that a tuning fork will vibrate in unison with certain air waves that beat against it, provided it has the structure and dimensions suitable for that kind of wave; to other waves that vibrate a little faster or slower it will remain forever a deaf-mute. If we had unlimited ingenuity and command of materials, it would be possible to construct a great many kinds of tuning forks, each of which would vibrate in unison with some one kind of wave movement, whether it were a high or a low musical tone, a rad or a blue wave of light. Each tuning fork would, so to speak, lead its own isolated life, moved to activity by those changes only to which its own particular structure compelled response." Patten expressed a belief in the correspondence of physiological structure to the abilities of sensation inherent in the physiological research of the time. Yet he remained very suspicious that other animals would have much different spheres of sensation—despite "strange stories told of the wonderful senses of the lower animals." William Patten, "The Organs of Sense and Their Limitations," *New York Times,* March 18, 1900.

38. Agamben, *The Open,* 39. As Agamben writes, the tick, *Ixodes ricinus,* "constitutes a high point of modern antihumanism and should be read next to *Ubu Roi* and *Monsieur Teste*" (45).

39. Heidegger, *The Fundamental Concepts of Metaphysics,* 215.

40. More generally, the whole turn in biology toward ethological themes, as William Morton Wheeler argued years earlier, can be understood as a realization of the limited perspective that physiological research and zoology, for example, had offered. See Wheeler, "'Natural History,' 'Œcology' or 'Ethology'?" 971–76. Wheeler delineated the difference between a botanical approach and a zoological approach to nature as follows: "While botanists and zoologists alike are deeply interested in the same fundamental problem of adaptivity, they differ considerably in their attitude, owing to a difference in the scope of their respective subjects. The botanist is interested in the effects of the living and inorganic environment on organisms which are relatively simple in their responses. The zoologist, however, is more interested in the expressions of a centralized principle represented by the activity of the nervous system or some more general and obscure 'archaeus' which regulates growth, regeneration and adaptation, carrying the type onward to a harmonious development of its parts and functions, often in apparent opposition to or violation of the environmental conditions" (974). Ethology is seen as continuing certain ecological emphases, as a science of conditions of existence and relations.

41. Jakob von Uexküll, "Bedeutungslehre," in *Streifzüge durch die Umwelten von Tieren und Menschen,* 137.

42. Bergson, *Creative Evolution,* 218–24.

43. Heidegger, *The Fundamental Concepts of Metaphysics,* 222. On Heidegger and his philosophy in relation to animality, see Matthew Calarco, *Zoographies: The Question of the Animal from Heidegger to Derrida* (New York: Columbia University Press, 2008), 15–53.

44. Heidegger, *The Fundamental Concepts of Metaphysics,* 236.

45. Ibid., 224. Interestingly, Heidegger used several examples from primitive animal life. He used protoplasmic creatures such as amoebas in his philosophy to demonstrate how a capacity is a primary force that gives rise to organs—as in the case of these single-celled creatures who can turn a mouth into a stomach and then into an intestine and finally into an anal tract, an example he picked up from Uexküll (224). Heidegger also referred to insect eyes, whose essence is not their physiological structure but their unraveling, unfolding with the environment (230–31). However, animals are captured in their environmental relationship and are not able to break out of this essential *Benommenheit* (239). For a critique of Heidegger's idea of the animal as poor in the world, see Ansell-Pearson, *Germinal Life: The Difference and Repetition of Deleuze and Guattari* (London: Routledge, 1999), 115–22.

46. Uexküll, "Bedeutungslehre," 119.

47. See Irenäus Eibl-Eibesfeldt, *Ethology: The Biology of Behavior,* trans. Erich Klinghammer (New York: Holt, Rinehart, and Winston, 1920), 1. For Eibl-Eibesfeldt,

however, ethology is a science of slowing down, of transforming intensive temporal movements into spatial structures "by means of motion picture film and sound tape if they are to become a preparation and a remaining document" (1).

48. Uexküll, "Bedeutungslehre," 118–19.

49. Ibid., 131.

50. Ibid., 132.

51. Ibid., 120–21. This example recapitulates the 1773 observation of H. S. Reimarus, who attributed a certain "artistic drive" to nature, expressed in the mutual becomings of animals: "How do the spider and the ant lion go about finding means of supporting themselves? Both can do no other than live by catching flying and creeping insects; although they are slower in their own movements than is the prey which they seek out. But the former already felt within the ability and the drive to artfully weave a net, before she as much as had seen or tasted a gnat, fly, or bee; and now that one has been caught in her net, she knows how to secure and devour it. . . . The ant lion, on the other hand, who can hardly move in the dry sand, mines a hollow tunnel by burrowing backward, in expectation of ants and other worms which tumble down, or buries them with a rain of sand which it throws up in order to cover them and bring them into his reach. . . . Since these animals possess by nature such skills in their voluntary actions which serve the preservation of themselves and their kind, and where many variations are possible; so they possess by nature certain innate skills—a great number of their artistic drives are performed without error at birth without external experiences, education, or example and are thus inborn naturally and inherited." Yet the writer interestingly notes that despite this innateness and determination, these animals must have a certain dynamism; otherwise they would remain examples of mechanistic repetition: "For if everything and all of their natural powers were to be determined completely, that is, would possess the highest degree of determination, they would be lifeless and mechanical rather than endowed with the powers of living animals." Reimarus, quoted in Eibl-Eibesfeldt, *Ethology*, 5.

52. Agamben, *The Open*, 42.

53. Jakob von Uexküll, *Niegeschaute Welten* (Munich: Paul List, 1957). Of course, Uexküll's ideas have problematic sides as well, for instance, a certain potential for solipsism in his emphasis on the closedness of the perceptual world (which, however can be addressed with the view on the dynamics of perception that unfolds in time). Also, the idea that there is a predefined score governing the actions of an entity could lead to problematic connotations if not read as expressing a virtual tendency.

54. Ansell-Pearson, *Viroid Life*, 118.

55. Deleuze and Guattari, *A Thousand Plateaus*, 51.

56. Ibid., 51–52. For example, for Marey, in analyzing animal movements the key question resides between the articulations of structure and those of function, where morphogenesis is primarily considered an anatomical and physiological process. Yet Marey notes the importance of tracking the particular speed of every animal, of finding its specific speed and slowness, so to speak. See "Locomotion comparée chez les différénts animaux," *La Nature,* 21st year, second half, nos. 1044–69 (1893): 215.

57. Gilles Deleuze, *Spinoza: Practical Philosophy,* trans. Robert Hurley (San Francisco: City Lights Books, 1988), 122–23. Hence, in the insect world we have very concrete examples of durations and slownesses that exceed those of the human. Consider, for example, the already mentioned tick, introduced by Uexküll, which was kept isolated for eighteen years. Or, for example, the often discussed "seventeen-year locust" (although not a locust but a cicada), which, as the name implies, is "emancipated" every seventeen years. Most of its development (from larva to nymph) takes place underground, and it shows up for only a couple of weeks to mate. Again, this cycle is opened up with a reference to mathematics and the duration of astronomic cycles in order to underline the otherwise perhaps incomprehensible durational accuracy of the insects. As Raymond Ditmars wrote: "It was at the end of the sixteenth year that the most marvelous of events transpired. This was the preparation of millions to emerge from the soil. To say marvelous was to use a weak term, even with the assertion that here was a manifestation of instinct, if instinct it was, that was more amazing than the fulfillment of astronomical prophecies. The latter were along mathematical lines and *must* transpire if the planets continued to move, but with the cicada there were billions of lowly forms, scattered over every type of soil, where storms had raged on one, droughts had burned another, where cold 'waves' had rendered the soil as hard as granite to a yard in depth, or a belt of Southern country had been bathed in mild winter sun—no matter how varying the conditions throughout the seventeen years, if embraced within the area of the swarm, the toiling multitudes would appear from the earth on time." Raymond L. Ditmars, *Thrills of a Naturalist's Quest* (New York: Macmillan, 1932), 25. Also, one might find an early example of interest in animal behavior as the defining feature in the work of the famous entomologist René Antoine Ferchault de Réaumur (1683–1757). Radically different from other natural historians of his time, such as Jan Swammerdam, Réaumur was interested not in morphological classifications but in behavior and structuring as the defining feature of life. Here, instead of structure, he was interested in grouping together insects that "clothe themselves" or ones that "do not undergo a metamorphosis." For a brief overview of Réaumur, see William A. Smeaton, "Réaumur: Natural Historian and Pioneer of Applied Science," *Endeavour,* n.s. 7, no. 1 (1983): 38–40.

58. On James and Deleuze and Guattari's plane of immanence, see David Lapoujade, "From Transcendental Empiricism to Worker Nomadism: William James," *Pli* 9 (2000): 190–99.

59. H. Maxwell Lefroy, assisted by F. M. Howlett, *Indian Insect Life: A Manual of the Insects of the Plains (Tropical India)* (Calcutta: Thacker, Spink, 1909), 3, quoted in J. F. M. Clark, "The Complete Biography of Every Animal: Ants, Bees, and Humanity in Nineteenth-Century England," *Studies in History and Philosophy of Biological and Biomedical Sciences* 29, no. 2 (1998): 266–67. However, Clark focuses on the systematic anthropomorphization of insects in the nineteenth century.

60. Heidegger, *The Fundamental Concepts of Metaphysics*, 203–5.

61. As noted earlier, ethology as a science is also, of course, part of this "slowing down" of the intensity of the world. Eibl-Eibesfeldt, *Ethology*, 1.

62. The nonhuman temporal duration of nature was also for Darwin the factor, or force, that separated the human world of creation from natural creation. See John F. Cornell, "Analogy and Technology in Darwin's Vision of Nature," *Journal of the History of Biology* 17, no. 3 (Fall 1984): 333. However, Cornell emphasizes Darwin's endeavor as one of anthropomorphization of the natural world.

63. Kontturi and Tiainen, "Feminism, Art, Deleuze, and Darwin," 253. Braidotti notes that the insect does not have a nervous system that could act as the site of memory, inscription, and hence institutions, being perhaps a perfect Nietzschean animal of forgetting. Braidotti, *Metamorphoses*, 149.

64. Deleuze, *Spinoza*, 124.

65. Cf. Deleuze and Guattari, *A Thousand Plateaus*, 257.

66. Heidegger, in his reading of Uexküll and his metaphysical meditations on animals, turns toward this closedness, an idea that an animal can open toward its captivation, its structuration, only with its environment, which it cannot bypass. See Heidegger, *The Fundamental Concepts of Metaphysics*, 257–60.

67. See Dyson, *Darwin among the Machines*, 15–34.

68. Samuel Butler, *Erewhon* (London: William Brendon and Son, 1918), 253.

69. Luciana Parisi, *Abstract Sex: Philosophy, Bio-Technology, and the Mutations of Desire* (London: Continuum, 2004), 186.

70. Ibid.

71. For an elaboration of the aesthetics of novelty in media ecologies with a Whiteheadian twist, see Matthew Fuller, *Media Ecologies: Materialist Energies in Art and Technoculture* (Cambridge, Mass.: MIT Press, 2005).

72. Ansell-Pearson, *Germinal Life*, 143. Deleuze and Guattari never tired of emphasizing the dynamics of machinic ontology, in which nothing works if it is not plugged in—and the plugging in, the movements of attaching and detach-

ing, are what constitute the parts. Deleuze and Guattari, *A Thousand Plateaus,* 4. Cf. Heidegger, who criticized Darwin for an overly rigid view of adaptation. There is no organism that adapts to a preexisting environment, Heidegger wrote; rather, the two enter into a mutual relationship, "the organism adapts a particular environment *into* it in each case, so to speak." Here, Heidegger's emphasis resonates with the machinic ontology of Deleuze and Guattari. Heidegger, *The Fundamental Concepts of Metaphysics,* 264. Italics in the original.

73. Ansell-Pearson, *Germinal Life,* 136.

74. See Lippit, *Electric Animal,* 100. Lippit argues that Bergson's cinematograph, Freud's unconscious, and ideas of genetics are continuing the idea of a radical nonhuman temporality that emerged with Darwin's theory of evolution. Cf. Ansell-Pearson, who argues that there is, however, an anthropomorphic bias in Darwin's idea of natural selection. Pearson, *Germinal Life,* 112–14. In "Analogy and Technology in Darwin's Vision of Nature," John F. Cornell analyzes Darwin's early interest in animal breeding and demonstrates how it affected his views of natural selection as well, consequently transporting a certain anthropomorphic bias into his view of nature.

75. Grosz, *The Nick of Time,* 111.

76. Here I am referring to Rodney Brook's insect robotics and, for example, to Craig Reynolds's boids programs from the end of the 1980s. See also Johnston, "A Future for Autonomous Agents," 473–516. Francisco J. Varela, "The Reenchantment of the Concrete," in *Incorporations,* ed. Jonathan Crary and Sanford Kwinter (New York: Zone Books, 1992), 320–38. Luciana Parisi discussed Butler in her mapping of the variations of symbiotic sex, alternative modes of evolution, and reproduction in the context of biotechnological emphasis on bacterial becomings. See Parisi, *Abstract Sex,* 185–87.

77. Whitehead, *Process and Reality,* 108.

78. Nonlinear media archaeology has been preeminently proposed by Wolfgang Ernst in "Dis/continuities: Does the Archive Become Metaphorical in Multi-Media Space?" in *New Media, Old Media: A History and Theory Reader,* ed. Wendy Hui Kyong Chun and Thomas Keenan (New York: Routledge, 2006), 105–23.

79. Heidegger, *The Fundamental Concepts of Metaphysics,* 234. Italics in original.

80. See Stengers, "A Constructivist Reading of Process and Reality," 95–96.

81. See Fuller, *Media Ecologies.*

82. Moira Gatens, "Feminism as 'Password': Re-thinking the 'Possible' with Spinoza and Deleuze," *Hypatia* 15, no. 2 (Spring 2000): 63. See also Gatens, "Through a Spinozist Lens: Ethology, Difference, Power," in *Deleuze: A Critical Reader,* ed. Paul Patton (Cambridge, Mass.: Blackwell, 1996), 162–87.

83. Eric Alliez, *The Signature of the World: What Is Deleuze and Guattari's Philosophy?* trans. Eliot Ross Albert and Alberto Toscano (New York: Continuum, 2004), 76. Alliez sketches elements, drawing from Deleuze and Guattari, Whitehead, and Raymond Ryuer, among others, for such a nonphenomenological approach to the becomings of science, art, and philosophy, which would recognize the earth as the "ground" of thought and sensation. Thought and sensation are contracted from the earth, which is the primary ontological *natura naturans,* and where concepts, affects, and percepts are about tracking the compositions, speeds, and slownesses of various expressions of the earth.

84. Alliez, *The Signature of the World,* 76.

85. See John Rajchman, *The Deleuze Connections* (Cambridge, Mass.: MIT Press, 2000), 132.

86. Uexküll, *Theoretische Biologie,* 38–39.

87. See Tom Greaves, "A Silent Dance: Eco-Political Compositions after Uexküll's Umwelt Biology," in *An [Un]Likely Alliance: Thinking Environment[s] with Deleuze/Guattari,* ed. Bernd Herzogenrath (Newcastle, England: Cambridge Scholars Publishing, 2008), 98–103.

88. Deleuze and Guattari, *A Thousand Plateaus,* 367–74.

89. Mark Hansen, "Becoming as Creative Involution? Contextualizing Deleuze and Guattari's Biophilosophy," *Postmodern Culture* 11, no. 1 (September 2000), http://www3.iath.virginia.edu/pmc/ (accessed April 10, 2009).

90. See Massumi, *Parables for the Virtual.*

91. Cf. Alliez, *The Signature of the World,* 69–84.

4. METAMORPHOSIS, INTENSITY, AND DEVOURING SPACE

1. Richard Marsh, *The Beetle: A Mystery* (Ware, England: Wordsworth, 2007), 111.

2. Sanford Kwinter, *Architectures of Time: Toward a Theory of the Event in Modernist Culture* (Cambridge, Mass.: MIT Press, 2002), 110.

3. William Morton Wheeler, "A Review of Die Metamorphose der Insekten," *Science* 29 (March 5, 1909): 384.

4. This did not, however, stop at least one review in 1831 of the earlier Rennie book *Insect Architecture* from making natural theological analogies between Rennie's analyses of the world of humans and the perfected design by deity. Despite the acknowledged functional uses of the knowledge of animals for "commerce, the arts, medicine, and domestic economy," the more fundamental teachings of insects were to be found through these reflections. The writer even quoted a proverb: "Find tongues in trees, books in living brooks, Sermons in stones, and good in every thing." Review of *The Insect Architecture, Magazine*

of Natural History 6 (1831): 40–41. According to the review, *The Insect Architecture* was distributed widely (with tens of thousands of copies) and hailed as a key popularization of insect research. As evinced by a number of natural theological teachings, God and his chain of being included the little beasts as well, which at times could even surpass in their capacities the human. William Paley's *Natural Theology; or, Evidences of the Existence and Attributes of the Deity* (1802) especially provided constant reference to the continuity from God to insects—and insects actually had their own special place: "But to return to insects. I think it is in this class of animals above all others, especially when we take in the multitude of species which the microscope discovers, that we are struck with what Cicero has called 'the *insatiable* variety of nature.'" William Paley, *Natural Theology; or, Evidences of the Existence and Attributes of the Deity,* 12th ed. (London: Printed for J. Faulder, 1809), http://darwin-online.org.uk/ (accessed April 20, 2009). Besides variation in enormous quantities, insects also proved inventive beings that came up with numerous solutions to problems of life, like breathing.

5. Harvey, quoted in James Rennie, *Insect Transformations* (Boston: Lilly and Wait, 1831), 289.

6. Kwinter, *Architectures of Time,* 110.

7. See Claudine Frank, "Introduction," in *The Edge of Surrealism: A Roger Caillois Reader,* trans. Claudine Frank and Camille Naish (Durham, N.C.: Duke University Press, 2003), 12.

8. Roger Caillois, "Letter to André Breton," in *The Edge of Surrealism,* 82–86.

9. See Ruth Markus, "Surrealism's Praying Mantis and Castrating Woman," *Woman's Art Journal* 21, no. 1 (Spring–Summer 2000): 33–39.

10. Linda Dalrymple Henderson, "The Fourth Dimension and Non-Euclidean Geometry in Modern Art: Conclusion," *Leonardo* 17, no. 3 (1984): 205.

11. Maurice Maeterlinck, *La vie de l'espace* (Paris: Eugène Fasquelle, 1928), 47–48.

12. Anne Friedberg, *The Virtual Window from Alberti to Microsoft* (Cambridge, Mass.: MIT Press, 2006), 118. See also Siegried Giedion, *Mechanization Takes Command* (New York: W. W. Norton, 1948), 360.

13. Jean Epstein, "Fernand Léger," in *Écrits sur le cinema tome 1 (1921–1947)* (Paris: Seghers, 1974), 115.

14. Jean Epstein, "L'intelligence d'une machine," in *Écrits sur le cinema tome 1,* 244; Gilles Deleuze, *Cinema 1: The Movement-Image,* trans. Hugh Tomlinson and Barbara Habberjam (London: Continuum, 2005), 25. In a way, as Sanford Kwinter argues, cinema embodies variations of perception. The problem of reconciling the two infinites of largeness (expressed via telescopy) and smallness (microscopy) presented a new ontological challenge to the unity of the world.

Similarly, much later, cinema and the technique of the montage presented a new perceptual world filled with "an infinity of different angles, an infinity of different distances, mise-en-scènes, perspectives, possible combinations with other objects, and positions in the chain of montage." Kwinter, *Architectures of Time,* 120. What is interesting is how the insect, as an object of the microscope, and later of photographic and cinematic vision, was a central figure in this variation of perception. Besides being the testing ground for new techniques of catching the "infinitely small," it was itself a vision machine that challenged the human eye.

15. Linda Dalrymple Henderson, "X Rays and the Quest for Invisible Reality in the Art of Kupka, Duchamp, and the Cubists," *Art Journal* 47, no. 4 (Winter 1998): 323.

16. Henderson, "The Fourth Dimension," 209. Italics mine.

17. Cited in Lippit, *Electric Animal,* 126. Italics in original. The idea that animals function as the forgotten part of the human being has been a recurring rubric in modern cultural theory. For example, Walter Benjamin referred to animals as "receptacles of the forgotten." See Kwinter, *Architectures of Time,* 174 n. 63. Rosi Braidotti provides another angle of approach to the neglected senses of the human being. What was a perversion in Freud's eyes is taken as a cue of "post-anthropocentric philosophy," that is, a cartography of new sensory realms beyond the visual—a cartography that is close to my aims in this book. In Braidotti's words: "The process of becoming-animal is connected to an expansion or creation of new sensorial and perceptive capacities or powers, which alter or stretch what a body can actually do. Nomadic thought actualizes different potentials in and of a body. In so doing, it is again attuned to our historical condition: for example, the superior olfactory capacity of dogs has been recognized in contemporary technological research. Smell has functioned as a potent indicator of well-being since antiquity. Nowadays it is being turned into a diagnostic tool and highly sophisticated 'electronic noses' are designed for diagnoses in medicine, as well as hygiene-control in the food industry." Braidotti, *Transpositions,* 103.

18. Deleuze and Guattari, *A Thousand Plateaus,* 260.

19. Lippit, *The Electric Animal,* 15.

20. Roger Caillois, "Surrealism as a World of Signs," in *The Edge of Surrealism,* 330. In addition, bestial worlds had already been touched years earlier by the poet Guillaume Apollinaire in his celebration of animal worlds: "Look at this lousy crowd / A thousand feet, a hundred eyes: / Rotifers and insects, mites / And microbes—all more wonderful / Than the seven wonders of the world / Or even Rosemonde's palace!" Guillaume Apollinaire, *Bestiary; or, The Parade of Orpheus,* trans. Pepe Karmel (Boston: David R. Godine, 1980), 26.

21. Consider Blossfeldt's words from 1932: "The plant may be described as

an architectural structure, shaped and designed ornamentally and objectively. Compelled in its fight for existence to build in a purposeful manner, it constructs the necessary and practical units for its advancement, governed by the laws familiar to every architect, and combines practicability and expediency in the highest form of art. Not only, then, in the world of art, but equally in the real of science, Nature is our best teacher." Karl Blossfeldt, *Art Forms in Nature,* 2nd series (London: A. Zwemmer, 1932), foreword.

22. "Jean Painlevé: La science au service d'une nouvelle vision du monde," *Thèses et mémoires en langue française sur les anarchismes,* April 4, 2007, http://raforum.info/these/spip.php?article135 (accessed April 20, 2009).

23. Frank, "Introduction to 'The Praying Mantis,'" in *The Edge of Surrealism,* 67.

24. See Gunning, "To Scan a Ghost: The Ontology of Mediated Vision," *Grey Room* 26 (Winter 2007): 95–96.

25. Friedrich Kittler's analysis of the Bram Stoker novel is also worth noting because it connects this vampyric tale to the emergence of the modern culture of technical media. Friedrich Kittler, "Draculas Vermächtnis," in *Draculas Vermächtnis: Technische Schriften* (Leipzig: Reclam , 1993), 11–57.

26. The notion of becoming is a central and complex idea that Deleuze and Guattari introduce in *A Thousand Plateaus.* They underline that the reality of the becomings is not constituted in the terms that are connected—for example, those of man becoming animal. Instead, what is real is the process of becoming itself, which "lacks a subject distinct from itself." Deleuze and Guattari, *A Thousand Plateaus,* 238. Becoming-animal is a process of creative involution that proceeds by alliances and the new assemblages produced by the pairings. Deleuze and Guattari's famous example is that of the wasp and the orchid. Becomings involve de- and reterritorializations of the terms involved. The process of alliances constitutes new blocs and relays that allow "a circulation of intensities" (10). The becoming-animal of the screen + animal is a new circuit that can be pinpointed in historical terms to a certain "phase" in the history of media technologies. This is why tracking such intensities of media technologies is a minoritarian approach to media history—a media archaeology of a kind. Patty Sotirin raises becomings as a central index of tendencies of life for Deleuze and Guattari. This index marks "what life does" as an active force of transversal powers that does not respect functional, organizational categories of royal science. It tracks the relations of bodies and their affects or the compositions a body might enter into. In this sense it refers to the molecular movements that are more transversal than molar planes. As Sotirin explains, all entities, roots, rocks, and insects, for example, do have their molar "insular configurations," but these molar definitions (such as body plans, functions, organs) do not sufficiently define what the body is capable of in a radical temporal framework.

See Sotirin, "Becoming-Woman," in *Gilles Deleuze: Key Concepts,* ed. Charles J. Stivale (Chesham, England: Acumen, 2005), 100. Incidentally, the notions of "mimicry" and masking are raised as key features of "play" as a cultural phenomenon both by Caillois in his book on games *(Les jeux et les hommes)* and even earlier, in 1938, by Johan Huizinga in his book *Homo Ludens: A Study of the Play Element in Culture* (Boston: Beacon Press, 1955). This aspect of play is intimately related to the tracking of the relations and thresholds of an entity and hence metamorphosis.

27. Walter Benjamin, "The Work of Art in the Age of Mechanical Reproduction," trans. Harry Zohn, in *Illuminations,* ed. Hannah Arendt (New York: Schocken Books, 1969), 235.

28. Ibid., 236.

29. Jean Epstein, "Le cinématographe vue de l'Etna," in *Écrits sur le cinéma,* tome 1, 134–35.

30. Erin Manning, "Grace Taking Form: Marey's Movement Machines," *Parallax* 14, no. 1 (2008): 85.

31. Väliaho, *The Moving Image,* 60–95.

32. Cf. Braidotti, *Transpositions,* 37.

33. Roger Caillois, "Mimicry and Legendary Psychasthenia," trans. Claudine Frank and Camille Naish, in *The Edge of Surrealism,* 96.

34. Ibid., 97.

35. Ibid., 99. Italics in the original.

36. Ibid., 100.

37. Ibid. Italics in the original. Here Caillois was referring to Minkowski's paper from the early 1930s titled "Le probléme du temps en psychopathologie" (The problem of time in psychopathology).

38. See Brian Massumi's ideas on the multiple dimensionality of body-in-movement in *Parables for the Virtual,* 204.

39. Denis Hollier, "Mimesis and Castration 1937," trans. William Rodarmor, *October* 31 (Winter 1984): 11.

40. See Roger Caillois, "The Praying Mantis: From Biology to Psychoanalysis," trans. Claudine Frank and Camille Naish, in *The Edge of Surrealism,* 81.

41. See Elizabeth Grosz, *Space, Time, and Perversion: Essays on the Politics of Bodies* (New York: Routledge, 1995), 200–201.

42. Caillois, "Mimicry and Legendary Psychasthenia," 99. Italics in the original.

43. Massumi, *Parables for the Virtual,* 191.

44. Hollier, argues, in *Mimesis and Castration,* 11–12, that Caillois emphasized the primacy of distinction (organism vs. environment) and was far from praising psychasthenia. This relates to a broader surrealist valorization of the

individual against the masses, a depreciation of the mass movements of the interwar period. The insect figure can be seen, then, as "registering" this tension between social insects and the more individual figures, such as the praying mantis found in Callois, Dali, and other surrealists. Jack J. Spector, *Surrealist Art and Writing 1919/1939: The Gold of Time* (Cambridge, England: Cambridge University Press, 1997), 152–53. Later, in 1958, Caillois noted, however briefly, that he did not regard the idea of returning to the inanimate as the key concern relevant to mimicry but wanted to focus more closely on the transrelations of insect mimicry and human simulacra. Roger Caillois, *Les jeux et les hommes: Le masque et le vertige* (Paris: Gallimard, 1967), 62–63 n. 1.

45. Manuel DeLanda, *Intensive Science and Virtual Philosophy* (London: Continuum, 2004), 72–73; James J. Gibson, *The Ecological Approach to Visual Perception* (Hillsdale, N.J.: Lawrence Erlbaum Associates, 1986).

46. Caillois, "Mimicry and Legendary Psychasthenia," 99.

47. Kwinter, *Architectures of Time*, 59.

48. Ibid., 60.

49. Bergson, *Matter and Memory*, 304.

50. Franz Kafka, "The Transformation," trans. Malcolm Pasley, in *The Transformation and Other Stories* (London: Penguin Books, 1992), 79.

51. Kwinter, *Architectures of Time*, 110–11.

52. Ibid.

53. In Kwinter's own words: "In Kafka, bodies are never personal, intimate objects but always public property; they are the surfaces through which so much communication and therefore social bonds are articulated.... The indifference and impassivity that accompanies sexual acts in Kafka merely literalizes the fact that the most intense bonds of connection and conjugation have already, historically, begun to take place at the expressive level of the human organism but to an ever greater degree at the level of the much more complex and global political and bureaucratic systems, of which individual men and women are mere points or relays" (ibid., 199).

54. Kwinter, *Architectures of Time*, 135–37.

55. Elizabeth Grosz, *Architecture from the Outside: Essays on Virtual and Real Space* (Cambridge, Mass.: MIT Press, 2001), 39. Italics in original.

56. Ibid.

57. Friedrich Kittler, in particular, in his earlier work insisted on the intimacy of the media technologies of modernity and Lacanian theory. See Friedrich Kittler, "Die Welt des Symbolischen—eine Welt der Maschine," in *Draculas Vermächtnis*, 58–80. See also Thomas Elsaesser, "Sigmund Freud as Media Theorist: Perception, Memory, and Data Management," in *Media Archaeologies*, ed. Erkki Huhtamo and Jussi Parikka (Berkeley: University of California Press, 2011).

58. Grosz, *Architecture*, 20–22.

59. Ibid., 38.

60. On subjectification and asignifying semiotics, see Guattari, *Chaosmosis*.

61. Mark B. N. Hansen, *Bodies in Code: Interfaces with Digital Media* (New York: Routledge, 2006), 126–37.

62. Jesper Juul, "A Dictionary of Video Game Theory," 2005, http://www .half-real.net/dictionary/ (accessed January 26, 2009).

63. Maaike Lauwaert, Joseph Wachelder, and Johan Van de Walle, "Frustrating Desire: On *Repens* and *Repositio,* or the Attractions and Distractions of Digital Games," *Theory, Culture, and Society* 24, no. 1 (2007): 89–108.

64. Caillois, *Les jeux et les hommes,* 61–62.

65. Ibid., 172–89. The temptation to read this as a version of sociobiological reductionism is clear, but one should not be fooled. Instead, we must remember Caillois's philosophical roots, which more clearly explain his insistence on the continuity between nature and culture. Although it stems from different ontological premises, I wish to underline the context of the book as part of recent theories of neomaterialism and the nature–culture continuum. In Caillois, the parallels between nature and culture stemmed from his ontological interest in the *Naturphilosophie* of romanticism. Caillois's idea of incorporating the ontological ideas from *Naturphilosophie,* a certain univocal ontology of continuity, as part of surrealism and a new scientific understanding of the world at the middle of the twentieth century, would in itself merit study. As Claudine Frank argues, Caillois's writings such as "Mimicry and Legendary Psychasthenia" engage in Schelling's way of breaking out of the boundaries that delimit the organic from the inorganic. Beyond the confines of modern biology, there is an ephemeral world of resemblances and connections where art, science, and insects meet. Frank, "Introduction," 12–14.

66. Mumford, *The Myth of the Machine,* 7.

67. Huizinga, *Homo Ludens,* 9.

68. Paolo Virno, *A Grammar of the Multitude,* trans. Isabella Bertoletti, James Cascaito, and Andrea Casson (New York: Semiotext(e), 2004), 81–84.

69. Brandon W. Joseph, "Interview with Paolo Virno," *Grey Room* 21 (Fall 2005): 30.

70. My argument resonates with the insistence on the animality, or bestiality, inherent in contemporary network culture as analyzed by Matteo Pasquinelli in *Animal Spirits: A Bestiary of the Commons* (Rotterdam: NAi Publishers, 2008). Pasquinelli draws a wider connection to nonhuman animality and elaborates this into contexts of political economic critique. He insists that the bestial and the flesh have been forgotten in contemporary code-centered media studies, and even if I find the point worth elaborating, his critique is too broad

and misses the inherent connections between certain notions of animality and, for example, software.

71. Huizinga quotes Plato on the topic of play and music, a passage that articulates how play is beyond representation or likeness as well as utility—and works instead through the mechanisms of capture of the senses (charm): "That which has neither utility nor truth nor likeness, nor yet, in its effects, is harmful, can best be judged by the criterion of the charm that is in it, and by the pleasure it affords. Such pleasure, entailing as it does no appreciable good or ill, is play." Huizinga, *Homo Ludens,* 160, quoting Plato in *Laws.*

72. See Jussi Parikka and Jaakko Suominen, "Victorian Snakes? Towards a Cultural History of Mobile Games and the Experience of Movement," *Game Studies* 6, no. 1 (December 2006), http://gamestudies.org/ (accessed April 20, 2009). Alex Galloway has referred to the gripping realism of gaming as a function of the action-element games require. Instead of catching the attention of the eye, they are catching the bodily faculties for action, control, etc. Between an audience and a diegetic character, the gamer is an ephemeral double entity, but I would argue that that the topological link of the gamer's body with the game is that of a perception-action wiring in Uexküll's sense. See Alexander R. Galloway, "Social Realism in Gaming," *Game Studies* 4, no. 1 (November 2004), http://www.gamestudies.org/ (accessed April 20, 2009). Elizabeth Grosz wants to underline the more ontological nature of capture inherent in arts. According to her recent claim, all art insists on contracting the senses. According to Grosz, "Each of the arts aims to make all of the other organs function even if it is just one organ. Music aims to make your eyes function like ears, makes the whole body into an ear, that resonates with music. The more we enjoy music and the louder it becomes, the more the body itself, our chest, torso, and our stomach, resonate as musical instruments. So the more absorbed we are in a particular work of art, the more all our other senses are directed to the one sense that is summoned up. Painting, to the extent that it's powerful and affective, makes us want to hear the paint, touch it, smell it, taste it, as well as to look at it. Each of the arts summons up something that all of the arts have in common, resonating with." Kontturi and Tiainen, "Feminism, Art, Deleuze, and Darwin," 253.

73. Caillois, "Mimicry and Legendary Psychasthenia," 99.

74. Kwinter, *Architectures of Time,* 136.

75. Caillois, *Les jeux et les hommes,* 63.

76. Uexküll, *Theoretische Biologie,* 174. The centrality of the perception-action coupling is found in Bergson as well. Perception is actually always to a certain extent a preparation for action, which points toward the close ties with Uexküll. According to Bergson: "Perception, therefore, consists in detaching,

from the totality of objects, the possible action of my body upon them" (*Matters of Memory*, 304). Perception eliminates from the plethora of images those that cannot be immersed as part of the action-sphere of the body of the perceiver. Furthermore, this signals that perception is never only of the perceiving body but of the tension fields among the body, the environment, and the multiple durations brought to the fore by memory.

77. Félix Guattari, *The Three Ecologies*, trans. Ian Pindar and Paul Sutton (London: Athlone, 2000).

INTERMEZZO

1. Rodgers, *Debugging the Link*, 122.

2. Emile Du Bois-Reymond, quoted in Laura Otis, *Networking: Communicating with Bodies and Machines in the Nineteenth Century* (Ann Arbor: University of Michigan Press, 2001), 49.

3. Kapp, *Grundlinien einer Philosophie der Technik*, 140–46.

4. Ibid., 307–11.

5. Esposito, *Bios*, 17.

6. Rodgers, *Debugging the Link*, 115–54.

7. See Jussi Parikka, "Mapping Noise: Techniques and Tactics of Irregularities, Interception and Disturbance," in *Media Archaeologies*.

8. Daniel Brewer, "A Review of Diderot's Dream," *Modern Philology* 90, no. 4 (May 1993): 548–52.

9. Denis Diderot, *Rameau's Nephew/D'Alembert's Dream*, trans. Leonard Tancock (London: Penguin Books, 1966), 168–69.

10. Otis, *Networking*, 50–52.

11. See, for example, Thomson Jay Hudson, *A Scientific Demonstration of the Future Life* (London : G. P. Putnam's Sons, 1896), 252. In his spiritist study Hudson also cites Henry Ward Beecher's religious ponderings from 1885, which express the willingness to keep alive views that seek unity in the multiplicity of the animal and spiritual "machine": "Who . . . designed this mighty machine, created matter, gave to it its laws, impressed upon it that tendency which has brought forth the almost infinite results on the globe, and wrought them into a perfect system? Design by wholesale is greater than design by retail" (252).

12. Albert-László Barabási, *Linked* (New York: Plume, 2003), 221.

13. Alex Galloway and Eugene Thacker, *The Exploit: A Theory of Networks* (Minneapolis: University of Minnesota Press, 2007), 109–12. In my view, a special role is reserved for insects. The focus on insects should be understood as a reflexive prism in the sense in which Foucault used the term in his lectures at the Collége de France in 1977–1978. Foucault, *Security, Territory, Population,*

276. Instead of giving a full-fledged account of the history of insects in modernity, my aim is to use the notion of insects as a prism that allows us to understand certain aspects relating to biopolitics, the emergence of the term *swarm,* and the centrality of even the early entomology for our current media theoretical considerations.

14. Cf. Bergson, *An Introduction to Metaphysics,* 45.

15. Cf. Erin Manning, "Grace Taking Form: Marey's Movement Machines," *Parallax* 14, no. 1 (2008): 82.

16. Michel Serres, *Angels: A Modern Myth,* trans. Francis Cowper (Paris: Flammarion, 1995), 30, quoted in Nigel Thrift, *Non-Representational Theory: Space, Politics, Affect* (London: Routledge, 2008), 56.

5. ANIMAL ENSEMBLES, ROBOTIC AFFECTS

1. Johnston, *The Allure of Machinic Life,* 25–27.

2. See David F. Channell, *The Vital Machine: A Study of Technology and Organic Life* (New York: Oxford University Press, 1991), 120–21.

3. William H. Laurence, "Science in Review: Cybernetics, a New Science, Seeks the Common Elements in Human and Mechanical Brains," *New York Times,* December 19, 1948.

4. N. Katherine Hayles, *How We Became Posthuman: Virtual Bodies in Cybernetics, Literature, and Informatics* (Chicago: University of Chicago Press 1999), 57.

5. Ibid., 62.

6. Ibid., 62–63.

7. Johnston, *The Allure of Machinic Life,* 8–9.

8. Ibid., 58–60.

9. Sleigh, *Six Legs Better,* 170.

10. John Lubbock had already experimented on bees' sense of direction and faculties of communication at the end of the nineteenth century. See John Lubbock, *On the Senses, Instincts, and Intelligence of Animals, with Special Reference to Insects* (Boston: Elibron / Adamant Media, 2004). The book originally came out in 1888.

11. Sleigh, *Six Legs Better,* 174–74.

12. Gilbert Simondon, *L'individuation psychique et collective* (Paris: Aubier, 1989, 2007), 125–26. As Alberto Toscano notes, what is missing in the mathematical notions of information is a focus on ontogenesis: the intensive (in)formations of individuation. Alberto Toscano, *The Theatre of Production: Philosophy and Individuation between Kant and Deleuze* (New York: Palgrave 2006), 144.

13. Adrian Wenner, "Division of Labor in a Honey Bee Colony—A Markov Process?" *Journal of Theoretical Biology* 1 (1961): 324–27.

14. For a good example, see the Web page Ant Colony Optimization, http://www.aco-metaheuristic.org/ (accessed April 6, 2009).

15. Steven Johnson, *Emergence: The Connected Lives of Ants, Brains, Cities, and Software* (London: Penguin, 2001), 59–60.

16. See Parisi, "For a Schizogenesis of Sexual Difference." For Parisi, this continuum extends to a schizogenetic analysis of gender as well.

17. Sleigh, *Six Legs Better*, 163.

18. The suggestions offered concerning the "ethnicities" of bees resonated with the European linguistic-political situation in the midst of unification after the Second World War, where Austrians and Italians could perhaps work together but communication was the problem. Again, talking about bees: "When the Austrian and Italian varieties are put together in a colony, they work together peacefully. But confusion arises when they communicate. The Austrian bee aroused by the wagging dance of an Italian bee will search for the feeding place too far away." William Laurence, "Bee Language: Study of Different Kinds of Bees Reveals Communication 'Dialectics,'" *New York Times*, August 12, 1962.

19. Sleigh, *Six Legs Better*, 168.

20. "Reading the Language of Bees," *New York Times*, January 12, 1947; "Bee Language Topic of Talk," *Washington Post*, April 10, 1949; Jacques Lacan, *Écrits I* (Paris: Éditions du Seuil, 1999), 295–96.

21. Tania Munz, "The Bee Battles: Karl von Frisch, Adrian Wenner, and the Honey Bee Dance Language Controversy," *Journal of the History of Biology* 38 (2005): 543.

22. Karl von Frisch, *The Dancing Bees: An Account of the Life and Senses of the Honey Bee*, trans. Dora Ilse (London: Country Book Club, 1955), 100–101, quote on 101.

23. Munz, "The Bee Battles," 547. See also the very interesting debate on animal communication with a special focus on Von Frisch at the Eighth Macy Foundation Cybernetics Meeting in 1951. Herbert G. Birch, "Communication between Animals," in *Cybernetics: Circular Causal and Feedback Mechanisms in Biological and Social Systems: Transactions of the Eight Conference, March 15–16, 1951, New York,* ed. Heinz von Foerster, Margaret Mead, and Hanks Lukas Teuber (New York: Josiah Macy Jr. Foundation, 1952), 134–72. Birch signals from the beginning his reluctance to address animal *communication* and indicates that he feels more comfortable if talking about animal interrelations. For him, communication is an issue of functions such as feeding, mating, migration, and so on (134). Despite the early reservations, the questions of anthropo-

morphism and differences with human communications are vividly addressed in the discussions.

24. Eileen Crist, "Can an Insect Speak? The Case of the Honeybee Dance Language," *Social Studies of Science* 34, no. 1 (February 2004): 12.

25. Von Frisch, *The Dancing Bees,* 119.

26. Bergson, *Creative Evolution,* 175.

27. Parisi, *Abstract Sex.*

28. Ibid., 15.

29. Ibid., 38.

30. Riskin, "The Defecating Duck."

31. Shaviro, *Doom Patrols.*

32. See William M. Tsutsui, "Looking Straight at Them! Understanding the Big Bug Movies of the 1950s," *Environmental History* 12 (April 2007): 237–53. In 1965 Susan Sontag published her key essay "The Imagination of Disaster," which set the agenda for understanding the monster insects as a trauma of the nuclear age. However, Tsutsui argues that the fear was much more mundane and had to do with the fear of uncontrollable insect swarms and infestation in the 1950s.

33. W. Grey Walter, *The Living Brain* (London: Gerald Duckworth, 1953), 3.

34. Ibid.

35. Ibid., 36.

36. Ibid., 77. Italics in original.

37. Ibid., 83.

38. Ibid.

39. Ibid., 94. This simple form of learning was also evident in Claude Shannon's maze-solving machine rat. It learned by trial and error but was able to remember the path through the maze on subsequent attempts. Claude Shannon, "Presentation of a Maze-Solving Machine," in *Cybernetics: Circular Causal and Feedback Mechanisms,* 173–80.

40. Walter, *The Living Brain,* 85–86.

41. Uexküll, *Theoretische Biologie,* 153.

42. See Ken Rinaldo's Web site, http://kenrinaldo.com/ (accessed April 23, 2009).

43. To quote Rosenblatt: "The 'coded memory theorists' are forced to conclude that recognition of any stimulus involves the matching or systematic comparison of the contents of storage with incoming sensory patterns, in order to determine whether the current stimulus has been seen before, and to determine the appropriate response from the organism. The theorists in the empiricist tradition, on the other hand, have essentially combined the answer to the third question with their answer to the second: since the stored information takes

the form of new connections, or transmission channels in the nervous system (or the creation of conditions which are functionally equivalent to new connections), it follows that the new stimuli will make use of these new pathways which have been created, automatically activating the appropriate response without requiring any separate processes for recognition or identification." F. Rosenblatt, "The Perceptron: A Probabilistic Model for Information Storage and Organization in the Brain," *Psychological Review* 65, no. 6 (1958): 387. See also Sherry Turkle, *Life on the Screen: Identity in the Age of the Internet* (London: Phoenix, 1997), 130–31.

44. See Herbert Simon, *The Sciences of the Artificial* (Cambridge, Mass.: MIT Press, 1969), 6–7, 14. However, alternative accounts were expressed as well. Earlier, in 1792, François Huber wrote in his *Nouvelles observations sur les abeilles* of the innateness of intelligence in bees: "If the worker does not have a model to work to, if the pattern according to which she cuts every cell is not something outside herself and Nature which directs her senses, then we have to admit that such work is directed by some kind of intelligence." Huber, quoted in Ramírez, *The Beehive Metaphor*, 27.

45. Simon, *The Sciences of the Artificial*, 24.

46. Ibid.

47. Friedrich Kittler, *Gramophone, Film, Typewriter*, trans. Geoffrey Winthrop-Young and Michael Wutz (Stanford, Calif.: Stanford University Press, 1999), 259.

48. Kittler, *Gramophone*, 258; Lacan, *Écrits*, 295–96. Lacan's ideas reinstate the hylomorphic idea of a fixed reality versus dynamic language. The language of human beings is based on the discourse of the other, where symbols work through their internal, dynamic relations—not through referring to reality. This implies a stagnant conception of the material and reality, which the neo-materialist mode of cultural analysis is trying to be rid of.

49. See Hayles, *How We Became Posthuman*.

50. Munz, "The Bee Battles," 539–40.

51. Von Frisch, *The Dancing Bees*, 80. Hence, "cinema in the bee state" (80) would be about hundreds of single pictures a second, according to Von Frisch.

52. Ibid., 82. See also Birch, "Communication between Animals," 142–43.

53. Birch, "Communication between Animals," 153.

54. Ibid. In the Macy conference discussions following the presentation in 1951, Birch posed the key question as follows: "How in the world does the bee translate this kind of orientation, based upon the polarization features of light, into the gravitational field itself?" Birch, "Communication between Animals," 153.

55. Munz, "The Bee Battles," 557–59. Wenner also planned to build an artificial bee in the 1960s but soon discarded the idea (554–55).

56. Von Frisch, *The Dancing Bees,* 121.

57. Ibid., 122.

58. Ibid., 122–23.

59. Ibid., 123.

60. Hayles, *How We Became Posthuman,* 134–37.

61. Wenner, quoted in Munz, "The Bee Battles," 557. According to Munz (559–64), the debate between Von Frisch and Wenner was settled with the synthesis offered by James Gould: both modes of communication (the dance language and the olfactory sense) were to be taken into account.

62. Translations of *L'individuation psychique et collective* and *L'individu et sa genèse physico-biologique* are both forthcoming from the University of Minnesota Press.

63. Gilbert Simondon, *Cours sur la Perception (1964–1965)* (Chatou, France: Les Éditions de La Transparence, 2006), 307.

64. Gilbert Simondon, "The Genesis of the Individual," trans. Mark Cohen and Sanford Kwinter, in *Incorporations,* ed. Jonathan Crary and Sanford Kwinter (New York: Zone, 1992), 317 n. 1.

65. In fact, this has been on the primary agenda of much of research into cybernetic culture and network society, from N. Katherine Hayles to Mark B. N. Hansen. See Hayles, *How We Became Posthuman;* Mark B. N. Hansen, *New Philosophy for New Media* (Cambridge, Mass.: MIT Press, 2004). Hayles and Hansen acknowledge the work by Donald MacKay as an early rethinking of the importance of embedded cybernetics. Hansen (76–85) draws in addition from the early work by Raymond Ruyer in his attempt to look for alternatives to Shannon- and Weaver-inspired perspectives, including that of Friedrich Kittler.

66. Gilbert Simondon, *L'individuation psychique et collective* (Paris: Aubier, 2007), 234.

67. Ibid., 88.

68. Ibid., 200.

69. Adrian Mackenzie, *Transductions: Bodies and Machines at Speed* (London: Continuum, 2002), 17. Mackenzie notes that the notion of transduction was also actively used in 1950s cell biology: "It named a specific event in which a virus carries new genetic material over into the DNA of bacteria" (17).

70. Ibid., 174.

71. Matthew Fuller, *Media Ecologies: Materialist Energies in Art and Technoculture* (Cambridge, MA: MIT Press, 2005), 18–19.

72. Simondon, "The Genesis of the Individual," 306. Italics in original.

73. Simondon, *L'individuation psychique et collective,* 27.

74. See Simondon, *Cours sur la Perception,* 309–10.

75. My suggestions resonate strongly with J. J. Gibson's ecological and

nonrepresentational analysis of perception, which he has initiated since the 1950s. Gibson's later ecological theories, which offer a more material understanding of perception and being-in-the-world than does, for example, *The Perception of the Visual World* (1950), are about the mutuality of the animal and its environment. In this sense it works on several similar premises as, for instance, Uexküll's ethology. Consider the illuminating opening of Gibson's *The Ecological Approach to Visual Perception:* "We are told that vision depends on the eye, which is connected to the brain. I shall suggest that natural vision depends on the eyes in the head on a body supported by the ground, the brain being only the central organ of a complete visual system." J. J. Gibson, *The Ecological Approach to Visual Perception* (Hillsdale, N.J.: Lawrence Erlbaum Associates, 1986), 1.

76. Toscano, *The Theatre of Production*, 144.

77. Ibid., 146. Toscano's recommendable reading of individuation highlights the importance of Simondon in thinking individuals and intensities—and also of the critique of code enacted by Simondon. In this passage, Toscano (142–47) explains the pre-individual tension of information, which is, contra mathematical information theory, unquantifiable. In other words, the receivers are not known in advance. This is an approach of potentials and relations in which the terms formed are secondary to individuation. As mathematical theories of communication systems suggest, there are systems between which messages travel, but Toscano outlines how Simondon sees this "between" as the primary (in)forming of the relational systems. A similar radical empiricist stance is also part of Deleuze and Guattari's philosophy and resonates, for example, with the work of William James.

78. See Johnston, *The Allure of Machinic Life*, 173; Christopher G. Langton, "Artificial Life," in *Artificial Life: The Proceedings of an Interdisciplinary Workshop on the Synthesis and Simulation of Living Systems Held September 1987 in Los Alamos, New Mexico,* ed. Christopher G. Langton (Redwood, Calif.: Addison-Wesley, 1989), 38–40.

6. BIOMORPHS AND BOIDS

1. Furthermore, Ansell-Pearson notes the importance of "sensibilia" as "pure sensory qualities," or art whose contrapuntal relations exhibit not solely predetermined functions but creative modes of aesthetic evolution. Ansell-Pearson, *Germinal Life*, 174.

2. Ibid., 177–78.

3. Andy Clark, *Mindware: An Introduction to the Philosophy of Cognitive Science* (New York: Oxford University Press, 2001), 143.

4. Quoted in Clark, *Mindware*, 91.

5. This approach has recently been underlined by Mark B. N. Hansen in *Bodies in Code.*

6. Clark, *Mindware,* 103.

7. See Parikka, *Digital Contagions.*

8. For Deleuze writing in the mid-1980s, this shift is to be understood in terms of technological objects' becoming "objectiles." In his book on Leibniz, Deleuze quotes the architectural theorist Bernard Cache and the idea of the technological object moving outside that of the "mold" or the "standard." The mass object (to which corresponds the mass media of broadcasting analyzed by Adorno as culture industry) is replaced by a continuum of variation. Instead of spatialized form-matter, we have "temporal modulation that implies as much the beginnings of a continuous variation of matter as a continuous development of form." Gilles Deleuze, *The Fold,* trans. Tom Conley (Minneapolis: University of Minnesota Press, 1993), 19. The mold becomes a site of persisting displacement and change, and the object becomes manneristic and is best understood through the concept of the event. This is the Leibnizian moment of the technological media culture of network society. Baroque mathematics informs us of the importance of the folds and curves persisting to infinity—a mathematics of irrational numbers and differential calculus that mark an alternative to that of the Cartesian coordinate system of points. Even though the 1980s were marked by the visual metaphorics of Cartesian cyberspace as the key model for the new technological object/space, it is more interesting and apt to look at digital culture in terms of folds and an ethology of relations, relationality. Luciana Parisi has addressed this brilliantly in her "Extensive Abstraction in Digital Architecture," in *The Spam Book: On Viruses, Porn, and Other Anomalous Objects from the Dark Side of Digital Culture,* ed. Jussi Parikka and Tony Sampson (Cresskill, N.J.: Hampton Press, 2009), 61–80. See also Anna Munster's take on the baroque inflections of contemporary digital arts and culture in *Materializing New Media: Embodiment in Information Aesthetics* (Hanover, N.H.: Dartmouth College Press, 2006). Because of the relational focus, animals and ethology are interesting figures to think with outside their normal "natural" habitats. Taking a look at digital technologies through animal bodies in their relationality does not neglect the mathematics of the digital but adds the element of ethology. Certainly recent decades have suffered enough from bad metaphorics relating to insects, evolution of cultural/technological/economic systems, and so on. However, I do not propose further analogies but rather offer a neomaterialist understanding of ethology and variation inherent in our digital network culture. An interesting perspective of the ethology of technology has been proposed by Pasi Väliaho in "Bodies Outside In," 7–19.

9. Paley, quoted in Dawkins, *The Blind Watchmaker,* 5.

10. Ibid.

11. Ibid., 31. "Our experience of electronic technology prepares us to accept the idea that unconscious machinery can behave as if it understands complex mathematical ideas. This idea is directly transferable to the workings of living machinery. A bat is a machine whose internal electronics are so wired up that its wing muscles cause it to home in on insects, as an unconscious guided missile homes in on an aeroplane" (37).

12. Ibid., 24. The point is a bit similar to the philosopher Thomas Nagel's famous question from 1974: "What is it like to be a bat?" Thomas Nagel, "What Is It Like to Be a Bat?" *Philosophical Review* 83, no. 4 (October 1974): 435–50. For Nagel the dilemma was set in a specific epistemological framework regarding the transportability of phenomenological lifeworlds and subsequently the mind-body problem. For Dawkins the question was one of technics, of engineering and design.

13. Richard Dawkins, "Computer Programs and the 'Evolution of Evolvability'" (1991), in *The Blind Watchmaker,* appendix, 329.

14. Nancy Forbes, *Imitation of Life: How Biology Is Inspiring Computing* (Cambridge, Mass.: MIT Press, 2004), 15–16; John Holland, *Adaptation in Natural and Artificial Systems* (Cambridge, Mass.: MIT Press, 1992). The first edition of Holland's book came out in 1975.

15. Indeed, for Darwin sexual selection was a realm of sensation and perception in itself and not reducible to reproduction: "—for instance, in the male possessing certain organs of sense or locomotion, of which the female is quite destitute, or in having them more highly-developed, in order that he may readily find or reach her; or again, in the male having special organs of prehension so as to hold her securely." Darwin, *The Descent of Man, and Selection in Relation to Sex* (Princeton, N. J.: Princeton University Press, 1981), 253. See also Grosz, *Chaos, Territory, Art,* 65–68. Grosz emphasizes the expressive nature of sexual selection instead of just its supportive role in natural selection. Indeed, the "media reality" of sounds, sights, and odors presents a much more material and intensive understanding of the relationality of nature and resonates strongly with Deleuze and Guattari's reading of ethology.

16. Richard Dawkins, "The Evolution of Evolvability," in *Artificial Life: Proceedings of an Interdisciplinary Workshop,* 201–20.

17. Ansell-Pearson, *Germinal Life,* 162–64.

18. Parisi, "Extensive Abstraction in Digital Architecture," 67.

19. Parisi turns toward Lynn Margulis–inspired notions of symbiotic environments, parasitism, and "spam architectures." See also Parikka, *Digital Contagions,* for an exploration of viral patterns as part of the media archaeology of digital culture.

20. Cf. Pierre Sonigo and Isabelle Stengers, *L'évolution* (Les Ulis, France: EDP Sciences, 2003), 117–18. Sonigo and Stengers offer apt tools for a critique of neo-Darwinism.

21. Kelly, *Out of Control*, 386. Kelly, a contributor to *Wired* and a chief figure of neo-Darwinist digital capitalism of the 1990s, explains natural selection: "It's a phenomenon of mobs distributed in space and time. The process must involve a population having (1) variation among individuals in some trait, (2) where that trait makes some difference in fertility, fecundity, or survival ability, and (3) where that trait is transmitted in some fashion from parents to their off-spring. If those conditions exist, natural selection will happen as inevitably as seven follows six, or heads and tails split" (386). In other words, despite being embedded in discourses of complexity, open-ended evolution, and the like, the neocapitalistic-become-neobiological trend of the 1980s and 1990s was keen on inevitabilities. However, Kelly is quick to add that natural selection does not amount to a single explanation of evolution as merely one of its functional composites. There is no one evolution, explains Kelly, in a neo-Darwinian language that promotes difference: "Evolution is plural and deep" (387). It would be interesting to analyze the notions of difference and change in the context of the new logistics of capitalism keen on tracking heterogeneities.

22. This was represented, for example, by quotes in books on artificial life, such as this one from Mark Ward, which gained rhetorical support from the Victorian naturalist Thomas Belt on the verge of the twenty-first century: "When we see intelligent insects dwelling together in orderly communities of many thousands of individuals, their social instincts developed to a high degree of perfection, making their marches with the regularity of disciplined troops, showing ingenuity in the crossing of difficult places, assisting each in danger, defending their nests at the risk of their own lives, communicating information rapidly to a great distance, making a regular division of work, the whole community taking charge of rearing of the young, and all imbued with the stronger sense of industry, each individual labouring not for itself alone but for all its fellows— we may imagine that Sir Thomas More's description of Utopia might have been applied with greater justice to such a community than to any human society." Mark Ward, *Virtual Organisms: The Startling World of Artificial Life* (New York: St. Martin's Press, 2000), 191–92. The quote is from Thomas Belt's 1874 book *The Naturalist in Nicaragua*, http://www.gutenberg.org/ (accessed April 7, 2009).

23. Steven Levy, *Artificial Life: A Report from the Frontier Where Computers Meet Biology* (New York: Vintage Books, 1992), 105.

24. Ward, *Virtual Organisms*, 192.

25. Will Wright has made references to this direction in interviews. See "Sims, BattleBots, Cellular Automata God, and *Go*," a conversation with Will

Wright by Celia Pearce conducted in September 2001, *Game Studies* 2, no. 1 (July 2002), http://www.gamestudies.org/ (accessed April 7, 2009).

26. Robert J. Collins and David R. Jefferson, "AntFarm: Towards Simulated Evolution," in *Artificial Life II: A Proceedings Volume in the Santa Fe Institute Studies in the Sciences of Complexity,* ed. Christopher G. Langton et al. (Redwood, Calif.: Addison-Wesley, 1991), 586–89.

27. Collins and Jefferson, "AntFarm," 589.

28. Ibid., 580.

29. Edward O. Wilson, "Pheromones," in *Nature Revealed: Selected Writings, 1949–2006* (Baltimore, Md.: Johns Hopkins University Press, 2006), 83. The piece was originally published in *Scientific American* in May 1963. Bruce Sterling's short story "Swarm" (1982) was clearly influenced by the enthusiasm for pheromones and the ideas of alternative organisms and living systems from us humans. The narrative also frames the biopolitical extraction of surplus from the living organism, highlighting that insect bodies and alternative living organizations are susceptible to biopolitical framing. In this sense it extends into a political economic critique of biopower through hinting at the passage from intensive living bodies to a profit.

30. Wilson, "Pheromones," 84.

31. Wilson does not deny the importance of the dance but sees chemicals as an important part of the organization of colonies (ibid., 89–90).

32. Wilson, "Pheromones," 86.

33. John Conway's Game of Life is an early example of such computational systems. See Martin Gardner, "Mathematical Games: The Fantastic Combinations of John Conway's New Solitaire Game 'Life,'" *Scientific American* 223 (October 1970): 120–23.

34. Johnson, *Emergence,* 59–63. However, Tracker was only about individual ants optimizing trails and paths, whereas the AntFarm was a colony-based parallel organism. A key digital feature was the Connection Machine computer, which was based on Danny Hillis's work at MIT during the early 1980s.

35. Levy, *Artificial Life,* 261.

36. See Howard Rheingold, *Smart Mobs: The Next Social Revolution* (Cambridge, Mass.: Basic Books/Perseus, 2002).

37. Alexander R. Galloway, *Gaming: Essays on Algorithmic Culture* (Minneapolis: University of Minnesota Press, 2006), 33.

38. Mitchel Resnick, *Turtles, Termites, and Traffic Jams: Explorations in Massively Parallel Microworlds* (Cambridge, Mass.: MIT Press, 1994).

39. "The most promising approaches to modelling complex systems like life or intelligence are those which have dispensed with the notion of a centralized global controller and have focused instead on mechanisms for the *distributed*

control of behavior." Chris Langton, "Artificial Life," in *Artificial Life: The Proceedings of an Interdisciplinary Workshop,* 21.

40. Langton, "Artificial Life," 3–4; Johnston, *The Allure of Machinic Life,* 174.

41. Resnick, *Turtles, Termites, and Traffic Jams,* 148. Italics in the original.

42. A similar point has recently been made by Jon McCormack, who has suggested that software is "a performance instrument" and that evolutionary programs open up modes of thought and experimentation with "computational phase-spaces." Jon McCormack, "Facing the Future: Evolutionary Possibilities for Human-Machine Creativity," in *The Art of Artificial Evolution: A Handbook on Evolutionary Art and Music,* ed. Juan Romero and Penousal Machado (Berlin: Springer, 2008), 445.

43. See Johnston, *The Allure of Machinic Life.*

44. "To illustrate, consider modelling a colony of ants. We would provide simple specifications for behavioural repertoires of different *castes* of ants, and create lots and lots of instances of each caste. We would start up this population of 'antomata' (a term coined by Doyne Farmer) from some initial configuration within a simulated two-dimensional environment. From then on, the behavior of the system would depend entirely on the collective results of all of the local interactions between individual antomata and between individual antomata and features of their environment. There would be no single 'drill-sergeant' antomaton choreographing the ongoing dynamics according to some set of high-level rules for colony behavior. The behavior of the colony of antomata would emerge from out of the behaviors of the individual antomata themselves, just as in a real colony of ants." Langton, "Artificial Life," 4. Langton had also worked on "vants," virtual ants, a simple rule-based search grid. See Levy, *Artificial Life,* 104–5.

45. See Andrew Goffey, "Intelligence," in *Software Studies: A Lexicon,* ed. Matthew Fuller (Cambridge, Mass.: MIT Press, 2008), 135.

46. Eric Bonabeau, Marco Dorigo, and Guy Theraulaz, *Swarm Intelligence: From Natural to Artificial Systems* (New York: Oxford University Press, 1999), xi.

47. Ibid., 85. See also Jason Palmer, "BT Injects Life into Its Network," BBC News Channel, August 7, 2008, http://news.bbc.co.uk/ (accessed April 7, 2009).

48. Bonabeau, Dorigo, and Theraulaz, *Swarm Intelligence,* 7.

49. Ibid., 107.

50. Ibid., 106.

51. "The model network used in the examples is obviously a simplification of reality: the 'ant routing' methods have to be tested on realistic, and therefore more complex, network models. Not only should more realistic traffic conditions be simulated, specific constraints should also be taken into account. In the considered examples, routing is limited to finding the shortest path from

one point to another under given network conditions. On the contrary, in the context of modern high-speed networks like ATM (Asynchronous Transfer Mode), routing is often complicated by the notion of guaranteed Quality of Services (QoS), which can either be related to time, packet loss or bandwidth requirements" (ibid, 105).

52. See Craig Reynolds's presentation notes, "Reactive Autonomous Characters" (2000), http://www.research.scea.com/ (accessed April 24, 2009).

53. See Galloway, *Gaming*, 32–33. In the game, the swarming crowds feed into the actual game play but are expressions of the very real informatic patterns as well.

54. Mark B. N. Hansen, *New Philosophy for New Media* (Cambridge, Mass.: MIT Press, 2004), 10.

55. Hansen, *Bodies in Code*, 2.

56. Craig Reynolds, "Flocks, Herds, and Schools: A Distributed Behavioral Model," *Computer Graphics* 21, no. 4 (July 1987): 30.

57. Matthew Fuller has explained software in terms of "conceptual proprioception" and a certain radical empiricism of relationality: "Each search, but also each piece of software, can usefully be approached as a transferral, a synthetic agglomeration of knowing, sensing, and doing. When you drive a car your mind fills out to the space occupied by the vehicle. You sense its shape in order to manoeuvre safely, or however. Equally, conceptual proprioception can be elaborated in order to negotiate the multiple levels of meaning-making in a search. The user mobilises and becomes infested with, composed through, flocks of sensorial, a billion symptoms, neurosis at the service of knowledge, or a simple slimy crawl of the switch-tongue at the point of slipping away into babble and the learning of language." Matthew Fuller, *Behind the Blip: Essays on the Culture of Software* (New York: Autonomedia, 2003), 94–95.

58. Langton, "Artificial Life," 32–33. Johnston, *The Allure of Machinic Life,* 179. It would be interesting to analyze such relationality in terms of Whitehead's "eternal objects," which relate to radical empiricism. From Whitehead's perspective, relations are eternal objects that have sensory qualities such as colors and tactility, along with more complex manners of relatedness. Shaviro, *Without Criteria,* 38–39.

59. Reynolds, "Flocks, Herds, and Schools," 29.

60. The often cited but continuously inspiring lines on Spinoza by Deleuze go as follows: "How does Spinoza define a body? A body, of whatever kind, is ·defined by Spinoza in two simultaneous ways. In the first place, a body, however small it may be, is composed of an infinite number of particles; it is the relations of motion and rest, of speeds and slownesses between particles, that define a body, the individuality of a body. Secondly, a body affects other bodies, or is

affected by other bodies; it is this capacity for affecting and being affected that also defines a body in its individuality." Deleuze, *Spinoza,* 123. For an elaboration of how to approach software as an ethological process, see Jussi Parikka, "Ethologies of Software Art: What Can a Digital Body of Code Do?" in *Deleuze and Contemporary Art,* ed. Simon O'Sullivan and Stephen Zepke (Edinburgh: Edinburgh University Press, 2010), 116–32.

61. Something similar has been suggested by Matthew Fuller in his take on media ecologies. Matthew Fuller, *Media Ecologies: Material Energies in Art and Technoculture* (Cambridge, Mass.: MIT Press, 2005).

62. See, for example, Christian Jacob and Sebastian von Mammen, "Swarm Grammars: Growing Dynamic Structures in 3D Agent Spaces," *Digital Creativity* 18 (2007): 54–64.

63. See Deleuze, *The Fold,* 19.

64. Casey Alt, "Objects of Our Affection: How Object-Orientation Made Computation a Medium," in *Media Archaeologies.*

65. Ibid.

66. Goffey, "Intelligence," 139.

67. Craig Reynolds, "Big Fast Crowds on PS3," *Proceedings of the 2006 ACM SIGGRAPH Symposium on Videogames* (New York: ACM, 2006), 113–21.

68. Ansell-Pearson, *Germinal Life,* 165.

69. John Protevi, "Deleuze, Guattari, and Emergence," *Paragraph* 29, no. 2 (2006): 19–39.

70. See Stengers, "Pour une approache speculative de l'évolution biologique," in *L'évolution,* 144.

7. SEXUAL SELECTION IN THE BIODIGITAL

1. James J. Gibson, *The Ecological Approach to Visual Perception* (Hillsdale, N.J.: Lawrence Erlbaum Associates, 1986), 16.

2. Ibid., 17.

3. Ibid.

4. DeLanda, *Intensive Science and Virtual Philosophy.* See also DeLanda's recent development of assemblage theory in *A New Philosophy of Society: Assemblage Theory and Social Complexity* (London: Continuum, 2006).

5. Fuller, *Media Ecologies,* 45.

6. Ibid.; Félix Guattari, *Three Ecologies,* trans. Ian Pindar and Paul Sutton (London: Athlone Press, 2000).

7. Ned Rossiter, *Organized Networks: Media Theory, Creative Labour, New Institutions* (Rotterdam: NAi, 2006), 174.

8. See Parisi, *Abstract Sex.*

9. See Braidotti, *Metamorphoses.*

10. See Simon O'Sullivan, *Art Encounters Deleuze and Guattari: Thought beyond Representation* (Houndmills, England: Palgrave Macmillan, 2006), 60–61. O'Sullivan points toward probeheads as "a name for more experimental, nontraditional art practices. Such practices might not seem to be defacialisations, but, with the systems of facialisation becoming increasingly complex (one thinks here of new communications technologies) then the lines of flight from these will themselves become increasingly complex and unfamiliar, as will the territories produced on the other side of the 'white wall'" (61).

11. Parisi, *Abstract Sex.*

12. Teknolust—The Movie Web site, director's statement, http://www .teknolustthemovie.com/ (accessed January 20, 2009).

13. Jackie Stacey, *The Cinematic Life of the Gene* (Durham, N.C.: Duke University Press, 2010). Referenced from the manuscript.

14. Matthew Calarco outlines the anthropomorphic underpinnings of contemporary philosophy in *Zoographies: The Question of the Animal from Heidegger to Derrida* (New York: Columbia University Press, 2008).

15. Casey Alt, "Objects of Our Affection: How Object-Orientation Made Computation a Medium," in *Media Archaeologies.*

16. Stacey, *The Cinematic Life of the Gene.*

17. See, for example, Ron Brinkmann, *The Art and Science of Digital Compositing* (San Francisco, Calif.: Morgan Kaufmann/Elsevier, 1999), 15–16.

18. Ibid., 16.

19. "Interview of Ken Rinaldo," August 2, 2006, http://www.we-make-money-not-art.com (accessed April 23, 2009).

20. Cf. Christopher G. Langton, "Artificial Life," in *Artificial Life: Proceedings of an Interdisciplinary Workshop,* 1–47. Langton's famous wording was that artificial life is focused on "life-as-it-could-be," not just the actual instantiations of life on earth.

21. See Alt, "Objects of Our Affection."

22. See Stacey, *The Cinematic Life of the Gene.*

23. "Remediation" is a term adopted from Jay David Bolter and Richard Grusin, *Remediation: Understanding New Media* (Cambridge, Mass.: MIT Press, 2000). Bolter and Grusin argue that new media are characterized by their particular style of remediating, or reusing, old media. Here I approach remediation as a tactic the SRAs use in their adaptation to the contours of human life—an adaptation that takes place via media forms such as television. In addition, remediation becomes a mode of repetition with a difference, connected in this text to multiplication as a mode of creating difference. Here every repetitious act (for example, cloning) is never a clear-cut repetition but summons a new

constellation and potential shift in the tension of forces. In *Teknolust,* repetition, multiplication, and remediation do not merely produce more of the same but also bring with them a qualitative change in concepts such as subjectivity.

24. Lev Manovich, "Database as a Genre of New Media," *AI and Society,* 1998, http://vv.arts.ucla.edu/AI_Society/manovich.html (accessed January 20, 2009).

25. Agent Ruby can be found at http://agentruby.sfmoma.org/indexflash .html (accessed April 7, 2009).

26. It is interesting to note that Hershman already used the idea of database identity and the mimicking of intelligence in the 1970s. Her four-year Roberta Breitmore performance (1974–1978) introduced the idea that one could construct an artificial person with the help of statistical behavioral and psychological data. Hershman adopted the identity of a database-defined person, Roberta, and many of Roberta's routines were repeated later in *Teknolust,* such as collecting various "souvenirs," including photographs, of the people she encountered. Hershman also evoked multiplication in the last performance of the work, in which several women played Roberta. See http://www.lynnhershman.com/ (accessed April 7, 2009).

27. On "medial will to power," see Fuller, *Media Ecologies,* 62–72.

28. A. M. Turing, "Computing Machinery and Intelligence," *Mind* 59 (1950): 433–60, http://loebner.net/Prizef/TuringArticle.html (accessed April 7, 2009). Thacker underlines the differences between Turing's mind-centered mode of intelligence and the networked intelligence inherent in biomedia computing. Eugene Thacker, *Biomedia* (Minneapolis: University of Minnesota Press, 2004), 103–7.

29. Other early AI programs included Simon and Newell's the Logic Theorist (1956) and the General Problem Solver (1957). The Manchester University Love Letter Generator (1953–1954) is an interesting example of automated confessions of love. See David Link, "There Must Be an Angel: On the Beginnings of the Arithmetics of Rays," *Variantology 2: On Deep Time Relations of Arts, Sciences, and Technologies,* ed. Siegfried Zielinski and David Link (Cologne: Walter König, 2007). The generator was designed by Christopher Strachey, and it works through variable scripts: the concrete words that are combined are independent of each other and stored as lists. Furthermore, as Link notes, "The software bases on a reductionist position vis-à-vis love and its expression. Like the draughts game that Strachey had attempted to implement the previous year, love is regarded as a recombinatory procedure with recurring elements, which can be formalised, but which is still intelligent enough to raise considerable interest should it succeed" (25).

30. Joseph Weizenbaum, "ELIZA—A Computer Program for the Study of

Natural Language Communication between Man and Machine," *Communications of the ACM* 9 (January 1966): 36.

31. See Hansen, *New Philosophy for New Media.*

32. In fact, Turing had already identified this problem having to do with language as a situated practice: "Of the above possible fields the learning of languages would be the most impressive, since it is the most human of these activities. This field seems, however, to depend rather too much on sense organs and locomotion to be feasible." Turing, "Intelligent Machinery," cited in Friedrich Kittler, "Code," in *Software Studies: A Lexicon,* ed. Matthew Fuller (Cambridge, Mass.: MIT Press, 2008), 44.

33. On language, order-words, and incorporeal transformations, see Massumi, *A User's Guide to Capitalism and Schizophrenia,* 27–32.

34. Cf. Deleuze, *Foucault,* 131.

35. Jan Eric Larsson, "The Turing Test Misunderstood," *SIGART Bulletin* 4, no. 4 (October 1993): 10.

36. "In 1900 speaking and hearing, writing and reading were put to the test as isolated functions, without any subject or thought as their shadowy support," writes Kittler, referring to the psychophysics of, for instance, Hermann Ebbinghaus, Paul Broca, and Karl Wernicke, who analyzed cultural practices to their minuscule constituent parts. Friedrich Kittler, *Discourse Networks 1800/1900,* trans. Michael Metteer and Chris Cullens (Stanford, Calif.: Stanford University Press, 1990), 214.

37. Lynn Hershman-Leeson, *Living Blog,* entry on October 2, 2005, http://lynnhershman.com/livingblog/ (accessed April 7, 2009).

38. Sadie Plant, *Zeros + Ones: Digital Women + the New Technoculture* (London: Fourth Estate, 1997), 81.

39. Joanna Zylinska, *On Spiders, Cyborgs, and Being Scared: The Feminine and the Sublime* (Manchester, England: Manchester University Press, 2001), 130.

40. Ibid., 130.

41. Braidotti, *Metamorphoses,* 118.

42. Ibid., 153–54.

43. Ibid., 149.

44. In Braidotti's writings, the Deleuzian notion of affect is well transposed into an ethical demand, or a desire: "Deleuze wants to cast this sense of intimate interconnectiveness as an ethos of ecological empathy and affectivity which also cuts across different species, that is to say different levels of *bios* and *zoe*" (ibid., 147).

45. See Reynolds, "Big Fast Crowds on PS3," 113–14.

46. See John Johnston, "A Future for Autonomous Agents: Machinic *Merkwelten* and Artificial Evolution," *Configurations* 10 (2002): 473–516.

47. For example, the Brooks mobots' "cockroach-like behavior" was based on three simple functions (or affects): to move, to avoid obstacles, and to collect small objects. Ibid., 489.

48. See Jeffrey E. Boyd, Gerald Hushlak, and Christian J. Jacob, "SwarmArt: Interactive Art from Swarm Intelligence," in *Proceedings of the Twelfth annual ACM International Conference on Multimedia* (New York: ACM, 2004), 628–35.

49. Johnston, "A Future for Autonomous Agents," 491.

50. See Deleuze and Guattari, *A Thousand Plateaus,* 257.

51. Deleuze and Guattari, quoted in Patricia Pisters, *The Matrix of Visual Culture: Working with Deleuze and Guattari in Film Theory* (Stanford, Calif.: Stanford University Press, 2003), 207. These ideas have been underlined in a feminist context by Braidotti in *Metamorphoses,* 153–60.

52. Pisters, *The Matrix of Visual Culture,* 207–8.

53. Stacey, in *The Cinematic Life of the Gene,* argues for a similar point with her use of the notion of "transduction" in the analysis of *Teknolust.*

54. See Väliaho, "Bodies Outside In," 7–19.

55. Ibid., 12.

56. Stacey, *The Cinematic Life of the Gene.*

57. Grosz, *Space, Time, and Perversion,* 200.

58. "It is in this sense that we make love to worlds: the universe of an other is that which opens up to and produces our own intensities . . . . The other need not be human or even animal: the fetishist enters a universe of the animated, intensified object as rich and complex as any sexual relation (perhaps more so than). The point is that both a world and a body are opened up for redistribution, dis-organization, transformation." Ibid., 193.

59. Caillois, "The Praying Mantis," 78–79. See also Grosz, *Space, Time, and Perversion,* 193.

60. See Braidotti, *Transpositions.*

61. As Parisi argues in her analysis of bacterial sex, foldings happen as perceptions between bodies: "As an act of selection, perception entails a collision of bodies that unfolds the virtual action of the environment on the body, affecting the capacity of reception and action of a body in the environment" (*Abstract Sex,* 178).

62. Parisi, *Abstract Sex,* 138.

63. Ibid., 61.

64. Stacey, in *The Cinematic Life of the Gene,* addresses the same issue of the SRAs as multiscalar figurations through the notion of "transduction," which she adopts from Mackenzie, *Transductions.*

65. Parisi, *Abstract Sex,* 197.

66. Green Porno is available online through the Sundance Channel, http://www.sundancechannel.com/greenporno (accessed April 7, 2009).

67. Again on this point I find an affinity with Stacey's analysis of *Teknolust* in *The Cinematic Life of the Gene.*

68. See Elizabeth Grosz, "A Thousand Tiny Sexes: Feminism and Rhizomatics," in *Deleuze and Guattari: Critical Assessments of Leading Philosophers,* ed. Gary Genosko, vol. 3, e-book version (Florence: Routledge, 2001), 1457. Deleuze and Guattari write about becomings: "Do not imitate a dog, but make your organism enter into composition with something else in such a way that the particles emitted from the aggregate thus composed will be canine as a function of the relations of movement and rest, or of molecular proximity, into which they enter. Clearly, this something else can be quite varied, and be more or less directly related to the animal in question: it can be the animal's natural food (dirt and worm), or its exterior relations with other animals (you can become-dog with cats, or -monkey with a horse), or an apparatus or prosthesis to which a person subjects the animal (muzzle for reindeer, etc.), or something that does not even have localizable relation to the animal in question (*A Thousand Plateaus,* 274). Furthermore, it is important to note the warning by Grosz that concerns the dangers of thinking in terms of "progression" in becomings ("A Thousand Tiny Sexes," 1461). Becoming-woman is easily thought of as the first step, followed by becoming-human, deterritorialized by becoming-animal, and so forth. We must argue against such "great chains of becoming."

69. Guattari, *Chaosmosis,* 120.

70. Ibid., 126.

EPILOGUE

1. Howard Ensign Evans, *Life of a Little-Known Planet: A Journey into the Insect World* (London: Andre Deutsch, 1970), 85–87.

2. "Two Hundred Crickets," *New York Times,* May 29, 1880.

3. Cf. Eugene Thacker, "Pulse Demons" *Culture Machine* 9 (2007), http://culturemachine.net/ (accessed April 18, 2009).

4. Mira Calix, *3 Commissions,* Milkfactory Web site, at http://www.themilkfactory.co.uk/ (accessed April 9, 2009). Paul Hegarty has also used insect sounds in *The Harvest.* The piece further underlines the thermodynamic process of the unrepeatable nature of temporality—decay. The recording itself is designed to decay through every playing.

5. Evans, *Life of a Little-Known Planet,* 88.

6. Graham Harwood, Richard Wright, and Matsuko Yokokoji, "Cross Talk: Using the Natural Environment as 'Eco Media,'" unpublished summary paper, March 2008.

7. Matthew Fuller, "Art for Animals," In *Deleuze/Guattari and Ecology,* ed. Bernd Herzogenrath (Basingstoke, England: Palgrave 2008), 266–86.

8. "CrossTalk." See the site for the Harwood-Wright-Yokokoji Ecomedia day in 2008 for practical assays in ecomedia at http://mediashed.org/ecomediaday (accessed April 9, 2009).

9. See the recent version of Dead Media by Garnet Hertz and ConceptLab, http://www.conceptlab.com/deadmedia/ (accessed March 31, 2009). See also "A Storehouse of Invention," *New York Times,* August 4, 1901. In the context of insect media, Hertz's Cockroach Controlled Mobile Robots have introduced a very concrete way of using the animal as part of the motility and coordination system of a robot. See http://www.conceptlab.com/roachbot/ (accessed April 10, 2009). The work demonstrates that insects have not been incorporated as models of technology, but it very concretely makes the insect body part of technological systems.

10. Tim Blackwell, "Swarm Granulation," in *The Art of Artificial Evolution: A Handbook on Evolutionary Art and Music,* ed. Juan Romero and Penousal Mechado (Berlin: Springer, 2008), 103.

11. Thacker, "Pulse Demons."

12. Hansen, *New Philosophy for New Media,* 11.

13. Rodgers, *Debugging the Link,* 122.

14. Hansen, *Bodies in Code,* 20.

15. Ibid., 85.

16. Johnston, *The Allure of Machinic Life,* 339–47.

17. See Alphonso Lingis, "Animal Body, Inhuman Face," in *Zoontologies: The Question of the Animal,* ed. Cary Wolfe (Minneapolis: University of Minnesota Press, 2003), 168.

18. Johnston, *The Allure of Machinic Life,* 353. For various approaches from the early 1990s onto adaption, swarm intelligence, software, but also robotics, see Varela and Bourgine, *Toward a Practice of Autonomous Systems.*

19. Alexander R. Galloway and Eugene Thacker, *The Exploit* (Minneapolis: University of Minnesota Press, 2007), 58–62.

20. Esposito, *Bios,* 112.

21. Matteo Pasquinelli, *Animal Spirits: A Bestiary of the Commons* (Rotterdam: NAi, 2008), 63. Pasquinelli's book, despite its bright analysis and call for a zoology of machines, remains short of offering the needed specificity in terms of the nonhuman animality of technical media culture.

22. See, for example, Esposito's account of Nietzsche in *Bios,* 101–9.

23. M. Fatih Tasgetiren, P. N. Suganthan, and Quan-Ke Pan, "A Discrete Particle Swarm Optimization Algorithm for the Generalized Traveling Salesman Problem," *GECCO'07,* ACM, July 7–11, 2007, 158–65.

24. Peter Tarasewich and Patrick R. McMullen, "Swarm Intelligence: Power in Numbers," *Communications of the ACM* 45, no. 8 (August 2002): 66.

25. Paolo Virno, *A Grammar of Multitude: For an Analysis of Contemporary Forms of Life,* trans. Isabella Bertoletti, James Cascaito, and Andrea Casson (Los Angeles: Semiotext(e), 2004), 49–71; Maurizio Lazzarato, "Art, Work and Politics in Disciplinary Societies and Societies of Security," *Radical Philosophy* 149 (May–June 2008): 26–32. See also Pasquinelli's *Animal Spirits* for a development of the ideas of Virno, Lazzarato, and others into a bestiary analysis of the post-Fordist culture of networks and networking.

26. Grosz, *Chaos, Territory, Art,* 82.

27. Guattari, *Chaosmosis,* 126.

28. Ibid., 128.

INDEX

affect(s), xiii–xiv, xxix–xxx, 56, 62,
71, 82–83, 103–5, 111, 119, 121,
145, 171, 173–76, 185, 187, 188,
192–94, 200–201, 233n23,
234n31, 239n57, 242n83, 266n44;
affective assemblages, xxiv;
affect-phrase (Lyotard), xxv; of
algorithms (software), 165–66,
169, 173, 176, 181; animal affects,
xvi, xxiv, xxv, xxvii–xxviii, xxix,
xxxi, xxxii–xxxv, 1–25, 27, 29,
32, 43, 49, 50, 79, 81, 88, 92, 95,
104, 113, 123, 127, 176, 191, 203;
assemblage and, xxv, xxvii, 74;
autonomity of (Massumi), 35,
214n68; biomolecular affect,
175; Grossberg on, xxii; media
and, xx–xxi, 59, 105–10, 165–66,
168, 178–79, 203; new materialism and, xxii; as potentiality, 79,
212n50, 227n46; relationality
and, xxvi, 44, 52, 58, 98, 100, 129,
175, 185–86, 212n50, 212n55,
213n58, 246n26, 262n60,
267n61; as temporal, 57, 85
affordance (Gibson), xiv, xxvi, 44, 62,
66, 71, 77, 94, 100–101, 104, 140,
169–73, 173, 176, 201
Agamben, Giorgio, xxiii, xxxi, 18,
63, 66, 68, 70, 219n50, 226n38,
236n38
Alice in Wonderland, xxx, 7, 67, 85
Alliez, Eric, 79–80, 242n83
Alt, Casey, 166, 175
amoebas, 65, 71, 93; Heidegger and,
237n45
animal studies, xxv–xxvi, 203
Ansell-Pearson, Keith, 71, 77, 209n31,
212n58, 236n36, 237n45, 241n74,
256n1
ant colony, 12, 154, 157, 202; optimization, 125, 159, 160–61, 261n44;
as superorganism (Wheeler), 51,
229n65
anthropomorphism, xix, xxxi, 8,
94, 127, 175, 188, 206, 214n10,

245n26, 246n46; devouring
(Caillois), xxxi, 85, 97–100, 110,
248n65
molar, 81, 86, 192, 193, 212n58,
245n26. *See also* molecular
molecular, xix, xxi, xxiv, xxvi, xxxv,
45, 60, 175, 177, 186–87, 191–93,
211n47, 212n58, 245n26, 268n68.
See also molar
Mongrel (art group), xviii
moths, x, xvi, xxxiv, 1, 98; moth
automata, 123
Müller, Johannes, 11–12, 64, 217n30,
234n24
Mumford, Lewis, 34, 88, 107
Munster, Anna, xx, 257n8
myograph, 13

nanotechnology, xxiii, 174
natura naturans (Spinoza), 233n20,
242n83
Naturphilosophie, 248n65
Negri, Antonio. *See* Hardt, Michael:
and Antonio Negri
neodarwinism, xxxiii, 30, 125–26,
144, 147–54, 163, 165, 171, 202,
259n20, 259n21. *See also* Darwin,
Charles
neomaterialism, xx, xxi, xxii, xxiii,
19, 32, 45, 184, 211n43, 232n8,
248n65, 254n48, 257n8. *See also*
nonrepresentational
Neumann, John von, 122
New AI. *See* Artificial Intelligence (AI)
new materialism. *See* neomaterialism
Nietzsche, Friedrich, xix, 54, 74, 77,
157, 179, 210n32, 216n17, 221n72,
240n63
non-Euclidean geometry, 46, 90, 99,
105

nonorganic life, xv, 119, 201, 211n46,
212n58
nonrepresentational, xxvi, 90, 100,
118, 137, 139, 143, 144, 169, 201,
255n75. *See also* neomaterialism

object-oriented programming, 147,
158, 162, 163, 166, 169, 175, 177,
194
olfactory sense, 66, 92, 138, 244n17,
255n61
order-words, 42, 182, 266n33
Origin of Species (Darwin), 5, 19,
35, 67

Painlevé, Jean, 88, 91, 94–97
Paley, William, 148, 214n8, 242n4
Parisi, Luciana, xxii, xxiii, 76, 173,
183, 189–93, 241n76, 252n16,
258n19, 267n61; critique of neo-
darwinism by, 151–53, 257n8
Pascal (programming language),
151–52
Pasquinelli, Matteo, 248n70, 269n21,
270n25
Peebles, Sarah, 195
perceptron (Rosenblatt), 135, 253n43
Pettigrew, James Bell, 16
phase space, 45–46, 227n46, 261n42
Phenomena (Argento), 144
pheromones, 154–56, 161, 260n29
photography, xix, 1, 7, 93, 96, 97,
230n69, 243n14, 265n26
Pisters, Patricia, 186
Plant, Sadie, 183, 266n38
Plato, xxvi, 117, 123, 249n71
Pliny, Elder, 5
Poincaré, Henri, 63, 90
*Population of an Old Pear-Tree; or,
Stories of Insect Life, The,* xxx, 8

Jussi Parikka is reader in media theory and history at Anglia Ruskin University, Cambridge, England, and director of the Cultures of the Digital Economy (CoDE) Institute. He is author of *Digital Contagions: A Media Archaeology of Computer Viruses* and coeditor of *The Spam Book* and *Media Archaeology*.